I, MICHELANGELO, SCULPTOR

Irving Stone is the author of:

BIOGRAPHICAL NOVELS

LUST FOR LIFE
(*Vincent Van Gogh*)
IMMORTAL WIFE
(*Jessie Benton Fremont*)
ADVERSARY IN THE HOUSE
(*Eugene V. Debs*)

THE PASSIONATE JOURNEY
(*John Noble*)
THE PRESIDENT'S LADY
(*Rachel Jackson*)
LOVE IS ETERNAL
(*Mary Todd Lincoln*)
THE AGONY AND THE ECSTASY
(*Michelangelo*)

BIOGRAPHIES

SAILOR ON HORSEBACK
(*Jack London*)
THEY ALSO RAN
(*Defeated Presidential Candidates*)
CLARENCE DARROW FOR THE DEFENSE
EARL WARREN

HISTORY

MEN TO MATCH MY MOUNTAINS

NOVELS

PAGEANT OF YOUTH
FALSE WITNESS

BELLES-LETTRES

WE SPEAK FOR OURSELVES
(*A Self-Portrait of America*)

WITH JEAN STONE

DEAR THEO
(*An Autobiography of Vincent Van Gogh*)

BEAUTY AND THE ARTIST

A heart of flaming sulphur, flesh of tow,
bones of dry wood, a soul without a guide
to curb the fiery will, the ruffling pride
of fierce desires that from the passions flow;

a sightless mind that weak and lame doth go
mid snares and pitfalls scattered far and wide;—
what wonder if the first chance brand applied
to fuel massed like this should make it glow?

Add beauteous art, which, brought with us from heaven,
will conquer nature;—so divine a power
belongs to him who strives with every nerve.

If I was made for art, from childhood given
a prey for burning beauty to devour,
I blame the mistress I was born to serve.

Head of Moses, 1513-1516. (*Courtesy of Fototeca Unione, Roma*)

I, Michelangelo, Sculptor

AN AUTOBIOGRAPHY THROUGH LETTERS

EDITED BY IRVING AND JEAN STONE

FROM THE TRANSLATION BY CHARLES SPERONI

DOUBLEDAY & COMPANY, INC.

Garden City, New York, 1962

Alinari photographs from Art Reference Bureau

Library of Congress Catalog Card Number 62-11312
Copyright © 1962 by Doubleday & Company, Inc.
All Rights Reserved
Printed in the United States of America
First Edition

CONTENTS

CAST OF CHARACTERS

Family

Lodovico Buonarroti-Simoni, father
Francesco Buonarroti-Simoni, uncle
Cassandra, Francesco's wife
Lionardo, brother
Buonarroto, brother
Giovansimone, brother
Sigismondo (called Gismondo), brother
Lionardo, nephew, son of Buonarroto
Francesca, niece, daughter of Buonarroto
Michele Guicciardini, married to Francesca
Cassandra Ridolfi, married to Lionardo

The Popes

Julius II (Giuliano della Rovere) 1503–1513
Leo X (Giovanni de' Medici) 1513–1521
Adrian VI (Adrian Florensz) 1522–1523
Clement VII (Giulio de' Medici) 1523–1534
Paul III (Alessandro Farnese) 1534–1549
Julius III (Giovanni Maria de' Ciocchi del Monte) 1550–1555
Marcellus II (Marcello Cervini) 1555
Paul IV (Gian Pietro Caraffa) 1555–1559
Pius IV (Giovanni Angelo de' Medici) 1559–1565

Emissaries and Agents of the Popes

Cardinal Alidosi of Pavia
Domenico Buoninsegni
Chamberlain Pier Giovanni Aliotti
Jacopo Salviati (relative of the Medici)
Francesco Peri, Salviati clerk
Figiovanni (Prior of San Lorenzo)
Lorenzo Pucci
Giovanni Spina
Atalante, in charge of the fabric of St. Peter's
Girolamo Tiranno, emissary for the Duke of Urbino

Apprentices and Assistants

Piero d'Argiento and Pietro da Pistoia
Francesco Urbino (his wife is Cornelia)

Bastiano, Malenotti of San Gimignano, and Pier Luigi Gaeta
Michele, Settignano stoneworker
Meo di Chementi, Cecone, stoneworkers
Lapo and Lodovico, stonecarver and bronzecaster
Donato Benti, sculptor, supervisor of quarrying in Pietrasanta
Stefano, miniaturist
Cagione and Matteo di Cucherello, Carrarese marble suppliers

Artists and Friends

Francesco Granacci, painter
Sebastiano Luciani (called del Piombo), painter
Baccio d'Agniolo, architect and woodworker
Giuliano da Sangallo, architect
Ammannati, sculptor and architect
Raffaello da Montelupo, sculptor
Bugiardini, painter, former apprentice of Ghirlandaio
Giorgio Vasari, painter and writer
Tommaso de' Cavalieri, Roman noble
Lionardo Sellaio (the saddlemaker)
Donato Giannotti
Giovanni da Ricasoli, Florentine noble
Vittoria Colonna

Friends, and sometime agents and business managers

Baldassarre, Giovanni Balducci, bankers
Giovan Francesco Fattucci, Chaplain of Santa Maria del Fiore, and
    emissary of Pope Clement
Pier Francesco Borgherini, Florentine merchant
Lorenzo, Filippo and Roberto Strozzi, Florentine merchants and
    bankers
Luigi del Riccio, agent of the Strozzi in Rome
Bonifazio Fazi, banker
The Altoviti family, Florentine bankers living in Rome
The Tornabuoni, Strozzi, Gaddi, Florentine bankers
Bartolomeo Angiolini, business manager
Messer Agniolo, Herald of the Signoria
Messer Soderini, Gonfaloniere of Florence
Rafaello da Gagliano, notary and relative of Michelangelo's stepmother
For transfer of funds, Silvestro da Montauto, the Quaratesi, Bartolomeo
    Bettini.
For the investment of his savings and real estate purchases, the
    Spedalingo, Director and business manager of the Hospital of
    Santa Maria Nuova in Florence.

ILLUSTRATIONS

INTRODUCTION

When I decided that the next book I would write would be a long-thought-about biographical novel of Michelangelo, I learned that although there were already some twenty-five hundred books, monographs and articles published about this archetype of the artist, in most of the languages of the world, no one had ever brought over into English the body of nearly five hundred letters written by Michelangelo Buonarroti, all of them fastidiously preserved.

The best of the Michelangelo biographers, from Grimm and Symonds down through the modern authorities, Berenson, Goldscheider and De Tolnay, had translated those particular letters or extracts needed to illuminate their work. But no one had ever started from letter number one, written on July 2, 1496, and translated straight through to the last known letter from his hand, dated December 28, 1563, just a short time before his death. This lack is the more inexplicable when one realizes that the entire body of the letters had been published in Florence, under the editorship of Gaetano Milanesi, in 1875, to celebrate the four-hundredth anniversary of the birth of Michelangelo, March 6, 1475.

I had the conviction that any novel about Michelangelo would have to be based squarely on his letters; and that I would have to read and study them for at least a year before beginning to organize the structure of the novel. The first task then was to find a copy of Le Lettere di Michelangelo Buonarroti in the 1875 Florentine edition. It took four months before a copy finally turned up in a rare books store in Rome, and was sent to my home in Beverly Hills. The second task was far more difficult:

to find someone who was capable of translating sixteenth-century Italian into its closest equivalent in English.

The choice lay close at hand: Dr. Charles Speroni, founder of the Italian Department of the University of California Los Angeles, and professor of Italian there. Tuscan-born, he is a devoted scholar of the language and literature of the Italian Renaissance, and an expert philologist. Once Dr. Speroni understood the purpose for which the translation was to be used, he undertook the difficult assignment.

With the full translation of the colorful letters before me, still a third problem arose. Milanesi, the editor, had not chosen to publish the letters chronologically, as they had been written, but rather had broken them up into categorical groups, the first to Michelangelo's father, the second to his brother Buonarroto, the third to his brother Giovansimone, the fourth to his brother Sigismondo (called Gismondo), the fifth to his nephew Lionardo, son of Buonarroto, the sixth to "Diverse People." Thus it was not possible to move forward in a continuous line through Michelangelo's life, as revealed by his letters; one had to double back five times, over the years, and then interweave the parts of the story.

What further complicated the situation was that many of the letters were undated, and others dated in error. Nearly three-quarters of almost five hundred letters had to be checked against all existing documents, as well as the painstaking researches of my illustrious predecessors, in order to fit them into an accurate and continuous narrative. Nor had Milanesi annotated more than a small proportion of the persons, places, or events to which Michelangelo referred in his letters. It was part of my job to try to document every last reference, no matter how obscure or lost in the mists of history.

Thus the book was born, though the primary purpose of these efforts was to secure for my novel the most complete and accurate statement of what Michelangelo thought, felt, suffered, and said, over the seventy-five years of his creative life.

When it came time to edit the translated *Lettere*, certain decisions had to be made. In order to understand their nature it was first necessary to know something about the mail system of Italy during the period. There was no government post. All letters had to be privately carried, either by friends or relatives, by employees of banking houses which had offices in several of the city-states, or lastly, by the private mule trains, such as the one that left Rome for Florence on Saturday morning, and would sometimes carry letters for a fee.

As a result, many letters were lost, stolen or destroyed. When Michelangelo had anything important to communicate, he wrote the same letter twice, to be dispatched at an interval of several days; and on occasion he sent off three versions of the same message. When he had received no reply for two or three months to an urgent demand for information, or an acknowledgment of money sent, he would sit down and again write the almost identical letter.

There seemed little point in reproducing in this book the duplications. Where there were fresh letters, with new material, and only a few phrases or lines repeated, those phrases and lines were deleted, the balance of the letter left intact. Where new writing appeared in a duplicated letter, that material was retained. The utmost care has been taken to make sure that everything of even the slightest interest or value has been preserved. All persons and places and art works referred to by Michelangelo are clearly identified in the notes. The editing, and the footnotes, are the responsibility of Mrs. Stone and myself.

Michelangelo had one idiosyncrasy in his letter-writing which will interest the reader. In the beginning years, when he was working on his giant projects, he wrote only sparingly about the actual processes of creativity; a man carving marble or painting frescoes for fourteen hours a day has little inclination to pour himself out in letters. Yet nothing in his life, not the tiniest thought or feeling, hardship or chisel stroke, was ever forgotten. As the reader gets deeper and deeper into the book he will find Michelangelo writing long, impassioned letters about the Tomb of Julius II, the bronze statue of Julius, the Sistine Vault, and the Medici Chapel, in which he tells the whole story of what transpired in those crowded, hectic, harassed, gloriously creative years. Thus the story of his life starts quietly, but works itself up to a tremendous and shattering climax.

The Michelangelo sonnets included here are from the excellent and faithful John Addington Symonds translation, first published in the 1870s by this English authority on the Italian Renaissance. Since Michelangelo rarely if ever dated his poems, the approximate time of their writing has had to be surmised from surrounding events; or from the mention of individuals and art works, emotions and philosophies conveyed by the lines themselves. These sonnets were selected for two reasons: because they shed the most light on his inner thinking and feeling, thus implementing the letters; and because they constitute, in our opinion, the best of his poetical writings.

The title of the book derives from Michelangelo's delightful habit, even when writing to his father or brothers, of signing his letters, *Your Michelangelo, Sculptor in Rome* . . . or Florence, or Bologna, wherever he happened to be living or working at the time. Truly he never wanted to be anything but a sculptor. The times and circumstances forced him to become painter, architect, engineer, poet. There was a brief period, when he was at the height of his fame in Rome, while in his late sixties, when he instructed his nephew in Florence not to address his letters to Michelangelo Buonarroti, Sculptor in Rome, because he was now known as something considerably more than a sculptor. But this conceit passed, and the last years of his life were spent with hammer and chisel in hand, a block of pure white Carrara marble before him.

Irving Stone

Summitridge Place
Beverly Hills
    February 11, 1962

THE STORY BEFORE THE LETTERS

Michelangelo Buonarroti-Simoni was born on March 6, 1475, in the living-quarters apartment of the city hall in Caprese, one of a scattering of Tuscan villages at the head of the Tiber Valley, where his father had been invited to serve for six months as "visiting Mayor in residence." Lodovico Buonarroti was some thirty-one years of age, but this appears to have been the first paid job he had held. Inheritor, along with his brother Francesco, of the dwindling Buonarroti fortunes, which had been founded around 1228 by the first Buonarroto on record, the wealth originating in money-changing and trade, Lodovico was the shepherd of a thinning flock of golden florins left in the family estate. Though the Buonarroti were as old a family as the Medici, Strozzi or Tornabuoni, and were fond of boasting that they had been paying taxes in Florence for three hundred years, Michelangelo's grandfather dissipated almost the last of the Buonarroti estate, leaving to the brothers Lodovico and Francesco only the family villa and farm at Settignano, and one house in Florence with a disputed title.

The Buonarroti family were old hands at politics. Starting in 1260, the family had provided councilors and captains for the Guelph party and army; from 1343 to 1469 a Buonarroti had ten times been a member of the Florentine Priori or City Council, the most honored position in the city; between 1326 and 1475 eight Buonarroti had been *gonfaloniere* or mayor of the Santa Croce quarter; between 1375 and 1473 twelve had been among the Buonuomini or Council of Santa Croce, including Lodovico and his brother, Francesco, who were appointed in 1473, two years before Michelangelo's birth.

The move of the Buonarroti family from Settignano to

Caprese had two important influences on Michelangelo's life. His mother, Francesca di Neri di Miniato del Sera, who was carrying Michelangelo at the time, was thrown from her horse while riding across the rugged mountains and was injured. At Michelangelo's birth, it was necessary to call in the wife of a stonecarver across the little valley from the Buonarroti villa to wet-nurse the baby. The accident may have contributed to Francesca's death, six years later.

Michelangelo was at the age when all sons of well-placed Tuscan families started their schooling. However he never saw the inside of a classroom until four years later; and then only because his father and new stepmother, Lucrezia di Antonio di Sandro Ubaldini, moved to a rented house in the Via dei Bentaccordi in Florence.

The intervening four years, from the ages of six to ten, were crucial in the development of Michelangelo's life; for he spent most of the time with the stonecutter's family which, for many generations, had helped cut and trim the building blocks for the palaces of the city of Florence. Instead of learning to read and write in Greek and Latin, as was the Tuscan tradition, Michelangelo was trained on the stonecutter's alphabet as he saw it before him each day: the various hammer and chisel strokes carved into a permanent stone block in the workyard. For the next eighty years there was rarely a day in which he was comfortable or happy without a hammer and chisel in his hands, and a block of stone before him.

At the age of ten, Michelangelo was entered in Master Urbino's grammar school in Florence, which he attended for the next three years. From a combination of having started four years too late, and having absorbed other and more exciting interests in the meanwhile, Michelangelo never developed into a good student. He did not learn to read either Latin or Greek; when the members of the Florentine Academy wrote a petition to Leo X, asking that Dante's bones be brought back to Florence from Ravenna, Michelangelo was the only one who signed his name in the Italian vulgate. Michelangelo was always drawing in the margins of his notebooks, and playing hooky to sketch different sketches. or the Masaccios in the Brancacci chapel of Santa Maria del Carmine. Discouraged over his instruction of Michelangelo, Master Urbino proved to be a better teacher than he had known; because Michelangelo later went to live in the Medici Palace, and was exposed to the brilliance of the Plato Academy, he proved to be a natural student of philosophy, religion and poetry.

Though the Buonarroti-Simoni family had been wealthy for about three centuries, they had never become patrons of the arts, nor even modest collectors. There is no record of any Buonarroti having built a chapel, commissioned an artist to decorate it with paintings and sculpture, or having bought works of art that might have been available as other first families of Italy had done.

It was apparently from his mother's side of the family, the Rucellai, that Michelangelo inherited his passion for art. The Rucellai were also a very old and wealthy family in Florence; they had built a chapel in Santa Maria Novella, with a Madonna and frescoes. They also had constructed one of the most magnificent palaces in Florence, filled with outstanding art works; and here in the courtyard the scholars of Florence met often for discussions of poetry, philosophy and the drama. Michelangelo had no contact whatever with his mother's side of the family; but their heritage ran strong in his blood.

Michelangelo was the second of five brothers. The oldest, Lionardo, became a monk while quite young, entered the service of Savonarola, and died in 1510. His younger brother, Buonarroto, was his lifetime friend, and the next youngest one, Giovansimone, his lifetime dependent. The youngest, Sigismondo, remained an unlettered farmer. Lodovico, the father, had plans for his sons to go into trade and re-establish the Buonarroti fortune. Lodovico Buonarroti was against

~~opposed~~ Michelangelo's becoming an artist, for the arts of painting and sculpture were little more than handicrafts, enjoying no
position and little money or respect in the community. It was
Lodovico's fear that if Michelangelo became an artist, it would
be the blow that would destroy ~~the last vestige of~~ the Buonarroti
social position. Nevertheless, it was Michelangelo who, at the
age of fifteen when he entered the Medici Palace, began to support
the Buonarroti family, a task he continued up to his death and
through a number of generations beyond it.

The only art work left from Michelangelo's childhood is a
satyr which he drew on the wall of the kitchen in the family villa
at Settignano. ~~According to De Tolnay, whose scholarly five-
volume work on Michelangelo is the authority in the field, this
drawing was made before Michelangelo entered Ghirlandaio's
studio.~~

At the age of thirteen, through the good offices of a young
friend and neighbor by the name of Granacci, who had been
borrowing drawings from Ghirlandaio's study for Michelangelo
to study and copy, Michelangelo was taken into the Ghirlandaio
studio as an apprentice. He had difficulty being admitted because,
as Ghirlandaio said, thirteen was too old an age at which to
begin an art apprenticeship. However, as the ~~warmhearted~~
Ghirlandaio soon admitted, Michelangelo had a ~~draftsman's fist~~ talent,
and before the first year was finished, Michelangelo had been
allowed to sketch and actually paint figures in the frescoes of
Death of the Virgin and Baptism of Christ in the murals which
Ghirlandaio and his ~~bottega~~ students were painting in the ~~choir~~ church of Santa
Maria Novella.

Michelangelo did not like mural painting. As late as 1508
he ~~announced categorically to~~ told Pope Julius II, "It is ~~was~~ not ~~my~~ his
trade." Nevertheless he did enjoy the days of hard sketching, and
it was Ghirlandaio, ~~according to the statement of Bernard
Berenson,~~ who first taught Michelangelo how to use a pen. "The
penwork in these early drawings, ~~and indeed~~ more than one trick
of shorthand of later date, ~~tell truthfully~~ show that Ghirlandaio was

the man who first put a pen into Michelangelo's hand and taught him how to use it."⟩

⟨ Michelangelo had not attempted to be admitted to a sculptor's studio in Florence because by the time he was ready to apply, the golden age of Tuscan sculpture, begun when Pisano unearthed the first Roman sarcophagi in the Campo Santo in Pisa, about 1240, had vanished. Now there was no sculptor left in Florence. ⟩Ghiberti, who had trained Donatello and the Pollaiuolo brothers, had died some thirty-three years before. Donatello, who had died twenty-two years before, had operated a studio for half a century, but his followers Antonio Rossellino had been dead nine years, Luca della Robbia six, and Verrocchio had just died. The Pollaiuolo brothers had moved to Rome some four years before, and Bertoldo, Donatello's favorite and heir to his vast knowledge and workshop, was old and ill. Andrea and Giovanni della Robbia, trained by Luca della Robbia, had abandoned stone sculpture for enameled terra-cotta reliefs.

SK ⫯P

⟨ A decisive piece of good fortune befell Michelangelo at the end of his first year of apprenticeship to Ghirlandaio, when he was fourteen years old. Lorenzo de' Medici, *Il Magnifico*, whose great-grandfather Giovanni di Bicci had been the patron of Ghiberti, and whose grandfather Cosimo had been the lifetime patron of Donatello, opened a sculpture garden and school on a piece of land off Piazza San Marco. Il Magnifico called in Bertoldo to re-create the golden era of Florentine sculpture. Lorenzo asked Ghirlandaio to send him his two best and most likely apprentices; Ghirlandaio could not and would not withhold this *great* magnificent opportunity from Michelangelo. Michelangelo spent a year in the sculpture garden under the fierce tutelage of dying Bertoldo, who by this time was old and dying.

Here Michelangelo first learned the art of handling stone, not as a cutter of building blocks of *pietra serena*, but of marble itself. Toward the end of the first year he caught the attention of Lorenzo, who toured the garden frequently, and admired a faun that Michelangelo was carving. Lorenzo made the comment that

Michelangelo's faun had more teeth than the aged figure would probably possess; and when *Il Magnifico* returned a day or two later, Michelangelo had not only knocked out a few ~~strategic~~ teeth, but had also aged and darkened the faun's gums. This incident is ~~reputed~~ believed to be the cause of Lorenzo's having invited Michelangelo to move into the Medici Palace "as a son of the family"; but there can be little doubt that Bertoldo, who was living in the palace, had long been speaking of his young apprentice's promise.

In the Medici Palace, Michelangelo enjoyed not only the admiration and love of *Il Magnifico,* but was tutored almost daily by Lorenzo's intimates, the Plato Academy, an assemblage of some of the most brilliant and creative minds in all Europe) Marsilio Ficino, who had founded the Plato Academy for Cosimo, Lorenzo's grandfather; Cristoforo Landino, tutor to Lorenzo's father, and the authority on Dante's *Divine Comedy;* Angelo Poliziano, magnificent scholar in Latin and Greek, translator of Homer's *Iliad,* and a superb lyric poet in his own right; Pico della Mirandola, who read and wrote in twenty-two languages, described as divinely gifted as a scholar; and Girolamo Benivieni, who taught Michelangelo how to write sonnets. (During the two years he lived in the Medici Palace, up to the time of Lorenzo's death, Michelangelo went to school to these great minds, and received an education at least equal to that which he might have ~~secured~~ received at the old ~~and venerable~~ universities of Padua or Bologna.

The two remaining works from Michelangelo's apprenticeship years are the Madonna of the Stairs, carved in 1491, and Battle of the Centaurs in 1492, both of which are now in the Casa Buonarroti in Florence. He was just about to take on a life-size block of marble when Lorenzo de' Medici died, and left Michelangelo's life, ~~as indeed the entire life of Florence~~, in ~~chaos~~ confusion. Michelangelo returned home to live but could find neither the will nor the opportunity to continue his carving.

It was during this period, when he was eighteen years old, that he spent the better part of a year dissecting corpses in the hospital of the monastery of Santo Spirito. Dissection of human bodies was illegal in Florence, and punishable by death. As a consequence, he had to steal into the Santo Spirito dead room at midnight, and be gone before first light. He sealed himself into the room, with a candle for his only illumination, and one of his stepmother's kitchen knives and a pair of scissors for his work. This long bout of dissection, in which he studied every part of the human anatomy, contributed to the power and the authenticity of his marble carving. There is evidence that Prior Bichiellini, the head of Santo Spirito, and an old friend, made it possible for Michelangelo to carry on these dissections.

After a while he was invited back into the Medici Palace by Piero, son of Lorenzo, with whom he had never gotten along. During this period he carved a Hercules from a nine-foot spoiled block which he had bought from the Duomo workyard. This Hercules has been lost.

On November 9, 1494, the Florentines, who disliked Piero de' Medici's arrogance and wild way of life, and incited by Savonarola, rose and drove the Medici out of Florence, sacking the Medici Palace. Michelangelo, as a sometimes-member of the Medici family, felt that his life was in danger and fled over the Apennines to Bologna. He was befriended and taken into the home of the Aldovrandi, one of the controlling families of the city in politics and wealth, and dedicated patrons of the arts. Through Gianfrancesco Aldovrandi, Michelangelo secured a commission to carve three figures to complete the Dell'Arca tomb in San Domenico. Here, during the next thirteen months, he carved a St. Proculus, a St. Petronius, and an Angel with Candlestick, still to be seen in the church of San Domenico in Bologna.

Back in Florence, Michelangelo went to see *Il Magnifico's* cousins, Lorenzo and Giovanni de' Medici who, before Michelangelo had left for Bologna, had offered him a commission to carve a young St. John. He had refused the first offer because he sensed that the Medici cousins, who were working to take the control of Florence away from Piero, were attempting to use him for political purposes. Now that this problem was gone he gratefully accepted the commission, bought a small block of Carrara marble, and carved a young St. John setting out for the desert to preach in the wilderness. This piece is lost. The Medici cousins did not commission a second work, so Michelangelo obtained a piece of marble for himself, and sculptured a Sleeping Child. The cousin, Lorenzo de' Medici, suggested that if he would bury his child in the earth for a while, so that it would take on color, he could send it to Rome and sell it as an antique cupid for a good price.

Michelangelo took this advice. After a time the Medici cousin sent the Cupid by mule train to Rome to an agent by the name of Baldassarre, who sold it to Cardinal Riario di San Giorgio, grandnephew of Pope Sixtus IV. The fraud was uncovered, and Cardinal Riario sent one of his young men to Florence to find the sculptor and bring him to Rome.

ROME

Christus, July 2, 1496

Lorenzo of Pier Francesco de' Medici in Florence.

Magnificent Lorenzo – Just to inform you that last Saturday we arrived safely, and we went immediately to see the Cardinal of San Giorgio to whom I delivered your letter. I have the impression that he was happy to see me, and he insisted that I go at once to see certain statues,[1] where I spent the rest of the day. Then, on Sunday, the Cardinal came to the new house,[2] and asked for me. I went to him, and he asked me what I thought of the things I had seen. I gave him my opinion, and there is no question that there are many lovely things. Then the Cardinal asked me whether I felt I could do something beautiful. I replied that I would not do anything as beautiful as what he had shown me, but that he would see what I could do. We bought a piece of marble for a life-size statue; on Monday I shall begin to work.

Last Monday I delivered your other letters to Paolo Rucellai,[3] and happened to meet the Cavalcanti[3] fellow. Then I delivered your letter to Baldassarre,[4] and I asked him for the statue of the sleeping child,[5] offering to return him his money. He answered very harshly, saying that he would rather break it into a thousand pieces, that the child belonged to him because he bought it, that he had papers to prove that he had paid the person who sent it to him, and that he had no fears of having to return it. Some Florentine compatriots tried to fix up matters, but they did not succeed. Now I plan to take action through the Cardinal, as Baldassarre Balducci[6] has advised me to do.

May God protect you from evil.

---

[1] Greek and Roman antiquities.

[2] Of Cardinal Riario di San Giorgio, now the church Chancellory.

[3] Florentines living and trading in Rome.

[4] Antique art dealer.

[5] Cupid sold through Baldassarre to Cardinal Riario; returned by him on discovery of the hoax.

[6] Banker and friend.

In the name of God, March, 1497
To the prudent young man Buonarroto of Lodovico Buonarroti
in Florence. Dear brother – The letter from you heartened me
greatly; especially upon learning about the deeds of your seraphic
brother Jeronimo,[7] who has the whole city of Rome talking about
him. They say that he is a rotten-to-the-core heretic; so much so
that it is logical he should come and prophesy in Rome for a
while, and later he will be canonized. And so, let all his people
be of good cheer. Brother Mariano also says very bad things about
your Prophet.

I think of you all the time, so be in good spirits and keep
your nose to the grindstone as you have been doing. I want you
to know that I gave two ducats to Balducci here in Rome so
that he could have Francesco Strozzi give them to you in Florence. There is no news except that yesterday seven paper[8] bish-
ops were created, and five were hung. My best regards to all of
you, and especially to my father Lodovico, whom I esteem as
such. Written in the dark. May God help you.

In the name of the Lord, July 1, 1497
Master Lodovico Buonarroti.
Most honorable and dear father – Do not marvel if I am not coming back, for I have not yet been able to settle my affairs with
the Cardinal, and I do not want to leave until I am fully satisfied
and rewarded for my labors; one must be patient with such important people, for they cannot be pushed.

I wish to inform you that brother Lionardo[9] came back
here to Rome. He says that he was forced to flee from Viterbo,

---

[7] (Jeronimo) Girolamo Savonarola.
[8] Legal offenders to be pilloried with paper mitres on their heads.
[9] His older brother, a monk in Savonarola's Dominican order.
  Probably driven out for his adherence to Savonarola, now ex-
  communicated.

and that his cloak was taken from him. He wanted to come to Florence, and so I gave him a gold ducat which he asked me for his journey. I am still up in the air and do not know how things will turn out. I hope to be with you shortly.

Remember me to my friends.

August 19, 1497

Dearest father – I wish to tell you that last Friday Buonarroto[10] arrived here. As soon as I found out, I went to call on him at the inn. He informed me about how you are getting along, and he told me that Consiglio, the mercer,[11] vexes you a great deal, that he is unwilling to settle on any sort of agreement, and that he wants to have you arrested. I suggest that you try to come to an understanding with him, and give him a few ducats at once; then let me know what you agree that you should give him. I shall send it to you. Although, as I told you, I have little money, I shall try to borrow some to avoid taking it from the bank.

Do not be surprised if occasionally I write you in an angry tone; at times I am quite upset by things that befall one who is away from home.

I agreed to make a statue for Piero de' Medici,[12] and I bought a piece of marble. I never began it, however, because he never kept his promise to me. For this reason I keep to myself, and I am sculpturing an image for my own pleasure.[13] I bought a piece of marble for five ducats, but it wasn't any good. I just threw that money away. Later I bought another piece, also for five ducats. So that you must realize that I too spend money and have my own troubles. In spite of all this, I shall

---

[10] A younger brother.

[11] A merchant demanding ninety florins for merchandise from Lodovico.

[12] Son of Lorenzo de' Medici, driven out of Florence. Now in Rome.

[13] A second Cupid, also lost.

send you what you may ask me, even if I should have to sell myself as a slave.

Buonarroto has a room and he is comfortable, and as long as he will want to stay here he will never lack for anything. I do not have the facilities of keeping him with me, for I am living in someone else's home. The important thing is that I shall see to it that he never lacks what he needs.

FLORENCE

1501–1506

Michelangelo returned home in the spring of 1501, after having carved the life-size Bacchus for his friend Jacopo Galli in Rome, and the Pietà now in St. Peter's, for the French Cardinal Groslaye of San Dionigi. He had remained in Rome long enough to see the Pietà installed in the Chapel of the Kings of France in the old St. Peter's, and arrived back in Florence in time to immerse himself in what was to prove the greatest sculpture contest since Giovanni di Bicci, founder of the Medici fortunes, had decided the contest for the doors of the Baptistery in favor of Ghiberti. The piece of marble to be worked was some seventeen feet high, but had been ruined by an earlier sculptor by the name of Duccio who had gouged so deeply toward the center of the column that the giant piece of Carrara marble had lain in the cathedral workyard for about eighty years, declared spoiled and useless by succeeding generations of Tuscan sculptors.

Michelangelo turned the block's deficits into assets by bold and imaginative designing. However, before the decision was announced he found it necessary to take a commission for the Piccolomini Altar in Siena, where he completed five figures, now in the cathedral: a St. Francis, which he recarved after the marble had been spoiled by Torrigiano, Michelangelo's boyhood friend, who had smashed Michelangelo's nose during a quarrel over their comparative drawing talents; two Popes, Pius I and Gregory the Great; and St. Peter and St. Paul. He was unhappy with this assignment because he could not do what he conceived to be his best work on small figures which were to be imprisoned in wall niches, and consequently returned to Florence homesick and discouraged, only to find that he had won the Florentine commission. For the following three and a half years he was immersed in the carving of the David, now in the Accademia in Florence.

This period of five years, from 1501 to 1506, after which Michelangelo returned to Rome in hopes of entering the service of Pope Julius II, was one of the most productive of his life. In addition to the David and the five small figures in the Siena Cathedral, he carved a Madonna for two merchants of Bruges, now in Notre Dame in Bruges; the Pitti Madonna, now in the Bargello in Florence; the Taddei Madonna, in the Royal Academy of London; and began a St. Matthew, one of twelve Apostles commissioned by the Signoria for the cathedral.

In addition to these ten marble sculptures, Michelangelo also did his first painting since he left the Ghirlandaio studio at the age of fourteen. The first of these is his only easel painting, the Holy Family, otherwise known as the Doni Madonna, in the Uffizi in Florence.

The second painting, which the artists of Europe for almost a century declared had revolutionized European painting and created a new era, was commissioned by the Signoria, or City Council, of Florence; or more properly, was dragged out of them by Michelangelo, working on Gonfaloniere Soderini, long-time head of the Florentine Council and an ardent admirer of Michelangelo's work. Michelangelo, who had no desire to paint, was eager for this commission to fill one-half of the vast east wall of the Council Hall of the Signoria, or City Hall, in Florence, only because Leonardo da Vinci, his rival and sometimes enemy, had a commission to paint the first half of the wall. Michelangelo completed his cartoons for the fresco, but left for Rome at the prompting of his friend Giuliano da Sangallo, architect to Pope Julius II, who wrote that the Pontiff was interested in the sculptor, and was sending him money for the journey. The cartoons for this vast mural did not so much disappear as disintegrate, for they were studied, pored over, copied, cut into parts and stolen by painters who thronged to Florence from all over the world to see what Michelangelo had created.

Though Michelangelo had worked mightily during his five years in Florence, and had earned through the David the reputation of being the first sculptor of Italy, he left for Rome almost empty-pocketed. All of the moneys he had earned had gone to the support of his father and brothers and other members of the Buonarroti family, and what had been left had been invested in a farm or two, so that the family would have some means of support while Michelangelo was away, and until he could secure a commission from Pope Julius II.

This commission, as Michelangelo envisaged it, was to be a gigantic sculptural tomb for Julius II, with thirty to forty larger than life-size figures. But soon after Michelangelo began to work, the Pope decided that it was bad luck to have one's tomb created while still alive; and an insulted Michelangelo fled back to Florence. The Pope, angry, insisted that Michelangelo return to Rome; Michelangelo refused, saying that he would do his work only in Florence. It was not until his friend, Gonfaloniere Soderini, told him, "We do not wish to go to war on your account," that Michelangelo gave in and went to Bologna, where Julius II was camped as commander of the Papal troops that had conquered the city.

ROME—FLORENCE

1496–1506

Rome, January 31, 1506

Most honorable father—I learned from one of your letters that the Spedalingo[1] has never returned to town. Thus, you did not close the farm deal as was your hope. It made me angry also, for I thought that by now it was yours. I have a feeling that he left town purposely to keep the money and the farm. If this should be the case, I will take my money out of his hands, and keep it elsewhere.

If my marbles[2] only arrived my work would progress satisfactorily here; but I seem to be very unlucky in this, for, since I have been here, we have not had two days of good weather. It so happened that several days ago, in spite of the bad weather, a boat was lucky enough to land; but as soon as I had the marbles unloaded, the river rose and covered them in such a way that I have not been able yet to start doing anything. I keep on making promises to the Pope[3] and giving him hope so that he may not become angry with me. I hope that the weather will settle, and that I will soon begin to work. May God grant it!

I beg you to take all those drawings, that is all those papers I put in that sack I told you about, and to make a bundle of them and send it to me with a driver. Be sure to wrap it well against the rain; and take care, when you wrap it up, not to damage a single sheet. Also tell the driver to be careful with it, for there are some very important things. Write me the name of the driver and how much I should give him.

I beg you to have the marble bas-relief of Our Lady[4] brought into the house and not to let anybody see it. If you should have to borrow money, go right ahead and do it, for if my marbles arrive,

---

[1] Director of the Hospital of Santa Maria Nuova and general business manager, who banked Michelangelo's funds for him in Florence.

[2] Ordered from Carrara for Pope Julius's Tomb.

[3] Julius II (1503–1513).

[4] Madonna of the Stairs, in Casa Buonarroti, Florence.

I shall soon send you money for this purpose and for yourself.

Who was the recipient in Lucca of the fifty ducats I sent for Matteo di Cucherello in Carrara?[5] I beg you to let me know whom Bonifazio[6] has in Lucca. I give you and Giovansimone[7] my clothes and my shirts. Pray to God that my things go well; and invest up to a thousand of my ducats in land, if that much money is left.

I beg you to send Piero d'Argiento[8] the letter I wrote him. It might be a good idea to send it through the Jesuates,[9] for often those monks go there.

Florence, May 2, 1506

Giuliano da Sangallo, Florentine Architect to Pope Julius in Rome.

Giuliano – I was informed by a letter of yours that the Pope was angry at my departure, and that His Holiness is ready to make the deposit and to do what we agreed upon; also, that he wants me to return and not to worry about anything.

About my departure, it is a fact that on Holy Saturday I heard the Pope say at the table, to a jeweler and to the master of ceremonies with whom he was conversing, that he did not want to spend another penny on stones, either large or small. This amazed me a great deal: just the same, before leaving, I asked him for part of the money I needed to continue the work. His Holiness answered me to return on Monday. I returned there on Monday, Tuesday, Wednesday and Thursday. At last on Friday morning I was turned out of doors, that is chased away. The man who sent me away said that he knew who I was, but that he had such orders. I was thrown in great despair. But this was not

---

[5] Carrarese quarrier and marble supplier.
[6] Agent for the transfer of funds.
[7] A younger brother.
[8] His houseboy and helper.
[9] Then known as the *Ingiesuati*.

the only cause of my departure: suffice it to say that it made me think that if I remained in Rome, my tomb would be made before that of the Pope.[10]

Now you write me on behalf of the Pope. Make His Holiness understand that I am as willing as I ever was to carry out the work, and if he wants by all means to make that tomb,[11] he should not mind where I carry out my work, as long as within the five-year period we agreed upon, it is set up in the place of his choice in St. Peter's, and it is as beautiful as I promised it would be: for I am sure that if it is carried out, there will be nothing like it in the whole world.

Now, if His Holiness wants me to proceed, let him set up said deposit, and I will have the numerous blocks of marbles I ordered from Carrara and those I have in Rome sent here, even if this should be against my interest. After I finish each piece, I could send it along, so that His Holiness would derive the same pleasure from my work as if I were in Rome. As for the money for the work, I will make out a written obligation to suit His Holiness, and I will give him whatever guarantee he asks of me, and the whole city of Florence will be my witness. I will do it better here and with more devotion, because I will not have to think about so many things. Nothing more.

---

[10] Michelangelo feared that he had made violent enemies in Rome.

[11] Of forty life-size or larger marble figures.

BOLOGNA

1506–1508

December 19, 1506

Buonarroto – Today I received one of your letters in which you recommend to me Piero Aldobrandini, and ask me to do for him what he will ask. I want you to know that he wrote me asking that I make for him a dagger-blade, and that I be sure that it be a very beautiful thing. To start with, I do not know how I will be able to please him: first of all because it is not my profession; in the second place, because I do not have the time to attend to it. Just the same, I shall try to please him as well as I can within one month.

I have heard everything concerning all of you, and especially concerning Giovansimone[1] I am happy that he comes to your shop[2] and that he is anxious to do well, for I am willing to help him as well as the rest of you. If God helps me, as he always has done, I hope that during this Lenten period I shall finish what I have to do here,[3] and then I shall return to Florence. Concerning the money you tell me Giovansimone wants to invest in a shop, it seems to me that he ought to wait four more months and make one grand splash. Tell him for me to continue to do well, and if he still wants the money, we will have to use the money we have in Florence, for as yet I do not have any to send from here. What they give me here for my work is little and uncertain. And furthermore something might happen to me that would cause my death.

As regards Giovansimone's proposed visit here, I do not advise it yet for I am lodged in a bad room. I have bought only one bed in which four of us sleep. If he insists on coming, let him wait until I cast the statue I am making. At that time I shall send Lapo and Lodovico, who are helping me, back to Florence, and I shall send Giovansimone a horse so that he may come here on horseback, and not like a dog.

Pray God for me that everything goes well.

---

[1] His third brother.
[2] The Strozzi wool shop where Buonarroto is working.
[3] A fourteen-foot bronze portrait of Julius II.

January 22, 1507

Buonarroto – I gather that Lodovico has contracted for Monna Zanobia's farm. I want you to know that if he has written me about it, I never received his letter.

As for Giovansimone, as soon as I have cast the statue I will by all means have him come here, and it will be much easier, for I will have become rid of all the expenses which I have now.

I think I shall be ready to cast my statue around the middle of Lent; so, pray God that it turns out well; for, if it does, I think I will be in luck with the present Pope. If I cast it at mid-Lent, and if it is a success, I hope to be in Florence during the Easter holidays. Tell Piero Aldobrandini that I had his blade made by the best master of these things here in Bologna. After I get it, if I think it is well done, I shall send it to him; if not I'll have it made over again. Tell him not to be surprised if I do not please him with the deserved promptness, for I have such a dearth of time that I cannot help it.

February 1, 1507

Buonarroto – I want you to know that last Friday evening at nine o'clock Pope Julius came to the house where I work and remained about half an hour to watch me working; then he gave me his blessing and left. He indicated that he is satisfied with what I am doing. Pray God that it turns out well, for, if that comes to pass, I hope to enter again into his good graces. I believe he will leave Bologna the coming Carnival; that's what the common people say. He does not leave things in good order here. As people say, there is something very suspicious going on; but one shouldn't look for it or write about it.

Also I inform you further that Friday morning I dismissed Lapo[4] and Lodovico[5] who were here at my service. I fired Lapo

---

[4] A Florentine stonecarver.
[5] A Florentine bronzecaster.

because he is shrewd and mean, and because he did not do what I expected of him. Lodovico is better, and I would have kept him two more months; but not to be shamed alone, Lapo incited him so much that both left. Both of them together are not worth three cents. Go to Messer Agniolo, the Herald of the Signoria,[6] for I wrote him everything; he is very kind and he will give you the details.

I have heard about Giovansimone. I am happy that he is attending the shops of your teachers and that he is striving to do well. If this thing turns out well, I hope to set you all up, if you are wise. Concerning the other farm which is next to Monna Zanobia's, tell Lodovico that if he likes it he should look into it.

February 8, 1507

Lodovico.

Most honorable father – I gather that Lapo and Lodovico have spoken to you. I deserve being rebuked as a bad person and as a sinner[7] as much as anyone and perhaps more. But I feel no guilt as regards them or anybody else; I am only guilty of this, that I do more than I should. Anybody with whom I have had anything to do knows how generous I am. And if anyone knows,

---

[6] Ruling Council of the Florentine city-state.

[7] Aldo Fortuna, the greatest of the Michelangelo archivists, who is now publishing his work in the new Il Vasari, Arezzo, 1958–on, maintains on the basis of his collateral evidence that Michelangelo had an affair with a Bolognese courtesan. He identifies the two sonnets on pages 32 and 38 as written to this girl; as does F. Filippini in Michelangelo in Bologna (Liceo Scientifico Righi, Bologna Annuario IV, 1926–27, p. 39), in which he traces the flower garland, the "dress which presses upon the breasts," the golden threads touching the neck, the close-fitting belt, as being the dress and jewelry peculiar to the Bolognese ladies of this period. There is, however, some difference of opinion among the authorities as to when the sonnets were written, Filippini claiming the year 1494–95, and Frey, the second visit to Bologna, 1507–08.

Lapo and Lodovico know it better than anybody else; for one of them during the last month and a half received twenty-seven ducats, and the other eighteen large ones, plus expenses. Therefore I beg you not to let them pull the wool over your eyes. As a matter of fact, their great resentment, especially Lapo's, the wretch, consisted in this: they had told everybody that they were the artists of this work. Lapo especially, but actually both of them, never realized that he was not the boss, until I fired him. That's the only thing that made him realize that he was working for me. And since he had been such a busybody and had begun to boast of the favor of the Pope, he was surprised when I threw him out like a dog. I regret that he owes me seven ducats. As a matter of fact, if he has any conscience, he ought to return to me the others he has received. And that's that. Go to see Messer Agniolo, take Granacci[8] along; then you will find out what scoundrels they are. However, I beg you to keep to yourself what I am writing you about Lodovico, for if I should not find another man to come here and found metal, I will try to bring him back; for to tell the truth, I did not throw him out of here. But since Lapo was too ashamed to return alone, he misguided Lodovico in order to make it easier for himself. Do not quarrel with Lapo, for there is too much shame involved.

Here is one of the things Lapo is grumbling about. Once I bought seven hundred and twenty pounds of wax. Before buying it I said to Lapo to see how cheaply he could get it. Lapo told me that we could not get it for one penny less than nine large ducats and twenty bolognini a hundred. And he told me to buy it at once, since we had found such a bargain. I told him to go back and see whether he could have those forty cents a hundred knocked off, and I would take it. He replied that the Bolognese people would be the last people in the world to take off a penny of what they ask. At that point I became suspicious and let the

---

[8] His oldest boyhood friend, who got Michelangelo apprenticed to Ghirlandaio.

whole thing drop. Later in the same day I took Piero[9] aside and said to him secretly to go and find out for what price he could get the wax. Piero went to see the same dealer as Lapo, and got the price down to eight ducats and a half. This is one of the strange things I did to Lapo. Indeed it seemed strange to him that I should catch that deception. He may have cheated me many times about which I know nothing, for I trusted him. I never saw a man who looked more honest than he.

———————◆◆———————

THE GARLAND AND THE GIRDLE

What joy hath yon glad wreath of flowers that is
around her golden hair so deftly twined,
each blossom pressing forward from behind,
as though to be the first her brows to kiss!

The livelong day her dress hath perfect bliss,
that now reveals her breast, now seems to bind:
and that fair woven net of gold refined
rests on her cheek and throat in happiness!

Yet still more blissful seems to me the band
gilt at the tips, so sweetly doth it ring
and clasp the bosom that it serves to lace:

yea, and the belt to such as understand,
bound round her waist, saith: here I'd ever cling.—
What would my arms do in that girdle's place?

———————◆◆———————

February 24, 1507

Buonarroto—Over fifteen days ago I sent Lodovico[10] a certain sum of money for a certain matter, and I have never received a reply. I am quite amazed. He is hardly the man to trust with an important matter when the next opportunity presents itself. I should

---

[9] Piero d'Argiento, now his assistant.
[10] Michelangelo is referring to his father.

think he would have written one hundred letters to be sure I received at least one. See that he lets me know by all means what he has done.

Yesterday I sent someone to see whether Piero Aldobrandini's dagger was finished. The smith has mocked me for a solid month, but the truth is that he could not have done otherwise, for in connection with the departure of the Court he had to work on the weapons of all the courtiers, and he was extremely busy. The Pope left early on Monday morning.

March 6, 1507

Buonarroto – With great difficulty this morning I was finally able to get delivery of the dagger; my Piero was so fed up with the countless times he had to call at the smith's, that he came within an inch of striking him on the head with it. The dagger will be brought to Florence by the goldsmith Chiaro di Bartolomeo. See that Chiaro gets paid for the carriage. If Piero does not like it, tell him to let me know, and I shall have another one made. Here in Bologna, since the court arrived, every artisan and every profession has gone up in reputation and rank. I too have had my own troubles, for after the arrival of the Court, this dagger-maker alone had more business than the whole city of Bologna ever had before. I have no time to write.

March 26, 1507

Buonarroto – Several days ago I received one of your letters, and from it I learned the whole story about the dagger and Piero Aldobrandini. I wish to tell you that, had it not been for your sake, I would have let him babble all he wanted. I want you to know that the blade which I sent was made to his specifications, for he sent me a paper blade and wrote me to have it made exactly like it; and so I did. Therefore, if he wanted a dagger, he had no business sending me the measurements of a rapier. If he should come to get the blade, don't give it to him; welcome him, and tell him that I gave it to a friend of mine: that's all.

I want you to know that it cost me nineteen carlini plus thirteen quattrini.

I hope to cast my statue within one month: therefore, pray God that my task will come to a good end, so that I may soon return to Florence. Remember me to Granacci. Here the plague is flaring up, and it is of the bad type, for, wherever it strikes it does not spare anybody. According to what they tell me it has struck forty homes.

March 31, 1507

Buonarroto – Know, then that I am well and that my work is proceeding all right: the Lord be thanked. The fact is that it is taking one more month than I had expected.

Concerning the setting up of a shop or a company for you, I want by all means to do it, but you must be patient until I come to Florence.

You tell me that Aldobrandini refused the dagger. Perhaps fate had not intended that he should carry it at his belt, all the more so since you were asked for it by a much more important man than he, Filippo Strozzi.[11] Therefore go and present it to him as a gift from you without mentioning the cost.

You will find enclosed a letter for Sangallo[12] in Rome. Give it to Baccio d'Agniolo;[13] he will find a good way to send it.

April 20, 1507

Giovansimone – I did not reply to a letter I received several days ago, because I did not have time. My statue here is coming along well, and so I hope it will come to a satisfactory conclusion: may God grant it. When this comes to pass, I shall come immediately to Florence, and I will do what I promised all of you,

---

[11] Michelangelo's friend, a leading Florentine merchant and banker.
[12] Giuliano da Sangallo, Michelangelo's friend, Julius II's architect.
[13] Florentine architect and woodworker.

namely to help you with what I have, in whatever manner you and father will want. Therefore, be of good cheer, go to the shop as often as you can, for I hope that you will soon have a shop of your own, and if you know the profession and how to manage, it will be very useful to you. So put your heart in it.

You write me about a certain physician friend of yours, who told you that the plague is serious business. There is quite an epidemic here, and these Bolognese people don't realize yet that it is deadly. For this reason I wish he would come here and speak to them with the voice of experience, for this would be very useful to these people.

This is all the paper I have. I hope to be in Florence soon.

April 20, 1507

Buonarroto—You tell me that my letters take a long time to get there; there is nothing I can do about it, for the postal service is a mess. I'd like you to go to the Herald[14] and tell him that since I have never received an answer concerning master Bernardino,[15] I have thought that Bernardino is not going to come here for fear of the plague. Therefore, I have hired a Frenchman in his place. I did this because I could no longer wait. Give my regards to his lordship the Gonfaloniere.[16] Remember me to Giovanni da Ricasoli.[17]

April 28, 1507

Giovansimone—I am sure Buonarroto informed you of my intention, and that is the way it is. God willing, as soon as I come to Florence, I will set you up in business by yourselves, or with a company, whichever will seem safest to us. So be of good cheer,

---

[14] Messer Agniolo, an officer of the Florentine city-state.

[15] A bronzecaster from Milan.

[16] Piero Soderini, permanent leader of the Florentine Republic, friend and admirer of Michelangelo.

[17] Florentine noble and friend.

for I am telling you the actual truth. I have finished my wax statue. Next week I will make the mold on it, and I think that in twenty or twenty-five days it will be finished. Then I will give the order to cast it, and if it comes out well, in a little while I will be in Florence.

May 2, 1507

Giovansimone – I wish to tell you that before the next two months have passed I will be in Florence: may God wish it so. Be of good spirits, you cannot imagine what a great and wonderful thing is in store for you. I want you to know that Bologna is bristling with weapons; for the last four days the city has been up in arms, with great confusion and danger, especially through the party of the Church. This was brought about by the exiles, namely the Bentivogli,[18] who tried to get back into the city with a multitude of people. However, I believe that the great courage and prudence of the papal Legate,[19] who took some strong measures, has again freed the city from them. In fact this evening at eleven P.M., the news came from their camp that they were retreating with little honor on their part. Nothing else. Pray God for me, and live happily, for I shall soon be there.

May 26, 1507

Buonarroto – On his trip here, master Bernardino brought me one of your letters. I hear you are all in good health, except Giovansimone. I hope soon to be there. It grieves me not to be able to help him. Also tell Lodovico that toward the middle of next month I think I will be able to cast my statue without fail; so if he wants to have a prayer recited or do something for its success, he should do it about that time. Tell him that I beg this of him.

---

[18] The ruling family of Bologna, expelled by the Pope's army. As soon as Julius II departed, they tried to retake the city.
[19] The Cardinal of Pavia, a friend to Michelangelo and emissary of Pope Julius II.

June 20, 1507

Buonarroto – I want you to know that it has not been cast yet, but this coming Saturday we will cast it at all costs; and, if it turns out well, as I think, within a few days I shall be in Florence.

July 6, 1507

Buonarroto – I want you to know that we cast my statue, but that I did not have too much luck with it. The reason was that master Bernardino, either through ignorance or through bad luck, did not found the metal well. Suffice it to say that my statue came out well as far as the waist; the rest of the material, namely half of the metal, remained in the furnace, for it was not fused; so that, in order to take it out it is necessary that I dismantle the furnace. That is what I am doing now, and I shall have it put together again this week. Next week we shall pour from the top, and I will finish filling the mould. I think that from this evil there will come a lot of good, but not without a great deal of suffering, fatigue and expense. I had so much faith in Bernardino that I would have believed he could fuse metal without fire; just the same, this does not indicate that he is not a good artisan and that he did not put his heart in this work. But he who works, at times fails. And he certainly did fail to my and his own detriment, for he is so ashamed that he does not dare lift his eyes anywhere in Bologna.

If this thing turns out well, I think that in fifteen or twenty days I will be all through and I will come to Florence. If it shouldn't come out well, I might have to try once more.

July 10, 1507

Buonarroto – Concerning my statue here, I think that although it met with some bad luck, it will turn out very well, although I know nothing about it yet. We have thrown in again from the top what was lacking, but I have been unable to see how it is coming along, for the clay is so hot that it cannot be uncovered. By next week I will know for sure. Master Bernardino left here yesterday. If he speaks to you, be civil with him.

THE SILKWORM

Kind to the world, but to itself unkind,
a worm is born, that dying noiselessly
despoils itself to clothe fair limbs, and be
in its true worth by death alone divined.

Oh, would that I might die, for her to find
raiment in my outworn mortality!
That, changing like the snake, I might be free
to cast the slough wherein I dwell confined!

Nay, were it mine, that shaggy fleece that stays,
woven and wrought into a vestment fair,
around her beauteous bosom in such bliss!

All through the day she'd clasp me! Would I were
the shoes that bear her burden! When the ways
were wet with rain, her feet I then should kiss!

———◆◆———

July 18, 1507

Buonarroto—My work could have turned out much better and
also much worse. As far as I can tell, the whole statue came out;
but I haven't yet uncovered the whole thing. I figure it will take
a few months time to clean it up, because it did not come out
very clean. Just the same we must thank God, for, as I say, it
could have been worse. If Salvestro del Pollaiuolo[20] or anyone
else should speak to you, tell them that I do not need anybody,
for I wouldn't want somebody or other to come out here and be
a burden to me. I have spent so much, that I hardly have
enough left for myself to live on, let alone support others.

August 2, 1507

Buonarroto—I did not write last week because I was unable. I
want you to know that the more I uncovered my statue, the
better it looked, and I see that it is not as bad as I thought it

---

[20] Nephew of the sculptor Pollaiuolo, an experienced caster.

would be. I feel the results were good, considering what might have happened; therefore, we have reason to be thankful to God. As far as I can tell, I think I will be busy at any rate for one month and a half cleaning it up. Remember me to my friends, Giovanni da Ricasoli, Granacci and Messer Agniolo.

August 19, 1507

Buonarroto – I think that my statue will be all right. The truth of the matter is that there is a great deal of hard work connected with it; yet I am sure that I am not going to run any more dangers, nor have any more excessive expenditures, for I have no other obligation than to leave it finished where it stands. You write me that in Florence it is very warm, and that things are expensive. I want you to know that here too it has been hot, for, since I have been here, it has rained only once; I don't think it has ever been so hot anywhere in the whole world. Here wine is as expensive as in Florence, but it is of the worst kind; and the same is true of everything else, so that it is not pleasant living here. I can hardly wait to get back to Florence.

September 29, 1507

Buonarroto – It is over a month since I received your last letter. I beg that either you or Giovansimone write me something. I do not write you because I do not have time. This because matters have become so complicated in connection with my work, that if it weren't for my haste, I would remain here for another six months. Just the same, I think I will have it finished by All Saints' Day or shortly later; I am hurrying things along so much that I hardly take time out to eat. Be of good cheer, and be patient until then. Nothing else.

October, 1507

Buonarroto – I haven't the time to answer your last letter, but I want you to know that I am well and that I shall soon have finished; I think my work will bring much honor upon me. I owe all of this to the grace of God. As soon as I am through here, I shall return to Florence and I shall take care of all the things you write me about, so that all of you, Lodovico and Giovansimone included will be happy.

I beg you to go and see Sangallo and to tell him that I think I shall finish soon.

I do not know what the date is today, but I know that yesterday was St. Luke's feast day. Figure it out yourself.

November 10, 1507

Buonarroto – I want you to understand that I am more anxious to return to Florence than you all are to have me back. Here I live in the greatest discomfort, and all I do is to work extremely hard day and night. The labor I am forced to do is such that if I were to make another statue I do not think I would be able to survive it, for it has been a tremendous enterprise. If this job had fallen into the hands of someone else, it would have been too bad for him. I believe that somebody's prayers have helped me and kept me in good health, for it was against the opinion of the whole city of Bologna that I should ever finish it. After the statue was cast, and even before, there was no one who believed that I would ever cast it. The fact is that I have brought my work close to a satisfactory conclusion, but I shall not have completed it until after the end of this month. Next month I will certainly be through, and I shall return. I shall not fail to do what I have promised all of you . . .

Give courage to Lodovico and to Giovansimone for me. Tend to learning and to running the shop properly so that when you need to, you will know how.

December 21, 1507

Buonarroto – I am enclosing a letter of great importance for the Cardinal of Pavia in Rome. Go to see Sangallo and see whether he has a good way of sending it. Tell him that I shall soon be there.

January, 1508

Buonarroto – Have patience and be of good cheer, for shortly I
will be there, and I will let you boys do what you want, either
with Lorenzo Strozzi or by yourselves, whichever way you think
will be more advantageous and safer.

I think that by all means I will leave within fifteen days, or
be just about ready to leave. I can hardly wait, for here I live in
such a wretched fashion that, if you knew, you would be sorry
for me. I do not know what the date is today, but I know that
tomorrow is the feast of the Epiphany.

January 18, 1508

Buonarroto – I thought I would be in Florence fifteen days ago,
because I was figuring that as soon as my statue was finished
they would set it up where it was meant to be.[21] Now they are
loafing and doing nothing about it, and I have orders from the
Pope not to leave until the statue has been set up. I feel like I
am stuck. I shall wait and see all this week, and if they give me
no further instructions, I will come regardless, without obeying
the orders.

---

[21] The statue was set in place February 21, 1508 on the facade of
the church of San Petronio in Bologna.

Three years after Michelangelo left Bologna, the Bolognese people pulled the bronze statue of Julius II off its niche on the facade of San Petronio, had it melted down and cast into a cannon called Giulia, to be used against Papal troops.

Back in Florence, the Signoria authorized Gonfaloniere Soderini to commission his friend, Michelangelo, to carve a giant marble Hercules (never begun) to match his David. Michelangelo went to see his friend Lorenzo Strozzi, who had bought his earlier Hercules and who also owned a prosperous wool shop. Strozzi agreed to accept from Michelangelo a modest sum in his brothers' names, so that they might share a little in the profits.

While waiting for a marble column from Carrara for the Hercules, Michelangelo resumed work on his St. Matthew. He was deep into the block, overjoyed to be using hammer and chisel on stone after the long bout with clay and bronze, when Gonfaloniere Soderini showed him a *breve* from the Pope summoning him to Rome, saying that he had good news for Michelangelo. This could only mean that he would be allowed to proceed on the tomb carvings.

Instead, Julius II ordered Michelangelo to paint the ceiling of the Sistine Chapel. Michelangelo cried out, "Painting is not my trade!" Nevertheless, he agreed to paint the Twelve Apostles, on the Pope's word that once the vault was properly decorated, he could return permanently to his marble carving.

Michelangelo assembled in Rome a *bottega* of his Florentine fellow artists, largely composed of those with whom he had worked at Ghirlandaio's. But after a year of trying to achieve what the Pope had described as "suitable decorations" he realized that he could never be content with the Pope's concept, dismissed his assistants, and evolved the sublime concept of Genesis for the vault. Judged from his drawings and designs, it was a task that would take forty years to complete . . . and make it impossible for Michelangelo ever to get back to marble sculpture.

ROME

1508–1515

May 13, 1508

Reverend Father in Christ, brother Jacopo Gesuato, Florence. Brother Jacopo – Since I have to have painted, or to paint myself certain things here,[1] I must inform you that I need a certain quantity of beautiful blues; and if you could help me to secure them now, you would be rendering me a great service. Therefore, try to send here to your brothers the quantity you have available, as long as they are beautiful. And I promise you to buy them for the right price.

July 2, 1508

Buonarroto – The bearer of this letter will be a young Spaniard[2] who is coming there to learn to paint. He has asked me to show him the cartoon I began in the Sala; therefore, see that he gets the keys,[3] and if you can help him in any way do it for my sake, for he is a fine young man.

Giovansimone is here. This last week he was ill; which, on top of my other troubles, worried me quite a bit. If he follows my advice he will soon return to Florence, for I do not think this air is good for him.

July, 1508

Buonarroto – I have learned from your letter how things are in Florence. I am very sorry to hear about them, all the more since I see that the family is in need, especially Lodovico, who you say should buy something to put on his back. I wrote Lodovico telling him that I had here marbles worth fourteen hundred large ducats, that I have a debt of one hundred forty large ducats on them, and that I am without money. I have to pay that debt, and I must live myself; furthermore, I have the rent to pay. So

---

[1] The Sistine Chapel ceiling.

[2] Probably the painter Alonzo Berruguete.

[3] To the Hall of the Council in the Signoria, where the cartoon is stored at this time.

1. Madonna of the Stairs, *circa* 1491. (*Courtesy of Alinari*)

2. Page from a letter of Michelangelo to the Supervisors of the Fabric of St. Peter's, 1560. (*Courtesy of Art Reference Bureau*)

that I have a lot of troubles, but I hope to get out of them soon and to be able to help you.

You write me to find some profession[4] for you. I wouldn't know what to find, nor what to look for. I will send for you as soon as I can. That's all.

July 31, 1508

Buonarroto—I am sending you the repudiation of Francesco's[5] inheritance which I had drawn up by a notary, and which Lodovico wants.

I inform you that on Tuesday morning Piero Basso[6] left here ailing, against my will. I did not like it both because I have been left all alone, and because I am afraid he may die on the way. He had developed such a fixation against the air of Rome, that I was unable to hold him back. In the present letter you will find one for Giovanni Michi,[7] who formerly wanted to come here and stay with me, and now writes that he is still willing. Therefore, I beg you to go to the San Lorenzo district, find him, and try to get a definite answer, for I cannot stay alone, and it is difficult to find somebody one can trust.

The family should bid for the lot of Nicolò della Buca, and ask for one month's time. Around the middle of August I have to send some money to Florence to purchase some blue, and I will send also the money for Nicolò. I enclose a letter for Granacci. Deliver it because it is urgent.

August, 1508

Most honorable father—I received a letter from a nun who says she is an aunt of ours. She says that she is very poor and in dire need, and she begs me to give her some alms.[8] For this reason

---

[4] Buonarroto's only job was apprentice in the Strozzi wool shop.
[5] His uncle, who had just died.
[6] Stonecutter who came to assist him in Rome.
[7] Florentine stonecarver.
[8] This relationship was never proved.

I am sending you five large ducats. Give her four and a half for the love of God. Give the other half to Buonarroto, and please tell him to buy for me from Francesco Granacci or some other painter, one ounce of lacquer, or as much as can be had for that much money.

I believe that the nun aunt is in the convent of San Giuliano. I beg you to try and find out whether she really is in great need of help, for I do not like the way she wrote me. For this reason I wonder whether I am being duped. In case you discover that the whole thing is a fraud, keep the money for yourself.

January 27, 1509

Dearest father – Today I received a letter from you, and it caused me much grief. It grieves me to know that you are so frightened. For, even if Cassandra[9] deprived you of all you have in this world, you would not lack a good livelihood, were I the only one to help you. I myself am quite concerned, for this Pope hasn't given me a single grosso[10] for a whole year, and I am not asking for any, for my work is not progressing in such a way as to make me think that I deserve anything. This is due to the difficulty of the work, and also to the fact that this is not my profession.[11] Yet I am wasting my time fruitlessly. God help me. If you need money, go to the Spedalingo and have him give you up to fifteen ducats; also, let me know how much you have left. During the last few days, Jacopo,[12] the painter whom I called here, left Rome. Since he complained about me here, I imagine that he will complain about me in Florence also. I want you to lend a deaf ear. That's all. He is a thousand times wrong.

---

[9] His Uncle Francesco's widow, who was bringing suit against the family because they refused the inheritance of debts left by Francesco.

[10] A small silver coin.

[11] Painting.

[12] Jacopo dell'Indaco, a fellow apprentice at Ghirlandaio's studio, brought to Rome to help on the Sistine fresco.

TO POPE JULIUS II

My Lord! if ever ancient saw spake sooth,
hear this which saith: Who can, doth never will.
Lo! thou hast lent thine ear to fables still,
rewarding those who hate the name of truth.

I am thy drudge and have been from my youth—
thine, like the rays which the sun's circle fill;
yet of my dear time's waste thou think'st no ill:
the more I toil, the less I move thy ruth.

Once 'twas my hope to raise me by thy height;
but 'tis the balance and the powerful sword
of Justice, not false Echo, that we need.

Heaven, as it seems, plants virtue in despite
here on the earth, if this be our reward—
to seek for fruit on trees too dry to breed.

———◆◆———

January, 1509

Most honorable father—I gather from your last letter that people
in Florence say I have died. It's of little import, since I'm still
alive. Therefore, let people say what they wish, and do not speak
of me with anyone for there are many bad individuals. I keep on
working as hard as I can. I have not received any money from the
Pope for thirteen months, but I think that I will certainly be paid
within the next forty days, for I will have spent all he has given
me. If he shouldn't give me any money, I'll have to borrow
some to return to Florence, for I am penniless. As a result I
cannot be robbed. The Lord knows what's best.

I have heard about Monna Cassandra. If I had any money,
I'd find out whether I could press that lawsuit here without
wasting too much of my time. I would have to name an attorney.
Inform me how things are going, and if you need any money,
go to the Spedalingo at Santa Maria Nuova, as I told you some

time ago. I have nothing else to tell you. I am dissatisfied here, not in very good health, and working very hard; without anyone to care for me, and without money. Yet I have the firm belief that God will help me.

July, 1509

Most honorable father – I wrote to you that I was not dead, although I had not been feeling too well. Through the mercy of God, now I feel very well.

I learned from your letter how the lawsuit is proceeding. It grieves me very much, for I know that when one deals with notaries one stands to lose or to be cheated, since they are a bunch of thieves. Since there cannot be a reasonable agreement, I urge you to defend yourself as well as you can, and above all, that whatever you do, you do it without anger; for the most important matter, if done with anger, is unimportant. When we have no money left to spend, God will help us.

Insofar as transferring the lawsuit here, if it can be done, I know that here it would cost Monna Cassandra much more than in Florence. She would even come to us and ask for mercy. But the truth of the matter is that I could not start anything until the Pope pays me. If you can come to an agreement, do not let trifles stand in the way. Do not worry if I do not reply, for many times I cannot.

August, 1509

Most honorable father – The evening I read your letter I received the worst news I have had during the last ten years. I thought I had settled their affairs:[18] namely, how they should hope to set up a good shop with my help. And, with this hope, that they should keep busy working hard and learning. Now I see that they are doing the opposite, especially Giovansimone. Had it been possible, on the very day I received your letter, I would have

---

[18] Buonarroto and Giovansimone.

jumped on horseback, and by now I would have straightened out everything. But since I could not do this, I will write him as I see fit, and if from now on he does not turn over a new leaf, I shall try to secure a leave from the Pope. I want you to believe that all the hardships I have endured have been no less for you than for myself, and that all I have bought I bought so that it may be yours while you are alive; for if it had not been for you, I wouldn't have bought it. Therefore, when you want to rent out the house or lease the farm, feel free to do so. Thus, with that income and with what I'll give you, you will live like a rich man. Were it not for the fact that summer is near, I would tell you to do it right now and to come and stay with me here. But this is not the appropriate time, for you wouldn't be able to endure it long here in the summer. I have thought of taking away from Giovansimone the money he has in that shop and of giving it to Gismondo;[14] let him and Buonarroto live together again as best they can. You ought to rent out those houses and the Pozzolatico farm, and, with that income and the help which I will give you, go and live in another place where you can keep someone to cook for you either in Florence or out of Florence, and leave that wretch holding his ass. I beg you to think only of yourself, and do anything you wish that would be best for you.

I have been told that here the lawsuit would cost me three times as much as in Florence. Furthermore, I do not have a single friend whom I can trust and I could not take care of this thing myself. Be as little afraid as possible, for it is not a matter of life and death.

August, 1509

Giovansimone – They say that if one does good to a good man, it makes him better, but if one does it to a bad man, it makes him worse. I have been trying for many years with good words and deeds to bring you to live honestly and in peace with your father

---

[14] His youngest brother.

and with the rest of us, and you are getting worse all the time. I do not say that you are a scoundrel, but you behave in such a manner that neither I nor the others like you any longer. I could tell you many things about your behavior, but I would only repeat what I have said before. To make it short, I can tell you as a fact that you have nothing in this world; for some time I have been paying your expenses and lodging for the love of God, believing you to be a brother of mine like the others. Now I am convinced that you are not my brother, for if you were, you would not threaten my father; on the contrary, you are a beast, and I will treat you as such. I want you to know that he who sees his own father threatened or struck is duty-bound to risk his life in reprisal. I repeat that you have nothing in the world; and if I hear the slightest thing about your behavior, I will come to Florence by the post, and I will show you how wrong you are and I will teach you to destroy your property, and set fire to the houses and farms you have not acquired. If I come there I will open your eyes to things that will make you shed bitter tears, and will make you realize on what you base your pride.

I want to say this once more: if you will strive to do good and to honor and respect your father, I will help you like the others, and presently I will have a good shop set up for all of you. What I lack in words I will make up with deeds.

I cannot help adding a few more lines. For the last twelve years I have been drudging all over Italy; I have borne every shame; I have endured every hardship; I have rent my body with all sorts of hard work; I have exposed my life to a thousand dangers; all this simply in order to help my family. And now that I have begun to improve the conditions of my family a little, you alone should be the only one to upset and ruin in one hour what I have done after so many years and so many hardships! By Christ's body this shall not be! I will rout ten thousand people like you if need be. Be wise, and do not tempt one who has other worries.

ON THE PAINTING OF THE SISTINE CHAPEL

I've grown a goiter by dwelling in this den—
as cats from stagnant streams in Lombardy,
or in what other land they hap to be—
which drives the belly close beneath the chin:

my beard turns up to heaven; my nape falls in,
fixed on my spine: my breastbone visibly
grows like a harp: a rich embroidery
bedews my face from brush-drops thick and thin.

My loins into my paunch like levers grind:
my buttock like a crupper bears my weight;
my feet unguided wander to and fro;

in front my skin grows loose and long; behind,
by bending it becomes more taut and strait;
crosswise I strain me like a Syrian bow:

  whence false and quaint, I know,
must be the fruit of squinting brain and eye;
for ill can aim the gun that bends awry.

  Come then, Giovanni, try
to succor my dead pictures and my fame;
since foul I fare and painting is my shame.

—— ✦✦ ——

1509

Dearest father—I learn from your last letter that the Spedalingo
has placed two farms in your hands: one of his own, the other
of somebody else. According to what you write me, the one of
Pian di Ripoli is very beautiful: I do not understand whether it
is beautiful because it is well kept, or because the soil is good.
Provided it is good, insofar as I am concerned I would like it for
the price, because it is comfortable, especially since it has a farm-
house. You are there on the spot, so do what is best. Whatever

you decide to buy, I shall be happy you have bought it. I shall come to Florence as soon as my painting is finished, which will be within two or three months.

September, 1509

Nothing is new with me here, and at the end of next week I'll have finished my painting, that is to say, the part I began.[15] After I unveil it I think I will be paid, and I shall try to get one month's leave to come to Florence. I do not know what will happen, but I really need a leave, for I am not too well.

September, 1509

Dearest father – I gather that the Spedalingo has been harassing you and feeding you a lot of words. Be patient, and pretend not to notice anything, until I arrive and settle everything. Do not worry if I do not write you more often, for I cannot, and furthermore, I lack a carrier to whom to give my letters. You too should not write me too often during the period I have to remain here, for I do not go out after my mail. The letters have to be brought here and that inconveniences others. Pray to God that my business here will come to a good end.

October, 1509

Buonarroto – I received the bread. It is good, but there is no reason to corner the market, for there would be little profit. I gave the boy five carlini, and he hardly wanted to give it to me. You inform me in your last letter that Lorenzo Strozzi will come and see me, and that I should give him a warm welcome. I don't think you are aware of how I live here, and so I excuse you. I shall do what I can. I hear that Gismondo is coming to attend to some business. Tell him not to count too much on me; not because I do not love him, like a brother, but because there is nothing I can do for him. It is understood that I should love

---

[15] The first half of the Sistine vault.

myself more than others, yet I can hardly provide myself with
what I need. I endure many hardships and bodily fatigue here;
I have no friends at all, and I do not want any. I hardly have
the time to eat what I need to keep going; so I do not want anybody to bother me, for I just couldn't take it at all.

September 5, 1510

Dearest father – This morning I received one of your letters, which
filled me with grief on learning that Buonarroto is ill. Should he
still be ill, I would come with the post next week, although that
would be very hard on me. This because I still have coming five
hundred ducats which I have earned; furthermore, I was promised another five hundred to put up the scaffolding and start the
other section of the work. Instead the Pope departed from
Rome[16] and left no instructions for me, so that I am penniless
and do not know what to do. If I leave, he may get angry and
I may lose what is rightly mine. I wrote him a letter, and I am
waiting for his reply. Just the same, if Buonarroto is in any danger, let me know, and I will leave with the post and be in Florence in two days. Men are worth more than money. Take all
precautions, and do not let money keep you from helping him.
Go to the Spedalingo at Santa Maria Nuova, and have him give
you fifty, or one hundred ducats, whatever is needed, and have
no qualms. Do not worry, for God did not create us to abandon
us.

September 15, 1510

Dearest father – I gave Giovanni Balducci[17] here in Rome three
hundred and fifty large gold ducats, and told him to have said
sum paid to you in Florence. When you receive them, take them
to the Spedalingo and ask him to take care of them for me the way

---

[16] August 17, 1510, Julius II left at the head of his army to drive
the French and Germans out of northern Italy.

[17] Friend and banker.

he has done in the past. There are left a few ducats of small denomination which I told you to take for yourself. If you need more, take what you need, even if you should spend everything.

I understand from your last letter how the matter[18] is going. I cannot help you in another way. Do not let that upset you, and do not mope over it, for even if a person loses his property, it is not the end of the world. I will make for you much more than you can ever lose; but I remind you not to trust such things too much, for they are fallacious. Nevertheless, do your best and thank God, for, since this hardship had to strike, it struck at a time when you could protect yourself better than you could have done in the past. Take good care of yourself and, rather than experience discomforts, let your possessions disintegrate, for I prefer to have you alive and poor. If you were to die, I wouldn't know what to do with all the gold in the world. And if those gossips or anyone else criticize you, let them talk, for they are ungrateful and heartless.

October 23, 1510

Buonarroto – I think that in a few days I shall have to return to Bologna because the Pope's Datary[19] promised me on his leaving Rome that as soon as he got to Bologna he would find work for me. He left one month ago, and I have not heard from him yet. I will wait all of next week. At that time, if nothing turns up, I think I will go to Bologna and will stop in Florence. And that's all.

October 26, 1510

Buonarroto – Yesterday I was given by the Pope's Datary five hundred gold ducats. Of these I gave Giovanni Balducci four hundred sixty-three and a half, so that he may empower Bonifazio[20]

---

[18] Probably still Monna Cassandra's suit against the family.
[19] Lorenzo Pucci, Florentine, later Cardinal de' Santiquattro, and an executor of Julius II's will.
[20] Agent for the transfer of funds.

in Florence to pay four hundred and fifty large gold ones. If he should not be able to pay them to you for up to ten days, be patient; after that period of time, insist that he give them to you, and take them to Santa Maria Nuova to the Spedalingo, who will credit them to my account like the others. Take along with you either Giovansimone or Gismondo, or both. Let me know exactly how much money I have there, and do not speak to anyone about this. If you see Michelagniolo Tanagli,[21] tell him that I thank him for the cheese.

January 10, 1511

Buonarroto – Several days ago I received a letter of yours, and from it I gather what your exact feelings are. Concerning the shop, I intend to do all I promised you as soon as I get back to Florence. Once I finish my work here and I am paid what is coming to me, there will be enough left to do what I promised you. Concerning the fact that you found someone who wants to advance you two or three thousand large ducats so that you can set up a shop, I can tell you that this is more money than I can offer you. It seems to me that you should by all means accept it, but be sure you are not deceived, because it is impossible to find someone who loves better others than himself. You tell me that this fellow wants to give you a daughter of his in marriage. I tell you that, once he has saddled you with his daughter, all his offers will come to naught. He will stick to his promise of giving a wife, and she will stick for a longer time than you will want. I also wish to tell you this: I do not think that through avarice it is a good idea to meddle with people who are more abject than you are. Avarice is a very great sin, and nothing contaminated by sin can come to a good end. It is my opinion that you string him along with fine words, and wait until I finish here, so that I may better see what my financial situation is at

---

[21] Friend who requested Michelangelo to find a carnelian or medal for him in Rome.

that time. This will be in about three months, more or less. Now do as you please.

January 11, 1511

Buonarroto – I arrived here safely on Tuesday evening.[22] The Lord be praised. Then I was given the money, just as they wrote me in Florence I would. You will find in this letter a first bill of exchange of two hundred and twenty-eight large gold ducats from Lanfredino Lanfredini.[23] Take it to the Spedalingo and have it credited to my account. Have him enter also the last money I sent him directly, and take the book and the papers. Then let me know the correct amount of my account. If you see Araudo, tell him to thank on my behalf the honorable Gonfaloniere.

Keep the chest locked, so that my clothes will not be stolen like those of Gismondo.

March, 1511

Dearest father – I do not trust Luigi Gerardini's property. If it were a safe bargain, it seems to me that it would have been sold by now. I do not understand why it should have been set aside for us more than for anyone else. Proceed cautiously.

October 3, 1511

Dearest father – On Tuesday I went to talk to the Pope. The fact is that I returned to see him on Wednesday morning, and I was paid four hundred gold ducats from the Apostolic Treasury. Of these, I am giving three hundred large ducats to the Altoviti[23] so that in Florence they may be paid to you by the Strozzi. See to it that the receipts are signed properly, and then take the money to the Spedalingo and have him take care of it as usual. Also remind him of the farm. If he strings you along, try to buy from

---

[22] Following his trip to Bologna, December–January 7, to obtain money from the Pope.
[23] Florentine bankers in Rome.

someone else; and if you see that it is a safe purchase, I give you permission to spend up to one thousand four hundred ducats. Take Buonarroto with you, and beg the Spedalingo to help us. Do your best to buy through him, for he is the safest.

I wrote you asking you not to let anyone touch my things, drawings or anything else. Pray God that I do myself honor here, and that I succeed in pleasing the Pope; for, if I please him, he will do us some good. And pray God for him too.

November 5, 1511

Most honorable father – I gather from your last letter that you gave to the mother and to the wife of Michele[24] six bushels of wheat at twenty-five cents a bushel, and that, as long as they need it, you will give them what you can. I ask you not to give them anything else.

I understand that you will send me my clothes very soon. Let me know how much you spent, and I shall send you immediately the money for the clothes and for the wheat at the same time.

I shall be very grateful to you if you will find out whether in Florence there is some young boy, son of good parents, but poor and accustomed to hardships, who would be willing to come here and live with me. He would do the various household chores, namely go shopping and run errands; and if he had time left over, he could learn. If you find some boy, let me know, for here one can only find rogues. With the grace of God, I am well and I work constantly.

January 5, 1512

Dearest father – Now you inform me that you are considering both Girolamo Cini's farm, and another farm at Pozzolatico. I should buy both of them, provided they have good security. I

---

[24] Relatives of a Settignano stonemason who assisted him.

have been reassured about the house.[25] I shall only have to pay rent as long as I remain there.

Buonarroto writes me about his wanting to get married. I'll tell you what I think: I am planning to free all of you in five or six months and make a gift to you of what you already have that belongs to me. Then you can do what you please. I will help all of you always in whatever I can. I strongly advise Buonarroto, however, not to get married for the rest of the summer. As long as he has waited so long, he will not be any older by waiting six months.[26] Buonarroto writes me also that Bernardino di Pier Basso[27] wishes to come here and stay with me. If he wants to come, let him come now, before I take on someone else, for I want to begin doing something. As for salary, I will give him what you wrote me, namely three ducats a month plus expenses. The fact is that I live simply at home, and that's the way I want it to remain. Tell him about it and tell him not to tarry. After eight days, if he does not like being with me, he will be free to return to Florence, and I'll give him all the money he needs for his journey.

January 20, 1512

Most honorable father – At first I sent for him[28] because I was promised that the matter of the house would be settled in a few days, and that I could start working. Later I realized that things would take a long time. In the meantime I am looking to see if I can find another house that will suit me in order to rid myself of the present one. I do not want to have any work started until I am settled.

---

[25] House in Trevi section of Rome, which Pope Julius let him use while working on the Tomb. Later written into the new Tomb contracts.

[26] Buonarroto is thirty-four.

[27] Son of his assistant of 1508.

[28] Bernardino.

As for the boy who came, that rogue of a mule driver cheated me of one ducat. He swore that the sum agreed upon was two large gold ducats. Actually the fare for all boys who come here with mule drivers is of no more than ten carlini. It made me angrier than if I had lost twenty-five ducats, for it is evident that it was the fault of the boy's father, who wanted to have his son travel respectably on muleback. I never had such good luck, not I! The other thing that the boy's father and the boy himself told me was that the boy would do everything; that he would attend to the mule and even sleep on the ground if he had to. Instead I have to look after him. That's all I needed. The shopboy I left here has been sick since the day I got back. It is true that now he is better, but he was on the point of death for nearly one month, so that I never went to bed. That, on top of many other troubles of my own. Now I get this dried-up shit of a boy who says that he does not want to waste his time, that he wants to learn. Back in Florence he told me that he would have been satisfied with two or three hours a day; now the whole day is not enough for him; he wants to draw the whole night! I need someone to take care of me: if he did not feel like doing it, they had no business making me spend all this money. But they are shrewd ones who have a goal in mind, and that's that. I beg you to have him taken out of my hands, for he has irritated me to the point that I am at the end of my patience. The mule driver has been paid so much money that he can very well take him back to Florence. Furthermore, he is a friend of his father's. Tell his father to send for him. I shall not be able to give one more penny, for I have no money. I will be patient to wait until he sends for him, and if he does not send for him, I shall turn him out of doors. Although I drove him out on the second day and then several other times, he does not think I am going to do it.

If you speak to the boy's father, break the news to him gently. Tell him that his boy is a good boy, but that he is too refined and not suited to do chores, and that he should send for him.

January 24, 1512

Dearest father – I am sending you one hundred large gold ducats, so that you can give them to Buonarroto and the others and have them give me an interest in the shop. If they strive to do well, I shall help them from time to time as I can. I am making a tremendous sacrifice to send the money I mentioned above. I do not think it is right for me to ask for more money, because I have no helpers, and I alone do not work much. As soon as I have this business of the house settled, I hope to start working hard.

January, 1512

Most honorable father – Several days ago I sent you one hundred large ducats out of those which I had saved here for myself to live on and keep working.[29] I beg you to take them to the Spedalingo and to have them credited to my account.[30] I have eighty ducats left here; I think they will last me four months, and I have to work for six more months before I will get any money from the Pope. Therefore I am sure I will be short of money, and I figure that I will need fifty ducats. Therefore, I beg you to send me back fifty of the hundred you promised you would return to me. You can keep the other fifty; with the understanding, however, that you have them ready at any rate in four months. I want to try and save the hundred I sent there to return them to the family of the Cardinal of Siena;[31] as you know they must be paid with the ducats in Santa Maria Nuova. I still have coming one thousand ducats from the Pope, and as soon as I finish my painting, if he likes it, I am sure I will get them. Therefore pray God for him, for his good and for ours.

Write me at once.

---

[29] On the second half of the vault.

[30] Apparently, the shop for Buonarroto does not materialize.

[31] The Piccolomini family, to whom he owes one hundred ducats advanced for unfinished work in Siena.

1512

Dearest father – I gather from your last letter that you have many things in your hands, but that they are poor buys; I believe it. It seems to me that it is impossible to buy anything without running some danger, except through Santa Maria Nuova. Therefore, it seems to me that we should wait another few months for the Spedalingo. Just the same, if in the meantime you should find a good and safe bargain, take it and do not let one hundred ducats more or less stand in the way. If you do not make a purchase from the Spedalingo or from anyone else, I hope to be in Florence for Easter Sunday, and we shall come to a decision together. I do not want the Spedalingo to have my money and torment us besides.

Give Buonarroto my apologies. I shall reply as soon as I can. I can't think of anything else.

1512

Dearest father – There has been some uneasiness here in Rome, and there still is, but not so much. It is believed that difficulties will be settled.[32] May God grant it. I have nothing else to tell you. This coming summer I shall be in Florence, come what may.

1512

Dearest father – I replied to you in my previous letter that I did not see how that farm on the way to Prato could have good security. You tell me again that the Spedalingo sent you to see one two miles away from Florence, but that it seems very expensive to you. I tell you that if we got a farm from him for fifty or one hundred ducats more than from another person, it wouldn't be so bad. But I have no hope, for I believe he is a real rogue. I wouldn't mind

---

[32] In the spring of 1512, alarm was so great over French success in northern Italy that the Pope took residence in the fortress castle of Sant'Angelo.

the one you are considering in the plain of Fonte in Valdarno, as long as it is good. Just the same, do as you please and buy what you like, for I will like what you like, wherever it may be, provided it has good security. God willing, this summer I shall come. You don't have to tell me about Francesco di Consiglio,[33] for, since his father never did a favor to you, I am not bound to do him one either: he who does ill has to take the consequences.

―――――――✦✦―――――――

ON ROME IN THE PONTIFICATE OF JULIUS II

Here helms and swords are made of chalices:
the blood of Christ is sold so much the quart:
his cross and thorns are spears and shields; and short
must be the time ere even his patience cease.

Nay let him come no more to raise the fees
of this foul sacrilege beyond report!
For Rome still flays and sells him at the court,
where paths are closed to virtue's fair increase.

Now were fit time for me to scrape a treasure!
Seeing that work and gain are gone; while he
who wears the robe, is my Medusa still.

God welcomes poverty perchance with pleasure:
but of that better life what hope have we,
when the blessed banner leads to nought but ill?

―――――――✦✦―――――――

1512

Dearest father – I told you about what I had found out here, and what I had been told; namely, how it was more dangerous than one might think:[34] I am referring to the farm near Prato. Concerning the contract you want me to send the Spedalingo, send me one just

―――――――――――――――――――――――――――――

[33] Son of the mercer who sued Lodovico in 1497.
[34] Threat of invasion of Florence by the alliance of Spanish troops and the ousted Medici.

as it should be drawn up; I will make a perfect copy of it and send it to you, for I do not know his name and would not know how to word it. If, after you make the purchase, the Spedalingo should refuse to give you the money, I will come there in person and make him give it to you. If you acquire any property, do not get it near the Arno or any other bad river. If you can bring him down to a reasonable price, take it; and even if it should be somewhat dishonest, but not excessively so, it would be wise to take it. Here we do not yet see the danger you people in Florence believe exists.[35] God grant us that everything will be all right.

1512

Dearest father – Since I wrote you I found out that the Spedalingo would scoff at a simple document written in my own hand; for this reason, I had a power of attorney drawn up and I am enclosing it in this letter and, as my attorney, you may be able to have him give you all the money you need to purchase the piece of property, including the tax; with the understanding that you will not spend on anything else a single penny of mine without my permission, nor take out more than is needed for the said purchase.

This summer I shall come without fail. At most, I shall tarry until September; but I do not believe I shall stay here that long.

1512

Dearest father – I do not know what to tell you, for a person who cannot see for himself is not in a position to pass good judgment. Therefore, do what you think best. I merely wish to remind you to be extremely careful about the security, for in these days one cannot afford to lose any money; for, if this came to pass, I don't think I could ever make up for it. Pray God that my things go well.

May, 1512

Dearest father – I learned from your last letter about the farm

---

[35] Danger of Medici return to power in Florence.

you had from Santa Maria Nuova, and how fine it is. I was very much pleased; and although it cost a lot, I believe you realize that it is worthwhile. I thank God that this matter is settled. Now I only have one left; and this is to have them[36] put up a shop; for, day and night, I don't think of anything else. Then I will have the feeling that I have met my obligations; and if I have a few more days left to live,[37] I shall want to spend them peacefully.

July 24, 1512

Buonarroto – I do not have time to reply to your letter, because it is late at night, and even if I had the time, I could not give you a definite answer until I am all through here. I will be in Florence in September, and I will do all I can for you, just as I have done until now. I toil and I suffer more than anybody ever did: I am not well, and I work hard; yet I have the patience needed to arrive at the desired goal.[38] You certainly can be patient for a couple of months, for you are ten thousand times better off than I.

July, 1512

Buonarroto – I gather from your letter that you are anxious to know where I would like you to purchase some property.

It seems to me that one should seek above all else good security; the location of the property is secondary, for I do not care. Whatever is all right with you, is all right with me. When you see Giovanni da Ricasoli, remember me to him.

August 21, 1512

Buonarroto – Since I do not have much time, I am replying briefly. As far as my returning to Florence is concerned, I will not be able

---

[36] Buonarroto and Giovansimone.

[37] He is thirty-seven.

[38] Completion of Sistine vault.

to do it, until I finish my work, which I think will be at the end of September. The truth is that it is such a great enterprise that I will not be able to tell for another fifteen days. Suffice it to say that, unless I die in the meantime, I shall be in Florence before All Saints' Day. I work as fast as I can, for I can hardly wait to get back there.

September 5, 1512

Buonarroto—I haven't written you for several days, for I did not have the opportunity. Now, hearing how things are in Florence, I think I should tell you how I feel about it. Since, as they say here, conditions are very bad there,[89] it seems to me that you should withdraw to some other town where you would be safe, and leave behind all your possessions, for life is worth much more than possessions. If you haven't the money to get away from Florence, go to the Spedalingo and have him give you some. If I were you, I would go to Siena. Once in Siena, I would take a house and stay there as long as things are unsettled in Florence. I believe that the power of attorney I sent Lodovico is still valid, and that he can still withdraw my money; therefore, if it is necessary, take it and spend all you need in such dangerous moments as the present. Save the rest for me. Concerning the events in Florence, do not get involved in them either by word or by deed, and do as one does when the plague strikes: be the first ones to flee. Nothing else. Let me know something as soon as you can, for I am greatly concerned.

September 18, 1512

Buonarroto—I learned from your last letter that Florence was in great danger, and that grieved me greatly. Now they say that the

---

[89] Spanish troops with Cardinal Giovanni de' Medici, as Julius II's legate, sacked Prato August 30. The next day Soderini resigned as Gonfaloniere in Florence.

Medici are back in Florence, and that everything is settled.[40] For this reason, I believe that the danger of the Spaniards is over. Therefore, live peacefully, and do not become friendly nor intimate with anyone, except God. Do not speak well nor evil of anybody, for one never knows how things end up; just mind your own business.

Concerning the forty ducats Lodovico took from Santa Maria Nuova, I wrote you the other day that if your lives are in danger, you could spend not forty ducats, but all. However, apart from this, I have not given you permission to touch them. I warn you that I do not have a grosso, and it wouldn't be exaggerating to say that I am without shoes and without clothes; furthermore, I shall not be paid what is still coming to me until I finish my work. I am suffering the greatest discomforts and hardships. Therefore, if you too should have to bear some discomfort, do not resent it, and as long as you can get along with your own money, do not take any of mine, except, as I said, in case of danger.

October, 1512

Dearest father—I read in your last letter that you brought the forty ducats back to the Spedalingo. You did well. If at any time you think they are in danger, please let me know. I finished painting the Chapel. The Pope is very satisfied with it. The other things are not turning out as well as I expected: I blame the times which are anything but favorable to our art. I shall not come to Florence for the feast of All Saints because I do not have what is necessary in order to do what I want.

October, 1512

Dearest father—I gather from your last letter that I should beware of keeping money in the house and of carrying it on my person,

[40] Returned September 14, Giuliano de' Medici is placed in command of the city. He is the youngest of *Il Magnifico's* sons, with whom Michelangelo grew up in the Medici Palace.

and also that in Florence it has been said that I have spoken evil of the Medici.

Concerning the money, I keep what I have in Balduccio's bank, and I only keep in the house and on my person what I need from day to day. With regard to the Medici, I have never spoken one word against them, except in that manner as is generally done by everybody in connection with the Prato affair;[41] for if stones could speak, they would have spoken about it too. Then, there have been many other things said, to which, when I heard them, I replied: "If it is true that they are doing what people say, they are acting wrongly"; not that I have believed such things: and may God grant that they are not so. Also during the last month someone who claims to be my friend told me many bad things about their deeds; so much so that I have rebuked him and told him that he is doing wrong to speak thus, and not to speak to me about them any more. Therefore I should like Buonarroto to try and discover in a subtle manner where he heard that I slandered the Medici, so that I may discover the origin of this rumor; and, if it should have originated with one of those who pretend to be my friends, that I may protect myself from him. I am not doing anything yet, and I am waiting for the Pope to tell me what to do.

October, 1512

Dearest father—One must have faith and ask for God's mercy and repent of his sins; for such adversities stem from nothing else, and especially from pride and ingratitude.[42] I never dealt with more ungrateful or more proud people than the Florentines. Therefore, if justice is coming, there is a good reason. I shall write a couple of verses for Giuliano de' Medici, and I shall enclose them in this letter: read them, and if you should like to take them to

---

[41] The Medici were blamed for the sack of Prato, though they maintained they tried to stop it.

[42] A levy was imposed by the new Florentine government, the Buonarroti share being sixty ducats.

him, do so. If they will be of no avail, give some thought to whether we can sell what we own, and go to live elsewhere. However, if they should treat our equals the way they treat you, have patience and trust in God.

You say that you have taken care of thirty ducats; take an additional thirty from mine, and send me the rest here. Take care of yourself and of your daily needs, and if you cannot have the same considerations as the other citizens of Florence, be satisfied with your daily bread, and live in the grace of God and poorly as I do here. I myself live miserably and do not care about honors and other worldly things; I live in the midst of the greatest hardships and of countless anxieties. I have been leading this sort of existence for about fifteen years, and I have not known one hour of well-being. I have done all I could to help you, and you have never acknowledged it or believed it. May the Lord forgive us all. I am prepared to continue doing what I have done as long as I live, provided I can.

ON DANTE ALIGHIERI

From heaven his spirit came, and robed in clay
the realms of justice and of mercy trod,
then rose a living man to gaze on God,
that he might make the truth as clear as day.

For that pure star that brightened with his ray
the undeserving nest where I was born,
the whole wide world would be a prize to scorn;
none but his Maker can due reward pay.

I speak of Dante, whose high work remains
unknown, unhonored by that thankless brood,
who only to just men deny their wage.

Were I but he! Born for like lingering pains,
against his exile coupled with his good
I'd gladly change the world's best heritage!

3. Bacchus, 1496-1497. *(Courtesy of Alinari)*

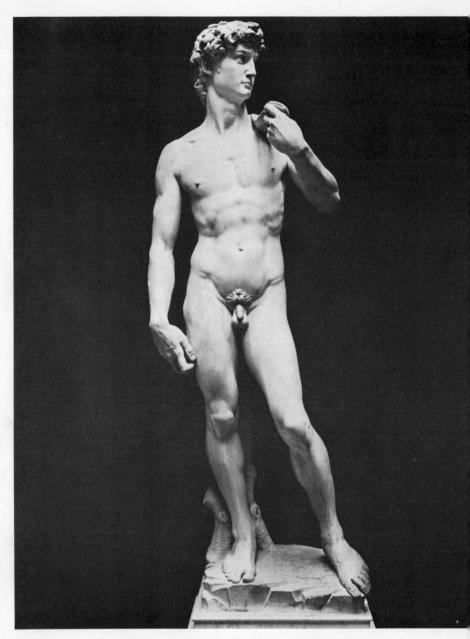

4. David, 1501-1504. (*Courtesy of Alinari-Brogi*)

October, 1512

Dearest father – I learn from your last letter that you are in favor again:[43] this makes me very happy. I want you to do me a favor: there is in Florence a young Spaniard named Alonso who is a painter. I understand he is ill; and since a Spanish relative of his who is here would like to know how he is getting along, he begged me to write to some acquaintance of mine and try to find out for him. Try to find out from Granacci who knows him, so that it is evident that I have wanted to do him a service.

1512

Dearest father – Now I would appreciate it very much if you could find out from the Spedalingo of Santa Maria Nuova whether he would be willing to sell some good property worth two thousand large ducats, for I have this money here at Balduccio's bank,[44] and I get no interest from it. The thought has occurred to me to spend them here to secure myself an income to help me carry out this work. But then I decided that as soon as I finish these statues,[45] I will come to Florence and do the rest there. Therefore, it seems to me that I should buy there.

1512

Baldassarre di Cagione from Carrara.

I am quite amazed at you, for, since you wrote me a long time ago that you had so many blocks of marble in readiness,[46] since the weather has been perfectly good for sailing, since you collected from me one hundred gold ducats, and since I did not fail you in anything, I do not understand what keeps you from doing what you

---

[43] Michelangelo's verses to Giuliano de' Medici seem to have worked.

[44] Payment for completion of the Sistine vault.

[45] Moses and the two Slaves for Julius II's Tomb.

[46] Marbles ordered in 1506 for the Julius Tomb.

are supposed to do for me. I beg you to load at once those marbles you say are ready, and to come as soon as possible. I only wish to remind you that you are doing the wrong thing in not keeping your promise, and in giving so much trouble to a man who is useful to you.

(February 21, 1513)[47]

July 30, 1513

Buonarroto – Michele the stoneworker came here to stay with me, and has asked me for some money for his relatives in Florence. So, go at once to Bonifazio, and he will give you four large ducats; give them to Meo di Chimenti, stoneworker, who works at Santa Maria del Fiore.

The mentioned Michele told me that you showed him how you spent about sixty ducats at Settignano.[48] I remember your telling me also here at the table that you had spent many ducats of your own. I pretended not to hear, and showed no amazement, for I know you. I believe that you have noted them down, and that you are keeping track of them so that some day you will ask us for them. I should like to know from your ungrateful self with what money you earned them; also, I should like to know whether you are taking into account those two hundred and twenty-eight ducats which you people took from my savings at Santa Maria Nuova, and whether you have forgotten the numerous hundreds I spent on the house and on all of you and the discomforts and hardships I have endured to help you. If you had enough understanding to know the truth, you would not say: I spent so much of my own. Furthermore, you wouldn't have come here to solicit my help. On the contrary, you would have said: Mi-

---

[47] Pope Julius II died on Feb. 21, 1513. He was succeeded by Cardinal Giovanni de' Medici, who was enthroned as Pope Leo X on March 19.

[48] The family farm.

chelangelo knows what he wrote us, and if he does not do it now, there must be some obstacle we are not aware of. And you would have been patient, for it is no good to spur a horse which is running as fast as he can, nay more than he can. But you and the rest of the family have never known me, and do not know me now. May God forgive you! For He has given me the grace to bear what I am bearing, or what I have borne, so that you may be helped. But you will become aware of this when you no longer have me with you.

I am informing you that I do not think I will be able to come this September, for I am so hard-pressed that I do not have the time to eat. Just the same, as I promised you, I want to give you one thousand large gold ducats, so that, with the others you have, you begin to be on your own. I want no share of your earnings, but I want to be sure that at the end of ten years, if I am alive, and if I should want them, you will give me, in money or in goods, these thousand ducats. I do not believe that this will come to pass, but should I be in need of them I'd want that money back. Concerning the four hundred ducats which you have of mine, I want you to divide them into four parts, and to take one hundred each: of these I make a gift to you. One hundred to Lodovico, one hundred to you, one hundred to Giovansimone and one hundred to Gismondo; with the understanding that you do nothing with them but invest them together in the shop. Nothing else.

For the period of the next twenty months there is not a single letter of Michelangelo's preserved, though it is a safe assumption that he continued to write to his father and brothers during this time. Those twenty months were comparatively peaceable for him. Giovanni de' Medici was now Pope Leo X, and he told Rome of his old friend, "Buonarroti and I were educated together under my father's roof." Michelangelo furnished the comfortable home he had bought in the Macello dei Corvi, and carved steadily on the Moses, Heroic Slave and Dying Slave.

In all probability he would have continued to carve on the Julius II tomb figures for many years; but Pope Leo, and his cousin, Cardinal Giulio de' Medici, soon became discontent at "the first sculptor of Italy" serving the Rovere family instead of the Medici. Despite Michelangelo's anguished pleas that he be allowed two more years, in which time he felt he could complete a modified version of the tomb, the Medici demanded that he design a facade for their uncompleted family church of San Lorenzo, in Florence, with many marble figures to make it one of the great churches of the world. To this end, Pope Leo granted Michelangelo another six months in Rome, in which to put his sculptural house in order, after which he was to depart for Carrara to choose, and have quarried, the pure white marble blocks and columns needed for his San Lorenzo facade.

March 31, 1515

Buonarroto–Enclosed you will find a bill of exchange for nine
hundred large gold ducats, which will be paid to me by Lorenzo
Benintendi. I think I am leaving tomorrow morning, but if this
letter gets to you before I arrive, try in the meantime to secure
a guaranty of payment.

April 28, 1515

Buonarroto–With the grace of God, I just arrived safely in Rome.[49]
I beg you to send me that woolen cloth[50] as soon as you can.
Buy that full color of which you showed me a sample, and, above
all, see that it is beautiful. Get five braccia[51] and send it with
the courier or with somebody else, as long as it arrives soon.
Address it either to me or to Domenico Buoninsegni[52] to the
palace of Cardinal de' Medici.[53]

May 19, 1515

Buonarroto–I received the wool material; it is good and beautiful.
The bill of exchange you sent me is not correct, for it reads that
the Gaddi[54] should pay me "ducati di camera,"[55] instead I have
large gold ducats coming. Therefore I refused to accept them, and
I am returning to you the bill of exchange in this letter. Have them
draw up a correct one.

June 2, 1515

Buonarroto–I received the money from the Gaddi, namely three
hundred and ninety-three large ducats. You write me that you

---

[49] From a visit to Florence.
[50] From the wool shop they had started.
[51] A unit of measure.
[52] Agent of Pope Leo X.
[53] Giulio de' Medici, cousin of Pope Leo X.
[54] Bankers in Rome.
[55] Ducats of the Apostolic Treasury.

would like me to help you here in Rome. I haven't got the courage to help you in such a thing, because I do not have the means; and if I did, I would foster my own things which are much more important.

You will find enclosed a letter addressed to Carrara. I beg you to send it secretly, so that neither Michele, nor anybody working at Santa Maria del Fiore, will know about it.

June 16, 1515

Buonarroto – I wrote the letter you wanted for Filippo Strozzi. See whether you like it, and give it to him. If it is not phrased quite well, I know that he will excuse me, for it is not my profession: I have no talent for such things. The main thing is that it will work. I'd like you to look up the Spedalingo of Santa Maria Nuova and have him take the necessary steps so that I will be paid here fourteen hundred ducats out of those which he has of mine, for this summer I must make a great effort to finish this work.[56] This because I think that after that I shall have to be at the Pope's[57] service. For this reason I bought around twenty thousand ducats' worth of brass to cast certain statues. I need money: therefore, if you could manage to have Pier Francesco Borgherini, who is in Florence, agree to have me get them here from his bank, I would appreciate it very much, for Pier Francesco is a friend of mine and would do things right. Do not talk about this, for I would like to be paid secretly.

July 7, 1515

Buonarroto – Although one cannot count on Michele for anything, still I think he knows this particular thing I am asking him, namely, whether I can expect any marbles this summer from Pietrasanta.[58]

---

[56] Tomb of Julius II.

[57] Pope Leo X, who was Giovanni de' Medici, son of Il Magnifico, and with whom Michelangelo lived in the Medici Palace in Florence while they were boys.

[58] Town near Carrara.

Domenico Buoninsegni informs me that he heard the road will soon be opened.[59] Nothing else. Take care of yourselves, and especially of your souls, for today that seems quite necessary.

July 28, 1515

Buonarroto – I have heard that the letter I wrote you for Filippo Strozzi has helped to alleviate the situation; I was very happy to hear that. When he comes to Rome, I will thank him.

August 1, 1515

Buonarroto – I know Michele is crazy, but I write him because I need a certain quantity of marbles and I do not know what to do. I do not want to go to Carrara myself because I cannot, and I cannot send anybody who will be satisfactory, for, if they are not crazy, they are traitors and wretches; just like that rascal Bernardino who cost me one hundred ducats while he was here, and on top of that he gossiped and complained about me all over Rome. He is a great rogue: keep away from him as you would from fire, and do not let him into the house on any account.

August 11, 1515

Buonarroto – I gather from your last letter that the Spedalingo told you he has not yet collected all my money. That does not sound good to me. I am afraid I'll have to quarrel with him. Since I returned from Florence I have not done any work. I have only attended to making models and to preparing the work, so that I can make one great effort and, by hiring a lot of workers, finish it in two or three years as I was forced to promise.[60] I made a large debt, and in doing so I counted on the money I have in Florence; thinking that I could have it when I wanted it, as logically one

---

[59] The Medici Pope wanted to open a road to the magnificent, unaccessible quarries at Pietrasanta, which had been ceded to Florence. It was not opened until Michelangelo built it himself.

[60] Under contract for Julius's Tomb.

does with one's savings. If now I should not, I would be in a fine fix. If he wants to pay my money, see that Pier Francesco Borgherini pays it to me here; the important thing is that I get it at once.

If Pier Francesco does not have a way to have that money paid to me here without his suffering a loss, I want you to put it immediately back in Santa Maria Nuova.

September 1, 1515

Buonarroto – Act as quickly as you can, and do not leave my money in the hands of others, for I do not trust anybody alive. You are lamenting about the way things are going in the shop; be patient, everywhere there is more grief than you imagine. I have been expecting these events for many years, and I always warned you that it was not the proper time to undertake such a thing. Yet, try all together to hold on to the capital and think of saving your souls. Reply to the father of Betto da Rovezzano that I do not have any marbles to be worked over; and that otherwise I would have accepted willingly. You will find enclosed a letter for Messer Antonio, secretary of the Marquis of Carrara.

September 8, 1515

Buonarroto – You write me in such a way as to make me believe that you think that I am more concerned with worldly goods than is becoming to me. The fact is that I worry about them more for your sake than for mine, as has always been the case. I do not believe in fables, and I am not at all a fool, as you think: and, if I am not mistaken, shortly you will appreciate more than you do now the letters I have been writing you during the last four years. And if I am deceived, I am not deceived by bad things, for I know that it is always a good idea to take care of oneself and of one's things. I recall that about eighteen months ago you wanted to take a certain step;[61] I wrote you that it wasn't time yet, and to let one year go by for the sake of precaution. A few days

---

[61] Open a wool shop.

later the King of France died: you wrote to me then, saying that
the King had died and that in Italy there existed no longer any
danger. You told me that I listened to monks and to empty talk,
and you made sport of me. You realize that the King didn't really
die, and that you would be much better off if you had heeded my
advice of several years ago; but enough of that. The fact is that
one should not make fun of anybody, and these days it does not
do any harm to live in fear and to tend to one's soul and body.

Do your best to live in peace, and if something cannot
be done, let it remain undone: if the times are bad, one must be
patient.

October 20, 1515

Buonarroto – When you sent me the first bill of exchange, the man
who cashed it made two per cent profit on it; the next time, he
lost on it; I had nothing to do with it, for I know nothing about
such things. I thought he was making the same profit. Concerning
the amount for which I am asking you now, do as you please,
provided it is paid to me when it is convenient for you. I want you
to know that I do not want to impose upon or bother at all Pier
Francesco Borgherini. I have to do a certain painting for him
and it might seem that I wanted to be paid in advance: therefore,
I do not want to feel indebted to him, for I like him and I do
not want anything from him; I want to serve him out of love,
not out of obligation: and if I can, I will serve him more willingly
than anybody I ever have served, because he is truly a fine young
man. If I am not mistaken, there is no Florentine like him here.
I understand that in Florence you will soon celebrate the concor-
dat.[62] I am very pleased, for our welfare is very dear to me.

November 3, 1515

Buonarroto – You say that the Spedalingo is complaining about me
saying that I have taken out so much money in such a short time. I

---

[62] Peace between Pope Leo X and France.

think he is a great fool to complain of such a thing, and even more since he offered to loan me in case of need five hundred ducats of his own. You ask me for some money, and you say that now things are settled and that people will begin to collect and to work. I laugh at your problem, and I am amazed that you write me so. I cannot give you the money because I have two years' work ahead of me before I am even with my employers; so much is the money I have received from them. Therefore, keep on temporizing and you will have enough to live on. Try to collect all you can; do not undertake anything new for the whole winter, and give nothing on credit. I must write you these things, since that's how I feel about them. I know very well that you will laugh at this. Nothing else.

November 9, 1515

Buonarroto—You tell me that you will go to see Pier Francesco's[63] office boy, and that you will have my money paid to me here. Pier Francesco says that he loses in the transaction. I do not want to cause him any hardships or woes, because I do not want to feel indebted to anyone. Therefore, if it is not convenient to him or to anybody else, I'd rather you left the money where it is. The Pope left Rome, and here they say he is going to Florence.

---

[63] Borgherini.

CARRARA

(PISA—PIETRASANTA—SERRAVEZZA)

1516-1519

Florence,[1] 1516

Lodovico in Settignano.

Dearest father – I marveled much the other day at what happened
to you when I did not find you home; and now, hearing that you
are complaining about me, and saying that I have driven you out
of the house, I marvel even more, for I am certain that from
the day I was born until now, I never intended to do anything
whatever, small or great, against you. All the hardships I have
borne, were borne out of my love for you. And since I returned to
Florence from Rome, you know that I have always cared for you,
and I have reaffirmed that what I have is yours. Only a few days
ago when you were sick I promised you that I would never fail
you, and do everything I could for you as long as I live; and this
I again affirm. I am truly amazed that you have forgotten everything so soon. Yet, you and your children have learned to know
me by experience for thirty years, and you know that I have always
thought of doing and actually have done you some good whenever
I have been able. How can you say that I drove you out of doors?
Don't you see what reputation you give me by letting people say
that I drove you out? That is all I need, besides the anxieties
caused me by other things: all because of my love for you! You
certainly are grateful to me for all this! But be it as it must, I'll
make myself believe that I have always given you only shame and
grief: and so, I ask you to forgive me, as if that were really the
case. Pretend to forgive a son of yours who has always lived in a
reprehensible manner, and who has done unto you all the bad
things that can be done in this world. And so, I ask you once again
to forgive me, the wretch that I am, and do not spread up there
the rumor that I have driven you out of the house, for it matters
to me more than you think: after all, I am your son!

The bearer of this letter will be Rafaello da Gagliano.[2]
I beg you, not for my love, but for the love of God, to come as far

---

[1] For a brief visit en route to Carrara to select marbles for Julius's
Tomb and the facade of San Lorenzo.

[2] A notary and relative of his stepmother.

as Florence because I must leave, and I cannot come up there to Settignano to tell you a very important thing which I must tell you. Since I have heard from the very mouth of Pietro, who stays with me, certain things that I do not like, I am sending him this very morning to Pistoia. He will never come back where I am because I do not want him to be the ruination of our house. All of you who knew that I did not know about his conduct, should have warned me long ago, and we would have avoided such a scandal.

I shall not go away until I talk to you and leave you in this house. I beg you to put aside your anger, and to come.

Carrara, September, 1516

Dearest father – I read in Gismondo's letter that you are all in good health, except Buonarroto who has an ailment in one of his legs. It grieves me, for I fear that the use of medicines will make things worse. I would merely keep it warm and take care of myself, and let nature take its course.

I have not done anything yet about my business here. We have started quarrying in many places, and, if the weather remains good, I hope to have all my marbles ready in two months. Then I shall decide whether to work them here, in Pisa, or whether to go back to Rome. I would have liked to work them here, but I have been caused some grief, so that I do not feel at ease here.[8] That's all.

Carrara, November 23, 1516

Buonarroto – I learned that Lodovico was on the point of death, and that according to the doctor's latest report, if nothing else happens, he is out of danger. That being the case, I will not come to Florence, because it is very inconvenient for me. Still, if there were any danger, I should want by all means to see him

[8] The Carrarese were frightened by his selectivity and feared cutting marble which Michelangelo would not buy.

before he died, even if I had to die with him. If he should have
a relapse, may God spare him and us, see that he does not lack the
things of the spirit and the sacraments of the Church; and ask
him whether he wants us to do anything for his soul. See that he
lacks no material things, for I have always worked hard for him,
to help him in his needs before he dies; likewise, see to it that
your wife[4] takes loving care of him and of his needs, for I will
reward her and all of you if need be. Do all you can, even if it
should cost us all we have. I have nothing else to say. Live in
peace, and inform me, for I am very concerned.

Carrara, March 13, 1517

Buonarroto—You inform me that you have sold my horse and that
you paid the money through Luigi Gerardini. You did well: save
the rest for me.

I am telling you that I do not believe I will come to
Florence for several months, because the Pope commissioned me to
do the facade of San Lorenzo,[5] as you probably have heard.

It is no longer necessary that I come to see to it that
Baccio d'Agniolo hurry up and finish the model,[6] for I have made
one here myself the way I want it . . . and I no longer need him.

Let me know with whom I should send your mule. I cannot
keep it because I have no way of providing oats, straw, or hay.

May Christ watch over you.

Florence, March 20, 1517

Domenico Buoninsegni in Rome.

Messer Domenico—I have come to Florence to see the model which

---

[4] Buonarroto married Bartolommea di Chezzo, March 19, 1516,
with a dowry of five hundred florins.

[5] In December, 1516, Leo X took him off the Julius II Tomb,
commissioning him to do the facade of the Medici Church in
Florence.

[6] A Florentine architect and woodworker making a model for the
facade.

Baccio has finished, and found that it is the very same one, namely, child's work. Tomorrow morning I am returning to Carrara; I agreed with La Grassa[7] that I shall make there a clay model according to the design and send it to him. I do not know how the thing is going to turn out. I think that after all is said and done I will have to do it myself. This thing bothers me because of the Cardinal[8] and the Pope. I cannot do anything else.

I wish to inform you that I got out of the company I wrote you I had formed at Carrara, for the sake of appearances, and that I have placed with the same fellows, an order for one hundred cartloads of marbles. I also placed an order with another company I formed, namely for another hundred cartloads, and they have one year's time to deliver them to me ready for shipment on a boat.

Carrara, April, 1517

Messer Domenico Buoninsegni – Since I wrote you last, I had a small model made by a man who is here with me:[9] small, so that I can send it to you.

Carrara, May 2, 1517

Messer Domenico Buoninsegni – I was unable to attend to making the model, as I wrote I would do. I had at first rough-hewn a small one in clay, which I thought would be useful to me here, and although it is all wrinkled up, I will send it to you anyway, so that you will not think this whole thing is a swindle.

Be patient and read what follows, for it is important. What I want to tell you is that I feel confident I can carry out the work of the facade of San Lorenzo in such a way that it will

---

[7] Francesco di Giovanni, an assistant.
[8] Giulio de' Medici, cousin of the Pope, with whom Michelangelo lived in the Medici Palace for several years.
[9] La Grassa.

be the architectural and sculptural mirror of all Italy; but it is necessary that the Pope and the Cardinal make up their minds soon as to whether they want me to do it. And if they want me to do it, they must reach some conclusion, namely, either they give me a contract for the whole work, and have complete confidence in me, or find some other way unknown to me.

I have ordered many marbles, and have paid out money here and there, and I have started quarrying in various spots. And in some places where I have spent good money, the marbles did not turn out the way I expected, for marbles are unpredictable, especially when it comes to the large blocks I need, and which I want to be as beautiful as possible. For instance, I had a large block cut, but then slips which could not be foreseen, occurred on the slope, so that I cannot get out of it the two columns I had expected, and thus I lose half of the money I have already spent in this enterprise. If I meet with only a few such mishaps in dealing with so many marbles, they will certainly amount to a few hundred ducats. I do not know how to keep accounts, and in the end I will only be able to show what I spent for the marbles I will deliver. I would gladly follow the example of Pier Fantini,[10] but I do not have enough balm to last till the end. Also in view of the fact that I am old,[11] I do not think it is worth wasting so much time just to save the Pope two or three hundred ducats. And since I am solicited from Rome about my work, I have by all means to reach a decision.

This is the decision. If I knew that I had been commissioned to do the job and the price, I would not care if I threw away four hundred ducats, because I would not have to account for them. I would choose three or four of the best men available, and I would give them a commission to supply all the marbles, of the same quality as those I have quarried until now, for they are

---

[10] A doctor in a well-known proverb who gave free service and medicines.

[11] He is forty-two at this time.

marvelous, even if I only have a few of them. I would order that the marbles I have now be shipped to Florence, and I would go there to work for the Pope and on my own project.

But since I have not made the above contract with the Pope, I cannot do it; and I could not if I wanted to, take the marbles to Florence, and then see myself forced to take them to Rome. I would have to go directly to Rome to work, for, as I said, they are urging me.

As for the cost of the facade, considering how I want to do it and carry it out, and, among other things, so that the Pope will not have to get mixed up with anything, it could not be under thirty-five thousand gold ducats. For such an amount I would agree to do the work and I would complete it in six years, with the understanding that within six months, in order to get the marbles, I would need at least another thousand ducats. If the Pope does not like to do this, it will be necessary either that the expenses I have encountered so far for the above-mentioned work be charged to me, to my own loss, and that I return the thousand ducats to the Pope, or that he keep here somebody who will go on with this undertaking,[12] for I want to get away from here.

As for the mentioned price, if, once the work has started, I ever realized that it could be done for less, I am so honest with the Pope and the Cardinal, that I would let them know with greater solicitude than if I were faced with a loss. Just the same, I prefer to underestimate.

Messer Domenico, I beg you to let me know definitely the intentions of the Pope and the Cardinal, and this will be a great favor you do me, which I must add to all the others you have already done me.

Carrara, 1517

Dearest father – I am sending Pietro,[13] who lives with me, to

---

[12] The actual quarrying.
[13] Urbano, his assistant-apprentice.

Florence to fetch the mule. I beg you to give it to him. After he gets back here with it, I shall come to Florence to spend the whole month of August in order to make the model of San Lorenzo,[14] and send it to Rome, as I promised. Nothing else.

Pietrasanta, March, 1518

Pietro Urbano in Florence.

Pietro – I understand from a letter of yours that you are well and that you are busy learning. That pleases me a great deal: work hard and do not let anything keep you from drawing and giving yourself every opportunity. I wish to tell you that I went as far as Genoa to look for some boats to ship the marbles I have at Carrara, and I took them to Avenza; but the Carrarese corrupted the owners of said boats and they are giving me so much trouble that I must go to Pisa to fetch some others.[15] Actually I am leaving today, and as soon as I have given the order to load the marbles, I shall come immediately. I imagine that will be within fifteen days.

Florence, March, 1518

Domenico Buoninsegni – The marbles which were quarried for St. Peter's came out very well, and worthy to be used in St. Peter's; they can be removed easily, and they are closer to the shore than the others; they are close to a place called Corvara; no road is required to be built from said place to the shore, except over that small marshy land which is near the shore. However, in order to secure marble suitable for statues, such as I need, the existing road has to be enlarged from Corvara to a couple of miles above Serravezza; furthermore, about a mile of it will have to be

---

[14] A larger wooden model, delivered to the Pope, December 29, 1517.

[15] Carrara is outraged because Leo X has ordered Michelangelo to open new quarries in Pietrasanta territory, under the control of Florence.

completely rebuilt, namely, it will have to be hewn out from the mountainside with picks as far as the spot where the marbles can be loaded. For this reason, if the Pope should have fixed only what he needs to get his marbles out, namely the section over the marsh, I shall not be able to tend to the marbles for St. Peter's, as I promised the Cardinal.[16] But should the Pope take care of the whole road, I shall do what I promised.

I know that you are wise and prudent, and that you love me: so, I beg you to fix things up with the Cardinal the way you see fit. If nothing comes of it, I shall return to Rome. I would not go to Carrara, for I would not be able to get there, in twenty years, the marbles I need. Furthermore, I have made many enemies there in connection with this matter. If I return to Rome, I shall be obliged to cast in bronze.[17]

I wish to communicate to you also that since I informed the workmen of the project, they have made great plans on this matter of the marbles, and I believe that the notaries, the arch-notaries, the purveyors, and the assistant-purveyors have already seen to it that the profits are doubled in that district. Therefore, think about it, and do all you can to prevent them from getting control, for then it would be more difficult to get the marbles from them than from Carrara.

I beg you to let me know soon what you think I should do, and remember me to the Cardinal. I am his representative here, therefore I shall do only what you advise me, in the belief that that is his intention.

If in my letters to you I should not write as correctly as one would expect, or if, sometimes, I leave out the main verb, please forgive me, for I have a bell ringing in my ears which does not let me think of anything I want.

---

[16] Giulio de' Medici, advisor of Pope Leo X.
[17] A part of the planned facade was bronzework, which Michelangelo hated.

Pietrasanta, March 29, 1518

Pietro Urbano – When the boatmen come to you bearing Donato's[18] letter, give each one of them the sum indicated in the letter I have given him written in my own hand.

Pay also the cart drivers at the rate of twenty-five soldi for delivery of one thousand large blocks, and twenty soldi for one thousand small ones. Keep a record of the people you pay and why.

Pay the ninety lire tax at the Contracts' office, and take the book and the papers.

Give Baccio di Puccione the money he asks of you, and make a note of it.

Buy some reeds, and have the vines in the orchard taken care of; and if you find either some soil or something else which is nice and dry with which to fill out the yard, have it done.

Buy twenty yards of strong rope, pay for it, and write it down.

Go to confession, keep on learning, and take care of the house.

Settle accounts with Gismondo, pay him, and have him give you a statement.

I am leaving you forty ducats today, March twenty-ninth.

Florence, 1518

Donato Benti, sculptor in Pietrasanta.

My dear Master Donato – Cecone[19] came to ask me for money; I refused to give him anything, because I do not know what they have done there: so I beg you to tell them to let me know what they have done. If they have something coming, I want to give it to them. I am not the man who would fail to abide by a contract.

---

[18] Benti, Florentine sculptor supervising the quarrying in Pietrasanta.

[19] A stonecutter. Michelangelo's spelling. Correctly Ceccone.

As for your things, Cecone tells me that you slow them down with the measurements, and that they cannot work. Furthermore, that the Pietrasanta men I hired to quarry, have left their jobs and are not doing anything. I do not believe all this. I shall soon be there.

Florence, 1518

Niccolò Quaratesi – Last night when we were at the Canto de' Bischeri, I was unable to give you a definite answer, since the fellow in behalf of whom you were speaking was present; I was afraid I might cause you some embarrassment. And although I shook my head several times, just the same I did not say flatly what I would have told you had we been alone. I am telling you now with this letter: for certain reasons I cannot take on a shopboy, all the more if he is from out of town. Therefore I told you that I was not going to do anything about it for two or three months, so that your friend would not leave his son here with the hope that I would employ him. Instead, he did not understand what I meant, and he replied that if I saw him, not only would I accept him under my roof, but even in my own bed. I am making it clear to you that I am not interested in this consolation. Therefore, give him a negative answer for me; I am sure you will know how to do it in such a way that he will go away in a good frame of mind.

Pietrasanta, April 2, 1518

Buonarroto – I should like you to let me know whether Jacopo Salviati[20] has had the Consuls of the Wool Guild reach a decision according to the sketch,[21] as he promised me; and if he

---

[20] Jacopo Salviati was a member of the Council of the Wool Guild; he was a banker and emissary for the Medici family, and was married to Lucrezia de' Medici, *Il Magnifico's* oldest child.

[21] Of a Pietrasanta road being built by the Wool Guild and the Board of the Duomo which Michelangelo wanted to superintend.

has not done so, beg him for me to do it. If you see that he is not going to do it, let me know, so that I may get away from here, for I have taken on an assignment that will drive me penniless, and furthermore it is not turning out as I had thought. Nevertheless, if they keep their promise to me, I will go on with this undertaking, with great expense and worry, and with no certainty for the time being.

Concerning the construction of the road here, tell Jacopo Salviati that I will do whatever his Magnificence wishes, and that he will not be deceived, for in such things I am not after my own interest, but after the interest and the glory of my masters and of my country. If I asked the Pope or the Cardinal to give me full control over the construction of said road, I did it only to be able to have it directed toward those places where the best marbles are to be found, for not everyone is a good judge of them. I did not ask for that authority in order to make money on the road, for such a thought never entered my head; as a matter of fact, I beg the Magnificent Jacopo to have the road built by Master Donato Benti, because he is very capable in such things, and, as I understand, conscientious.

All I ask for is the authority to determine its course and its bed as I see fit, because I know where the best marbles are located and also what kind of road is required for the transit of carts. Furthermore, I think I can save money for those who are having it built. Also, beg his Magnificence to ask his men in Pisa to do me the favor of finding the boats to ship my marbles from Carrara. I went to Genoa and I brought four boats to the shore to have the marbles loaded. The Carrarese have corrupted the owners of said boats, and decided to beset me, so that I haven't concluded anything, and today I may go to Pisa and secure other boats. So recommend me to him as I said, and write me.

Pisa, April 7, 1518

Buonarroto – As I wrote you, I was being prevented from shipping my marbles. In Pisa, through the intercession of Jacopo

Salviati, and for a fair charge, I turned them over to a ship owner who will serve me. Therefore, give my regards to his Magnificence and offer him my thanks. I received a letter from him, but I do not answer it because I am not up to it; however, within fifteen days I shall be in Florence, and I hope to reply by word of mouth much better than I could do in writing. I hope the road and everything else will come out all right. Now I am leaving for Pietrasanta. Francesco Peri[22] is giving me one hundred ducats which I am to take to the Commissary of Pietrasanta for the road.

Pietrasanta, April 18, 1518

Buonarroto – I heard that no decision has been reached yet:[23] I am really upset. For this reason, I am sending to Florence a helper of mine with the single purpose of his waiting the whole day of Thursday to see whether the decision is taken, and of bringing me the news on Friday morning. If what I am asking for is granted, I will go on with this undertaking; if it is not granted, I will mount on horseback at once, and I will go to see the Cardinal de' Medici and the Pope. I will tell them how I feel about it, and I will give up my work here and return to Carrara, for I am entreated to return there as one entreats Christ.[24] The stoneworkers I brought here from Florence know nothing about quarries or marbles. They have cost me already more than one hundred and thirty ducats, and they haven't yet quarried one single slab that is any good. Furthermore, they try to work for the *Opera*[25] and for others with the money they receive from me. Since I have been here I have wasted about three hundred

---

[22] Employee of Salviati in Pisa.

[23] On awarding him supervision of the road.

[24] The Carrarese, out of favor with Leo X, were unable to sell their marble.

[25] The Board of Works of the Cathedral in Florence, which wanted marble paving blocks.

ducats, and to date I do not see anything that will do for me. It would be easier to resuscitate the dead than to try to tame these mountains and to make this town art-conscious. If the Wool Guild gave me, for what I am doing here, one hundred ducats a month, besides the marbles and the granting of the road contract, it wouldn't be doing the wrong thing. Therefore, plead my case with Jacopo Salviati, and write me via my helper; the uncertainty is wearing me down.

The boats I hired in Pisa never came. I think I was duped: that's how all I do turns out. Cursed a thousand times be the day and the hour I left Carrara! This is the cause of my utter ruin, but I shall return there soon. Nowadays it is a sin to do well.

Florence, May, 1518

The Captain of Cortona.[26]

Captain – While I was in Rome the first year Leo was Pope, there came the painter Master Luca da Cortona.[27] I met him one day near Monte Giordano, and he told me that he had come to talk to the Pope, and that he had come close to losing his head for the love of the Medici family, and that he had the impression that now they did not give him recognition for it. In the course of our conversation, he asked me for forty giuli, and he indicated to me where I was to send them for him, namely, to the shop of a shoemaker, and so I did. Later, after several days, he came to my house in the Macello dei Corvi district,[28] which I still occupy, and found me working on a marble statue seven and a half feet tall, which represents a man standing with his arms behind his back.[29] He told me his woes, and he asked me for another forty giuli, saying that he wanted to leave. I went up to my room, and came back with forty giuli, which I gave him in the presence of

---

[26] A town between Arezzo and Perugia.
[27] Luca Signorelli, the famous painter.
[28] Which he bought in 1513.
[29] The Heroic Slave.

5. The Great Flood. Section of the Sistine Chapel Ceiling, 1508-1509.
(Courtesy of Alinari)

6. Creation of Man. Section of the Sistine Chapel Ceiling, 1511.
(Courtesy of Alinari-Anderson)

a Bolognese housemaid of mine. He took the money, and went away. I have never seen him since. At that time I was in poor health, and before Master Luca left my house, I complained in his presence of not being able to work. He said to me these words: do not worry, the Angels will descend from Heaven, they will seize your arms and will help you.

I am writing you this because, if these things were repeated to him, he would recall them, and he would not say he has returned the money to me . . . and furthermore you also believe he has returned it to me; that I am a real rogue. Your Lordship may think what he wishes: I swear that my money has not been returned to me.

Florence, July 15, 1518

Cardinal Giulio de' Medici in Rome.
Most Reverend Monsignor – In the hope that during the course of this year I will get a certain quantity of marbles for the facade of San Lorenzo in Florence, and unable to find suitable rooms to work them either within San Lorenzo or in its vicinity, I decided to buy a piece of land near Santa Caterina from the Chapter of Santa Maria del Fiore, in order to build a suitable site for myself. This lot cost me about three hundred large gold ducats. I had to work two months to get the Chapter to sell it, and had to pay sixty ducats more than it is worth. They made me understand that they were sorry, but that they could not deviate from the directive of the Papal Bull concerning sales. Now, if the Pope makes Bulls enabling one to steal, I beg your most Reverend Lordship to have one made for me also, for I need it more than they do. And if such Bulls are not made, I beg your Lordship to see to it that justice is done to me as follows: the said lot I purchased is not sufficient for my needs; the Chapter owns a certain amount of land behind my lot: wherefore, I beg your Lordship to have them give me another piece of land whereby I am repaid the excess I disbursed for the lot I purchased.

As for the construction, the beginning of anything is always difficult . . .

Serravezza, August 12, 1518

Buonarroto – If I shouldn't be there in time to pay the taxes on the lot I purchased, see that you fix things in such a way that I avoid delinquency until I return. I think that my business here will turn out well, but I am having a lot of trouble. I am sending Michele to Florence to buy certain things from the Opera. If he needs a mule to carry them back here, help him find one, and keep the cost down to a minimum.

Serravezza, August, 1518

Buonarroto – Of the stoneworkers who came here, only Meo[30] and Cecone are left: the others returned to Florence. I gave them four ducats, and I promised to give them money continuously for their living expenses, to see if they would please me. They worked only a few days and spitefully at that, so that that little wretch Rubecchio[30] practically ruined a column I had quarried. But what hurts even more is the fact that they are returning to Florence, and, in order to remove the blame from themselves, they give me and the marble quarries a bad name; so that, if I should later want other men, I wouldn't be able to find any. Actually, Meo and Cecone would have remained and done their best, but they could not do anything all alone, and so I dismissed them.

Sandro[30] left here too. He spent several months here with a mule and a colt living pompously, and busy fishing and flirting. He wasted one hundred of my ducats: he left here a quantity of marbles from which I am supposed to choose those I can use. I cannot find from among them twenty-five ducats' worth of marbles, for they are terrible. Either through malice or ignorance, he has treated me very badly. I think I'll stay here one more month.

Serravezza, September 16, 1518

Buonarroto – I learn that you have in your hands a good farm

---

[30] Florentine stonecarver.

located not far from Fiesole, and also that Pier Francesco Borgherini has spoken to you of the house. I say, then, concerning Pier Francesco's house, that I am willing to buy it at an honest price, provided the air is not bad.

If you think it is good, I am also willing to buy the farm; however, if you can hold out until I return there, I would prefer it. I plan to be back within fifteen or twenty days.

You tell me that Cecone has recovered from his ailment, and that if I want him to come here he will do so gladly. Reply to him that winter is starting, and it rains all the time, and that it is impossible to stay up in the mountains working. Therefore, I do not think it would be a good idea for him to come now, for we would be wasting our time and our money.

Serravezza, September, 1518

Berto da Filicaia in Florence.[31]

Berto – I trust in your indulgence, and I thank you for the favors and courtesies I have received from you; I am ever at your complete disposal. The road is practically finished; there is only a small amount of work left, namely, there are certain rocks to be cut, or rather tunnels to be dug out. One of these is where the road that comes out of the river runs into the old road at Rimagno; the other tunnel is just beyond Rimagno on the way to Serravezza: here, there is a large boulder that sits across the road; and the third one is at the edge of Serravezza going toward Corvara. There are also a few places that must be leveled out with the pick. Everything would be finished in a couple of weeks if we only had a few good stonecutters. I have not gone out on the marsh for about a week; at that time they were doing a rather poor job of filling it. If they kept on working, I imagine that by now they have finished. As for the marbles, I had the column which I had hewn out taken down safely to the canal, and it is about thirty-five yards from the road. Taking it down was

---

[31] A friend who went with him to Pietrasanta to retrieve his broken column.

more of an enterprise than I had anticipated; a few workers were hurt in the process, and one of them had his neck broken and died immediately; I myself came near losing my life. The other column had been almost completely hewn out, when I noticed that there was a vein cutting across it; I had to work back into the hill the whole thickness of the column in order to avoid that vein, and I hope that now everything will be all right. We are still hewing away. The terrain where we are quarrying here is very rough, and the workers are very poor at this type of work. Therefore, it will take quite a bit of patience for a few months, until we have tamed the mountains, and the men have become more skilled. Then we shall proceed more rapidly; the main thing is that I shall do at all costs what I promised, and if God helps me I shall do the most beautiful work ever done in Italy.

After I wrote the above, I received a reply from those men who, six months ago, began quarrying a certain amount of marbles at Pietrasanta. They neither want to work, nor return to me the one hundred ducats I gave them. For this reason I am planning to come to Florence to see the officers of justice and ask for payment of damages. I hope that the Magnificent Jacopo Salviati will help me to obtain justice.

Serravezza, 1518

Buonarroto – I would like you to find out the measurements of the lot of Santa Caterina and its price. Do this in a hurry because I must write Giovanni da Ricasoli who is holding it for me.

If I were sure to get it, I would wait a few months before buying Pier Francesco's house. However, the contract should be drawn up now, and I am ready to make the deposit on it now. If not, let us not talk about it any more.

Serravezza, September, 1518

Pietro Urbano – If your finger has healed, and you think you should come here with Michele, you may come; and bring me two shirts. If you do not think you should come, send them with Michele, and let me know how you are.

Florence, September, 1518

The Most Reverend Monsignor de' Medici in Rome.[32]

Most Reverend Monsignor—We are quarrying away at Pietra-santa for the marbles of San Lorenzo, and upon finding the Carrarese more humble than they usually are, I gave the order that a large quantity of marbles be excavated, so that by the time the first rains come, I hope to have a large number of blocks in Florence, and I think I will be able to keep my promise to the last detail. May God grant it, for all I care in the world is to please you. I think that within one month I shall need one thousand ducats. I beg your Most Reverend Lordship not to fail me with the money.

Further, I wish to inform your Most Reverend Lordship that I have sought but never found a house large enough to carry out in it this enterprise, namely, the marble and bronze statues.[33] Recently, Matteo Bartoli found for me an admirable site, which is well suited for the building of a room for such work: this is the Square before the church of Ognissanti. According to what Matteo, who is one of the administrators, tells me, the monks are willing to sell me their rights to it; the whole city is happy over it. No one else has anything to say about it, except the officers of the Torre, who are in charge of the wall along the Arno River,[34] against which are built all the houses of Borg'Ognissanti. As for them, they will give me permission to build my room against that wall. The only thing that remains to be done is this: the monks would like Your Most Reverend Lordship to write them a letter saying that this matter meets with your pleasure. Therefore, if your Lordship would be so kind as to have someone write a couple

---

[32] Cardinal Giulio.

[33] For the facade of San Lorenzo.

[34] Principally of the defense towers in the city's defense wall.

of lines to the monks or to Matteo, I would appreciate it.[35]

Florence, December 21, 1518

Lionardo, saddle maker, at the Borgherini's shop in Rome.

My dear friend Lionardo – I am full of grief at not being able to do what I should like to do; such is my bad luck. Eight days ago Pietro, who lives with me, returned in the evening from Porto Venere with Donato Benti, who is working for me in Carrara in connection with the loading of the marbles; they had left a loaded barge in Pisa, but it never got here because it has not rained yet, and the Arno River is bone-dry. There are four other barges in Pisa which we hired for these marbles; as soon as it rains, they will be loaded and they will come here, and I shall begin to work hard. All this makes me the unhappiest man in the world. Metello Vari is also after me for the statue I agreed to make for him.[36] The marble for his statue is also in Pisa, and will come on the first shipment. I never replied to him, and I have decided to stop writing even you until I start to work. I am overcome with grief, and I feel I have become a cheat against my wishes.

I have readied a lovely room here, where I shall be able to have twenty statues at one time. I cannot cover it because there is no lumber in Florence, and none will get here until it rains. I have come to the conclusion by now that it will start raining only when it can do me some damage.

Do not tell the Cardinal anything else, for I have already made a poor impression on him.

Florence, December 22, 1518

Francesco Peri at the Salviati[37] in Pisa.

My dearest Superior – I have not come to settle accounts, as you

---

[35] Michelangelo does build this studio.

[36] The Risen Christ. Now in Santa Maria sopra Minerva, Rome.

[37] Offices of Jacopo Salviati.

wrote me several times I should do, because I have not been well. Now I am well and strong, and as soon as I receive an important answer I am expecting from Rome I'll mount on horseback and come. Since you have been so patient with me, I beg you to be patient a few more days.

I am aware of the services you have rendered me and of all the trouble I have caused you. I am obliged to you in eternity, and, although it is of little importance, I place myself and all I have completely at your service.

————◆◆————

A PRAYER FOR AID

Oh, make me see Thee, Lord, where'er I go!
If mortal beauty sets my soul on fire,
that flame when near to Thine must needs expire,
and I with love of only Thee shall glow.

Dear Lord, Thy help I seek against this woe,
these torments that my spirit vex and tire;
Thou only with new strength canst re-inspire
my will, my sense, my courage faint and low.

Thou gavest me on earth this soul divine;
and thou within this body weak and frail
didst prison it—how sadly there to live!

How can I make its lot less vile than mine?
Without Thee, Lord, all goodness seems to fail.
To alter fate is God's prerogative.

————◆◆————

Florence, December 26, 1518

Donato Benti—I wrote you through Domenico called Zucca, Andrea's partner, that I would come there right after the holidays. Now it so happens that Francesco Peri is here, and he tells me that he wants to stay here four or six more days. Since I have to settle accounts with him in Pisa, I have waited here in order to go to Pisa with him, and then come to Serravezza. Because of my delay here, I am sending you ten large ducats so that if the time to load has arrived, you go right ahead with it. Francesco Peri promised me that the freight of all the marbles you take to Pisa will be paid there. Recently he has informed me of your hard work, although I already knew about it and appreciated it. I thank you for it and I am deeply obliged to you. I am certain that if the present Pope lives this enterprise will bring you a great deal of good.

Florence, 1519

Messer Domenico Buoninsegni – I gather from your letter that Bernardo Nicolini wrote you that I got somewhat angry with him because of a paragraph of yours which said that the Lord of Carrara attacked me and the Cardinal[38] complained about me. I became angry with him because he read said passage publicly in a merchant's shop as if I were standing trial, and so as to inform the people why I was being sentenced to death.

You will tell me that I would do well to allocate the San Lorenzo marbles to others. I have already allocated them three times, and every time I was cheated. This because the stone-hewers here do not know anything about marbles, and when they realize that they do not succeed, they leave. Thus, I have wasted several hundred ducats on them. And for this reason I have had to start them out myself, showing them the grain of marbles, what damages them, and which are the bad ones; and even how one should quarry, for I am skilled in such things.

Serravezza, April 20, 1519

Pietro – Things turned out very badly. Saturday morning we started with all precautions to lower a column; everything was in perfect readiness, but we had only lowered it about one hundred feet when a lewis-ring snapped, and the column fell into

---

[38] The Medici were preparing to postpone the facade because of waning funds.

the river and was smashed into a hundred pieces. Donato had ordered this lewis-ring from his godfather Lazzero, who is a blacksmith. As for its being adequate, I can say that if it had been a good one, it would have hoisted four columns, and judging by its appearance you wouldn't have doubted a thing. After it broke, we became aware of the fraud, for it was not solid through and through, and there was not enough iron in its thickness as there is in the rib of a knife. All of us who were around came close to losing our lives, and furthermore, a lovely column was ruined. This past Carnival I left Donato to take care of these iron implements; I told him to go to the ironworks and to get good soft irons, instead you see what he did to me. When you think that these hoisting machines are twice the size of those used at the *Opera*, there is no doubt that if they were made of good iron, they would hold an infinite weight. One must be patient. I shall be there for the coming holidays and, God willing, begin to work.

FLORENCE

1519–1533

May, 1519

Pietro – You must go to Messer Giovan Badessa[1] in Pietrasanta, and have him give you the contract[2] which I properly drew up with the Carrarese; with Pollina, with Leone and with Bello. This contract concerns eight pieces of marble which they must block out for eight statues:[3] four of nine feet and four of ten feet, of the width and thickness specified. Said contract reads that around the middle of May I will give the mentioned Carrarese thirty large gold ducats, provided, by that time, they have hewn out four of the blocks, two of nine feet and two of ten. If they have not blocked out the four pieces of marble, do not give them any money. If they have blocked them, and they are as is specified in the contract, give them thirty ducats just as the contract reads: give them the money in Pietrasanta. Then, in Carrara, have them give you a note, signed before witnesses, stating that you went there at mid-May to take money to the said workmen in fulfillment of the contract.

You will see Marco, who collected two ducats to roughhew the block I had at Sponda, and make of it a statue of three or four feet. See if he has roughhewed it, and if you can have him take it to the shore, and put it on a boat together with another block which is on the beach and which I got from Leone. Marco will find the boats to ship them to Pisa as usual. There is also a blocked-out statue of three and a half feet which I got from Cagione.[4] For the drawing up of the mentioned contract, Ser Giovan Badessa has received three barili; pay him the balance, which I think may be as much as one ducat. Do the best you can.

September 17, 1519

Pietro – I am sending you the doublet, a pair of stockings, the cloak, and the felt with a fellow called Turchetto, who works in

---

[1] A notary.
[2] Of April 13, 1519.
[3] For the facade.
[4] A Carrarese quarrier.

Buonarroto's shop. I would have come there to see you,[5] but I am so busy, that I cannot leave; just the same, if it is necessary that I come, let me know. Whenever you feel well enough to come here, send a trustworthy person to fetch the mule, and write me what I must give him, and I will pay him.

1519

Meo – I am again urged to work, and to send someone to quarry again for marbles to replace the blocks which are not good. Therefore, I beg you to be in San Lorenzo Square a little earlier than usual tomorrow, so that we may look over a couple of pieces of marble which are there, and see whether there are any flaws before the sun bothers us.

1519

Domenico Buoninsegni – I am ever ready to risk my person and my life for Cardinal de' Medici, if the necessity arises. I am referring to the previous marbles which we contracted at Carrara. You know the Cardinal's will about this far better than I do. Therefore, let me know what you think I should do, and I will do it. I have no means of riding there myself, nor have I money to spend. If I had a way, I would do what I thought would be useful and pleasing to the Cardinal.

June, 1520

Cardinal Bernardo Dovizi in Rome.[6]

Monsignor – I beg you, most reverend Lordship, not as a friend or servant, for I am not worthy of being either, but as a low, poor and crazy man, that you have Sebastiano,[7] the Venetian painter, now that Raphaello is dead,[8] share in the works at the Palace. And if it should seem to your Lordship that kind offices are

---

[5] Pietro became ill at Carrara in August.

[6] Long-time Medici tutor and trusted companion to Leo X, who made him a Cardinal. He superintended all festivities.

[7] Luciani, friend and portrait painter.

[8] Raphaello died April 6, 1520.

wasted upon a man like me, I am of the opinion that on certain
rare occasions one may find some satisfaction in being kind even
to fools; in the same way that a man who is tired of eating capons
finds pleasure in eating onions, for the sake of a change of food.
You do favors to important men every day. I beg your Lordship
to try to do a favor to me: it will be a very great favor, and the
said Sebastiano is a talented man. If your favor should be wasted
on me, it will not be so on Sebastiano, for I am certain he will
prove a credit to your Lordship.

1520

Sebastiano Luciani[9] in Rome.
In the year 1516, while I was at Carrara to get marbles for the
construction of Pope Julius's tomb, Pope Leo sent for me in
connection with the facade of San Lorenzo which he wanted to
build in Florence. So, on the fifth of December I left Carrara
and went to Rome. When I arrived there, I made a sketch for
said facade, and upon that, Pope Leo gave me the commission to
have marbles quarried at Carrara for the work. After I returned
to Carrara from Rome on the last day of that December, Pope
Leo sent me through Jacopo Salviati one thousand ducats to
quarry the marbles for the work. This money was brought to me
by a servant of his called Bentivoglio. I received it around the
eighth of the following month, January; and that is how I made
out the receipt. Then, the following August, upon the Pope's
request that I send him a model of the work, I came from
Carrara to Florence in order to make it. Thus, I made it to scale,
of wood with wax figures, and I sent it to him in Rome. As soon
as he saw it, he had me go to Rome. And so I went, and took
upon myself the contract of said facade, as is indicated by the
document I signed with His Holiness. Then, in order to do what
His Holiness wanted, I had to take to Florence the marbles which I
was to take to Rome for the tomb of Pope Julius: and when I

[9] Apparently for delivery by Sebastiano to Michelangelo's business
manager in Rome.

finished working them, I took them back to Rome. The Pope promised me that he would pay for the tax and the shipment costs, which amount to about eight hundred ducats, although it is not in the contract.

On February sixth, 1517, I returned from Rome to Florence, and, since I had contracted at my own expense the facade of San Lorenzo, and since Pope Leo was to have me paid in Florence four thousand ducats on account of said work, as is written in the contract, around the twenty-fifth, I received from Jacopo Salviati eight hundred ducats and I made out a receipt; then I went to Carrara. But since there they abide by the contracts and commissions made earlier for the marbles of said work, and since, furthermore, the Carrarese were bent on harassing me, I went to have the marbles excavated at Serravezza, a mountain at Pietrasanta[10] under the rule of Florence. After I had blocked out six columns of about twenty-five feet each, and many other pieces of marble, and after I started there the present-day quarrying, for no quarrying had ever been done there before, on March twentieth, fifteen hundred and eighteen I came to Florence in order to secure the money for the transfer of said marbles. Thus, on March twenty-sixth, fifteen hundred and nineteen, the Cardinal de' Medici had the Gaddi of Florence pay me five hundred ducats for Pope Leo's work, and I properly made out a receipt for said money. Then, during this very same period of time, the Cardinal, on behalf of the Pope, stopped me from continuing the above-mentioned work, for, they said, they wanted to free me from the chore of shipping the marbles, and they wanted to deliver them to me in Florence, and make a new agreement. That's how things are standing even today.

Now, since at that time the *Operai*[11] di Santa Maria del Fiore sent a large number of stonecutters to Pietrasanta, or rather

---

[10] Roman engineers under the Caesars had tried to open quarries there and failed.

[11] Directors of Duomo works.

to Serravezza, to take over the quarry I had started and taken possession of the marbles which I had excavated for the facade of San Lorenzo, in order to use them for the floor of Santa Maria del Fiore; since Pope Leo wanted me to proceed with the facade of San Lorenzo, and the Cardinal de' Medici had commissioned the marbles of said facade to others rather than to me, and had turned over to them what I had started at Serravezza, without taking me into account, I complained bitterly, for neither the Cardinal nor the workmen could take over my things before the contract with the Pope had been broken. And upon calling off the contract for the facade of San Lorenzo in agreement with the Pope, either His Holiness or myself would be entitled to the quarry, the marbles and the tools. After this had been settled, either party could do what he wished with it.

Now, concerning this matter, the Cardinal told me to show how much money I received and how much I spent, and that he wants to release me, so that he can take whatever marbles he wishes from the mentioned quarry at Serravezza, both for the *Opera* di Santa Maria del Fiore and for himself.

Therefore, I have shown that I received two thousand three hundred ducats, as I have indicated in this letter, and also that I spent eighteen hundred of them. Of these, about two hundred and fifty were spent for shipping up the Arno River the marbles for Pope Julius's tomb. To send them to Rome will cost more than five hundred ducats. I do not reckon the wooden model of the facade which I sent him to Rome; I do not reckon the period of three years I wasted in this work; I do not reckon the great insult put on me by being brought here to do the work, and then see it taken away from me; and for what reason I have not yet learned. I do not reckon my house in Rome, which I left, and where marbles, furniture and blocked-out statues have suffered upwards of five hundred ducats. Not taking into account the above things, of the twenty-three hundred ducats only five hundred remain in my possession.

Now this is the agreement: let Pope Leo take over the

quarry I started with the mentioned marbles which have been excavated, and I will keep the money I have left. Furthermore, I will be completely free. I have decided to have a brief drawn up to send to the Pope for his signature.

Now you know how the whole thing stands. I beg you to make out for me a rough copy of said brief, and that you fix the matter of the money I received for the work at San Lorenzo in such a way that I can never be asked for it; and also, that you make clear how in exchange for the money I received, Pope Leo is taking over the mentioned quarry, marbles, tools, . . .

March, 1521

Giusto di Matteo, shoemaker in Pistoia.

Giusto – I learn from your letter that Masina's husband, Giulio Forteguerri, would sell the house he owns here on Via Mozza, if he could get twenty soldi to the lira. It must be a year since I spoke to you about it, and since I never heard anything further on this matter, I started to build in an orchard I own near there. Now, if Giulio and Masina are to sell the mentioned house, I shall take it and give up the construction I started. So I beg you to let me know how much they want for it, and if the price is fair, I shall not back out.

February, 1522

The prudent youth Gherardo Perini[12] in Pesaro.

All your friends, dearest Gherardo, rejoice with me, the more so the ones who you know love you most, upon hearing that you are in good health and well. We, your friends, are also well, and we all send you our best.

February whatever day it may be, according to my housemaid.

Your most faithful and poor friend

---

[12] A friend mentioned by Aretino in one of his attempted blackmail letters.

Ser Giovan Francesco Fattucci, Chaplain Santa Maria del Fiore in Florence.

My dearest Ser Giovan Francesco[13] – Since, as you know, the first tailor cannot take care of me, and since the last one I have gone to is your friend, I beg you to tell him not to behave with me next Sunday the way he did the last, when he refused to see how the coat fitted me. Had he done so, he might have fixed it so that it would look well. These last few days I have been wearing it, and it was very tight on me, especially around the chest. I wonder whether he did not do a good job so that he could save some of the cloth for himself, although actually he looks like an honest man. Well, that is past, but for the next clothes he is to make me, I beg you to tell him to keep his eyes open when he takes my measurements, for I shouldn't want to change tailor again.

It is eleven o'clock, and every hour seems a year to me.

Your most faithful sculptor on Via Mozza, next to the corner.

June, 1523

Most honorable father – In a letter of yours I received this morning I get a good piece of news, namely it seems to me that you are not satisfied with the contract[14] we made recently among ourselves. I am even less satisfied with it, and I beg you to make the others agree, for I am always ready to cancel it. I have no way of paying the money to Gismondo, and I wouldn't have agreed to the contract if you hadn't promised me to help pay him. Therefore, without going to any notaries, come when it is convenient for you and get me out of a quandary, for I am more in need of money than of your farms.

---

[13] Florence friend who took over Michelangelo's business and contract matters with the Pope. Later, he went to Rome for him.
[14] June 16, 1523, in which Michelangelo agreed to pay Gismondo five hundred florins in two years as his share of their mother's inheritance.

June, 1523

Lodovico – I do not reply to your whole letter, but only to those things that seem to matter; I scoff at the others. You say that you cannot get your payments at the bank because I have had the account put in my name. This is not true, and I must reply to you on this point because I want you to know that you are deceived by somebody whom you trust, and who, perhaps, has cashed your payments and made use of them, and makes you believe this for his own convenience. I have not had the account set up in my name at the bank, nor could I do it if I wanted; but it is true that, in the presence of Rafaello da Gagliano, the notary said to me: I shouldn't want your brothers to make an agreement with the bank, and then after the death of your father you would not find the money here. Then he took me to the bank where—and this cost me fifteen grossoni—he had a condition placed on it that no one could touch it as long as you were alive. And as you know, the contract says you are the usufructuary as long as you live.

I have explained to you about the contract,[15] and said to have it canceled when you want, since you do not like it. I have explained to you about the bank money, and you can see it when you like; I have always made and unmade contracts exactly as you wanted: I do not know what else you want of me. If I bother you alive, you have found the way to remedy that, and thus you will inherit the key of the treasure-trove you say I have. And you will be acting wisely, for the whole city of Florence knows that you were wealthy and that I always stole from you, and deserve to be punished. You will be greatly praised for that. Go on shouting and saying of me what you wish, but stop writing me, for you prevent me from working, and I still have to make good what you have received from me during the last twenty-five years. I would prefer not to have to tell you this, but I cannot help it.

---

[15] With Gismondo.

Take care of yourself for we die only once, and cannot return to earth to remedy our misdeeds. You have waited until death to do such things! God help you.

July, 1523

Bartolomeo Angiolini[16] in Rome.

My dearest friend Bartolomeo—I received in your letter a letter from the Cardinal:[17] I am amazed that you had him write for such a trifling matter. I am anxious to oblige His Most Reverend Lordship, and I shall do my very best and as soon as I can.

I have many commitments, and I am old[18] and indisposed; so much so that, if I work one day, I must rest the following four days. For this reason, I hesitate to give a definite promise. I shall try very hard to oblige at all costs. I have nothing else to say.

1523

Fattucci in Rome.

Ser Giovan Francesco—Two years have passed since I returned from Carrara where I had commissioned the excavation of marbles for the Cardinal's tombs.[19] At that time he told me to find some means whereby I would complete the tombs quickly. I sent him in writing the various plans I had for them, as you well know since you read them; namely, that I would make them on contract, by the month, by the day, and even as a gift; in whatever way was agreeable to His Lordship, for I was anxious to make them. No one of my suggestions was accepted. They said that I was not willing to work for the Cardinal. Later, when I was

---

[16] A friend who handled his affairs in Rome.

[17] Grimani, who wanted one of Michelangelo's works in any medium.

[18] Forty-eight.

[19] The tombs for the Medici Chapel, commissioned in 1520. Pope Leo X died December 1, 1521, and Cardinal Giulio failed to advance the project since then.

approached again by him, I offered to make models in wood of exactly the size of the tombs and place on them all the statues in clay and lopping, made to size and finished exactly as they would be; and I showed him that this would take a short time and cost little. This was when we wanted to purchase the Caccini's yard. Nothing came of it, as you know.

Later, as soon as I learned about the Cardinal's trip to Lombardy,[20] I went to see him. He told me to get some men and to hasten securing the marbles, and furthermore that I should do my best and show him a few concrete results, without asking him anything else. Also, that if he lived for a while, he would have the facade made too, and that he left to Domenico Buoninsegni the commissioning of all the money that was needed. When the Cardinal left, I wrote Domenico Buoninsegni all these things, and I told him that I was ready to do everything the Cardinal wished. I kept a copy of this for myself, and I wrote everything in front of witnesses. Domenico called on me at once, and he told me that he had no commission whatever. Finally, upon the Cardinal's return, Figiovanni told me that he had asked about me. I went to see him immediately. He said to me, "We should like to see something good on these tombs, something fashioned by your own hands." He did not say that he wanted me to make them. I left, and I told him that I would return to speak to him when the marbles had arrived.

Now you know how in Rome the Pope[21] has been told about this tomb of Julius, and how a decree has been drawn up to have him sign it and start proceedings against me, and request of me what I have received in connection with this work, along with both damages and interest; and you know that the Pope gave permission to do this if I refuse to make the tomb. So, unless I want to invite trouble, I must make it as it has been or-

[20] France had invaded Lombardy. Cardinal Giulio was the Papal legate for Pope Adrian VI.

[21] Adrian VI received complaints against Michelangelo from the heirs of Julius II over his failure to complete Julius's tomb.

dered. And if the Cardinal de' Medici now, as you tell me, has decided once again that I make the San Lorenzo tombs,[22] you see that I cannot, unless he frees me from this Rome matter. If he frees me, I promise to work for him gratis as long as I live; it is not that I want to be freed because I do not wish to make the tomb of Julius,[23] for I would gladly make it, but in order to serve him. If he does not want to free me, and if he wants something done by my hands for the tombs, while I shall be working on Julius's tomb, I shall do my best to find time to make something which he will like.

November 25, 1523

Domenico called Topolino, stonecutter in Carrara.

My dearest Master Domenico – You undoubtedly heard that the Medici Cardinal was made Pope:[24] I am sure the whole world rejoiced at the news. I am sure that art, here, will benefit very much as a result. Therefore, do what is expected of you well and faithfully, so that we may do ourselves honor.

1524

Pope Clement VII in Rome.

Most Blessed Father – Since mediators very often are the cause of great scandals, I have summoned up courage to write without their aid to your Holiness about the tombs of San Lorenzo here in Florence. I do not know what is preferable, the evil that does good, or the good that hurts. Crazy and mean as I am, I am sure that if I had been allowed to continue, as I had begun, by

---

[22] For the Medici Chapel in Florence.

[23] Michelangelo had already carved for Julius's tomb seven figures: Moses (San Pietro in Vincoli, Rome), the Heroic Captive, or Slave, and Dying Captive, or Slave (Louvre, Paris), the unfinished Atlas, the Young Giant, Bearded Giant, Awakening Giant (Accademia, Florence).

[24] Pope Adrian VI died September 14, 1523, and Giulio de' Medici became Pope Clement VII November 18, 1523.

now all the marbles needed for said works would be in Florence properly blocked out, and for less money than has been expended on them thus far. The various blocks would be as lovely as those I have already brought here.

Now I see that things are taking a long time, and I have no idea how they will turn out. Therefore, I wish to clear myself with your Holiness, for, since I have no authority in the matter, if anything should happen that your Holiness does not like, I do not think I should be held responsible. For this reason, if your Holiness wishes me to do anything, I ask that he place no superiors over me in my profession, that he trust me, and that he give me a free hand; then he will see what I can do, and how I discharge my duties.

Stefano[25] finished and uncovered the lantern of San Lorenzo's Chapel; everyone likes it, and I hope your Holiness will like it also when he sees it. We are having the ball made; it will be about two feet high. To make it different from others, I thought of making it faceted, and that's what we are doing.

1524

Giovanni Spina[26] in Florence.
My dear Giovanni—Since the pen is ever more courageous than the tongue, I am writing you what these days I have not dared tell you by word of mouth: and this is that, in view of our times which are contrary to my profession, I do not know whether from now on I can hope for an allowance.[27] Even if I were certain never to get it again, I would not stop for this reason, working for the Pope, and doing all I could for him, but I would no longer run a house because of the debt you know I have, for I have a place where I could return with less expense. And, furthermore,

---

[25] Stefano di Tommaso, miniaturist who assisted him on the Medici Chapel.

[26] Florentine banker acting as agent for Clement VII on the Medici projects.

[27] From the Medici Pope Clement for his services.

you would be relieved of the rent problem. If my allowance should be continued, I shall remain here as I have done in the past, and I shall do my best to do my duty. Therefore, let me know what you think about it, so that I may attend to my business.

January, 1524

Fattucci in Rome.

Messer Giovan Francesco – I gather from your last that His Holiness our Lord wished that the design for the Library[28] be done by me. I have received no information, and I do not know where he wants to erect it. And although it is true that Stefano spoke to me about it, I did not pay close attention. When he returns from Carrara I will inquire, and I will do what I can, although it is not my profession.

As for the pension[29] you write me about, I do not know how I will feel about it a year from now. For this reason I do not wish to promise something I might regret later.

January, 1524

Fattucci in Rome.

Ser Giovan Francesco – Since the Pope made you my administrator,[30] I beg you to treat me well, as you have always done, for you know that I am more indebted to you for your services, than, as we say in Florence, the crucifixes of Santa Maria del Fiore are to Noca the hosier.[31]

January, 1524

Fattucci in Rome.

Messer Giovan Francesco – You ask me how I fared with Pope Julius. I tell you that if I were to ask for damages and interest,

---

[28] The Laurentian Library for the Medici collection of books and manuscripts.

[29] Clement VII gave him a lifetime pension of fifty ducats a month.

[30] Appointed by the Pope to deal for Michelangelo with Julius's heirs over the unfinished tomb.

[31] Andrea di Cristofano, shoemaker to Pope Leo X.

7. The Heroic Captive, 1514-1516. (*Courtesy of Alinari*)

8. Atlas, *circa* 1519. *(Courtesy of Alinari-Brogi)*

I think that what I am owed is more than what I owe. For, when he sent for me in Florence—I think it was during the second year of his pontificate[32]—I had agreed to paint half of the Sala del Consiglio in Florence: I was to get three thousand ducats for it.[33] As all of Florence knows, I had already made the cartoon; I felt I had already earned half of the sum. And of the twelve Apostles I was still to make for Santa Maria del Fiore,[34] I had roughhewn one,[35] and I had already brought to Florence the greatest part of the marbles. But since Pope Julius took me away from here, I was never given anything for either one of the two works. Then, when I was in Rome he commissioned me to make his tomb. I think it was the second year of my stay with him, after many sketches, I made one that he liked, and we made an agreement on it: I agreed to make it for ten thousand ducats; and since I figured it would take one thousand ducats' worth of marbles, he had this sum paid to me by the Salviati of Florence, and he sent me to Carrara for the marbles.

I remained at Carrara eight months to have the marbles blocked out, and then I returned to Rome, and I began to work on the pedestal and the statues. When I had finished paying for the shipment of these marbles, and all the money I had received for the work was spent, I furnished the house I had on St. Peter's Square with beds and equipment at my own expense, trusting in the commission of the tomb, and sent for workmen from Florence, and I paid them in advance with my own money. After eight or nine months the Pope changed his mind, and refused to go on with it. Since I was faced with a large expense, and since His Holiness refused to give me money for the work, one day I complained to him about this; he became angry, and had me expelled from his chamber. I felt insulted, and I immediately left Rome.

---

[32] Spring, 1505.
[33] The cartoon of the Battle of Cascina.
[34] Commissioned in 1503 for the Choir Chapel of the Cathedral.
[35] A St. Matthew.

The things with which I had my house stocked went to waste; and the marbles which I had brought to Rome lay on St. Peter's Square until Pope Leo was elected: and both lots were injured and pillaged. Among those of which I can give an account, Agostino Chigi[36] took two ten-foot blocks of mine from Ripa, which had cost me over fifty gold ducats; and these could be repossessed, for I have witnesses. But to return to the marbles, from the time I went to get them and remained at Carrara, until I was expelled from the Palace more than a year went by. I never received a penny for my time; as a matter of fact, I spent several tens of ducats of my own. After seven or eight months, during which time, as the Pope was angry with me, I had to live practically in hiding, since I could not remain in Florence, I was forced to go to Bologna and ask for his forgiveness.

The first time the Pope went to Bologna I was forced to go there with a rope around my neck[37] to beg his pardon; wherefore he ordered me to make a seated figure of him in bronze, which was about fourteen feet high. He kept me there nearly two years. Pope Julius asked me how much said statue would cost; I told him that casting in bronze was not my profession, and that I thought I could cast it for one thousand gold ducats, but I did not know whether I would succeed. He answered: "Go, start working; you shall cast it over and over again till it succeeds, and I will give enough to make you happy." Then he sent for Messer Antonio Maria da Legna,[38] and told him to pay me one thousand ducats upon request. I found it necessary to cast the statue twice. I can prove that I spent three hundred ducats for wax, that I had numerous helpers, and that I paid Master Bernardino, who was chief of the artillery of the Signory of Florence, thirty ducats a month plus board, and I kept him several months.

---

[36] Sienese banker who built a magnificent palace (later the Farnesina) in 1509.

[37] Under coercion.

[38] A Bolognese banker.

Suffice it to say that finally, after having raised with great difficulty the statue in its place, I found that at the end of two years of work I had four and a half ducats left.

I never received anything else for my time spent there working; and all the money I was paid in said two years were the one thousand ducats with which I had said I would cast it. These were paid to me in various installments by Messer Antonio Maria.

After I had raised the statue on the facade of San Petronio I returned to Rome, but the Pope still refused to let me complete the tomb, and he insisted that I paint the vault of the Sistine; I agreed to do it for three thousand ducats. The first design of said work consisted of twelve Apostles in the lunettes,[39] the remainder being a certain space filled with ornamental details, as is customary.

After I had begun said work, I said to the Pope that the Apostles alone would make a poor effect. He asked me why, and I told him that the reason was that the Apostles had been poor themselves. Then he gave me a new commission, namely that I do what I wanted; and he told me that he would remunerate me, and that I should paint down to the frescoed histories[40] below. During that period of time, I had practically finished the vault, when the Pope returned to Bologna.[41] Twice I went there to get the money which I had coming; I wasted all that time, and I did not accomplish anything. One day I was complaining about this with Messer Bernardo da Bibbiena[42] and Atalante,[43] saying that it was impossible for me to remain in Rome any longer. Messer Bernardo told Atalante to remind him, for he

---

[39] Crescent-shaped openings in a vault which often are frescoed.
[40] By Ghirlandaio, Botticelli, Pinturicchio, Rosselli, Signorelli, Perugino.
[41] To direct his military campaign.
[42] Friend of the then Cardinal Giovanni de' Medici.
[43] A pupil of Da Vinci, one of the superintendents of the fabric of St. Peter's.

wanted by all means to have me paid. He saw to it that I was given two thousand ducats Camera, and the first thousand of the ducats for marbles which they advanced me for the tomb. As a matter of fact, I expected more in view of the time I had lost and the work I had done. Since with this money Messer Bernardo and Atalante had resuscitated me, I gave one hundred ducats to the former, and fifty to the latter.

Then Pope Julius died. At the beginning of Leo's pontificate, Cardinal Aginensis[44] wanted to enlarge the tomb, to make the work larger than the drawing I had made at first; and so we signed a contract. And since I did not want them to include in the account the mentioned three thousand ducats which I had received, showing them that I had much more coming, Aginensis told me that I was a swindler.

January, 1523

Giovanni Spina – The bearer of this letter is Antonio di Bernardo Mini[45] who lives with me; you will pay him fifteen gold ducats for the models of the tombs of San Lorenzo's sacristy, which I am making for Pope Clement.

January, 1524

Piero Gondi[46] – The poor man,[47] who is ungrateful, has this nature, that if you help him in his needs, he says that what you gave him was superfluous to you; if you find him a job for his own good, he says that you were forced to do so, and that you set him to do it because you were incapable of doing it yourself; and whatever benefits he receives, he ascribes to the necessities of the benefactor. When the benefits he receives are evident, and cannot be denied, the ingrate waits until the benefactor makes

---

[44] Lionardo Grosso della Rovere, cousin of Julius II.

[45] His assistant, 1521–31.

[46] An intimate friend.

[47] His assistant, Stefano.

some public mistake, which gives him the opportunity of maligning him, and winning credence, in order to free himself from the obligation which he has. This has always happened to me. No one ever had anything to do with me (I am referring to workmen) to whom I did not do good with all my heart. Then, because of some peculiarity of my temper, or some madness, which they say is part of my nature, and which hurts no one except myself, they have begun speaking evil of me and slandering me. Such is the reward of all honest men.

I am writing about the conversations held last night, and about Stefano. Until now I have never assigned him to a place where, if I could not be there myself, I could not have found someone else to place there. I have done everything for his own good, and not for my own interest; and this I did also the last time. I have undertaken to benefit him, and cannot renounce it. Let him not believe or say that I do it for my necessities, for, God be praised, I do not lack men. And if recently I have pushed him more than usual, it is because I myself have more obligations than usual. For this reason it is necessary for me to know whether he wants, or he is capable of doing, what I want him to do, so that I may attend to my own affairs. Since it was not clear to me what he intends to do, last night I asked you to be a sort of mediator and inform me of his opinion. I should like you to find out how much he wants per month to supervise the helpers and teach them how to make the mortar and whatever I may order.[48] I shall pay the helpers myself. Do not be amazed if I write you this, for it is important to me for various reasons, and especially for this one: if he left without justification and I put someone else in his place, I would be proclaimed among the Piagnoni[49] as the greatest traitor who ever lived, even though I were right.

---

[48] To stucco the inside of the Medici chapel which he had to finish before he could decorate it.

[49] The "Hired Weepers," a nickname for the followers of Savonarola and their successors.

Therefore, I beg you to do me this favor. I am bold enough to bother you with this, because you show that you love me.

February 6, 1524

Giovanni Spina – The bearer of this letter is the miniaturist Stefano. Give him fifteen ducats for the models,[50] which as I told you in a previous one, I am making for Pope Clement.

July, 1524

Fattucci in Rome.

Messer Giovan Francesco – After I received your last letter I went to see Spina to find out whether he has the commission to pay for the Library, as well as for the tombs. Since he does not have it, I did not begin the work, as you advise me to do, for one cannot get along without money. If this work has to be done, I beg you to see to it that Spina is authorized to pay me, for it would be impossible to find a better suited man, or one who could handle such matters with greater solicitude and tact.

As concerns my beginning to work, I must wait for the marbles to arrive; and I do not think they will ever come, so badly has the whole thing been handled! I could write things that would amaze you, but nobody would believe me. All I can say is that this business is my ruination; for, if my work had progressed farther than it has, perhaps the Pope would have settled the matter of the tomb,[51] and I would be free from so much grief. But it is true that one who spoils things can show more progress than one who fixes them up.

Yesterday I ran across a man who told me to go and settle accounts, otherwise on the last day of this month I shall incur the penalties.[52] I did not think there were other penalties than

---

[50] Of the Medici Chapel.

[51] Julius's tomb. The Medici Popes would not allow him time to work on it. The heirs pushed for completion. As time went on, finances were disputed, with both sides claiming restitution.

[52] Taxes.

those of hell, or two ducats of income tax, if I opened a silk shop or a goldbeater shop, or I loaned out money upon usury. We have been paying taxes to Florence for three hundred years: at least if I had been just once in the service of the Proconsolo![53] And yet one must pay. They will take everything from me because I have no other means, and I shall come to Rome. If that matter of mine were settled,[54] I could sell something and buy some bank notes to pay for the taxes, and I could remain in Florence.

August 8, 1524

Giovanni Spina – The bearer of this letter is Niccolò de Giovanni called the Deaf. Pay him three ducats on account for the hard stone which he has undertaken to quarry for the Library of San Lorenzo. Pay this amount for the time being; and after he delivers the first cartloads we shall see the work he does, if the price is right, and how good the stone is. As for the three ducats, I vouch for him.

August 29, 1524

Giovanni Spina – After I left you yesterday, I began thinking about my affairs; and seeing that the Pope has his heart set on this work of San Lorenzo, and how His Holiness urgently requires my service, and that he has of his own free will given me a good provision in order that I may serve him with more convenience and speed, and seeing furthermore that if I do not accept it I will be delayed, and that I have no good reason not to serve him, I have changed my mind; and whereas until now I did not ask for the allowance, now I do, believing that this is much wiser for more reasons than I care to write; and especially in order to return to the house in San Lorenzo which you took

---

[53] Rector of the Guild of Judges and Notaries.
[54] Dispute over Julius's tomb.

for me,[55] and settle down there like an honest man. For, if
I do not return there, it gives rise to gossip and does me great
damage. Therefore, I should like you to give me the amount of
salary which is due me from the time it was set up for me until
now: and if you have the power to do so, I beg you to tell
Antonio Mini, who lives with me and is the bearer of the present,
when you want me to come for it.

December 24, 1524

Fattucci in Rome.

Messer Giovan Francesco – I gather that you will soon finish and
return here; and that you can hardly wait. I beg you not to delay,
for my business cannot be settled properly unless I am present in
Rome myself. It is almost one year now since I began writing you
that if you had only my business to settle in Rome, you let it go
and come back here, for I did not want people to say that I kept
you there. When I saw that you were not coming back, I had
Messer Dino write you that your mother was not well, and that
you should hurry back to see her. Recently, I sent word to you
through Ricciardo del Milanese that you come back by all means
and let my business go unheeded; and a few days ago I sent you
the same message with Lionardo the saddle maker.[56] Now I beg
you once more: if you have nothing else to do in Rome except
take care of my affairs, let them go and come back immediately.

April 19, 1525

Giovanni Spina – It seems to me that there is no reason to send
a power of attorney about the tomb of Pope Julius, because I do
not want to plead. There cannot be any pleading if I confess
that I am in the wrong. I'll pretend to have sued and lost, and
that I have to pay: and this is what I am ready to do, if I can.

---

[55] He moved out of the house provided for him, and gave up his
pension in the spring of 1524, complaining of interference and
trouble with superiors.

[56] A friend in Rome.

Therefore, if the Pope is willing to help me in the matter, seeing that I cannot finish the said tomb of Julius either because I am old[57] or ill, he would do me a very great favor. As an intermediary, he might express his desire that I repay what I have received to make it, so as to free me from this burden, and to enable the relatives of Pope Julius to have it made by any master of their choice. In this way His Holiness our Lord could be of great assistance to me; and also in seeing to it that I be made to give back as little money as possible, always consistent with justice. Furthermore, he might propound some of my arguments, as, for instance, the time I spent in Bologna for the Pope, and other times wasted without any compensation, as Ser Giovan Francesco, who is informed of everything, knows. As soon as I have found out how much I have to give back, I will decide what to do with my property. I will sell, and I will do everything so that I can repay the money; then I shall be able to think about the orders of the Pope and to work. As it is, worries hardly let me live, let alone work. There is no other solution which is safer for me, or more agreeable, or that can put my mind more at ease; and it can be done amicably, without a lawsuit. I pray to God that the Pope will be willing to settle it thus, for it seems to me that it does not concern anybody else. So, I beg you to write to Messer Jacopo Salviati as convincingly as you can, in order that this matter receive the proper attention, and I may work.

1525

Fattucci in Rome.
Ser Giovan Francesco—So that people will not believe that I am to make a new tomb, with the two thousand ducats mentioned in the contract,[58] I should like you to explain to Niccolò that the said tomb is more than half done, and that of the six statues

---

[57] Fifty.
[58] Never drawn.

mentioned in the contract four are completed, as you know since you saw them in my house in Rome. As the contract shows, they are giving me the house.

April, 1525

Sebastiano Luciani in Rome.
My dearest friend and companion[59] Sebastiano—Here not only I, but many others who love you and know you through your good fame, are waiting for a painting which you made for Anton Francesco degli Albizzi. We think it is finished, and we are looking forward to seeing it.

May, 1525

My dearest Sebastiano—Last evening our friend Captain Cuio Dini and certain other gentlemen were so kind as to ask me to go to have supper with them. I had a very good time, for I set aside my melancholy, or, if you wish, my mad mood. Not only did I enjoy the wonderful supper, but I enjoyed even more the conversation. Furthermore, my delight in the conversation increased when I heard Captain Cuio mention your name. But this was not all: my joy became boundless when, talking about art, the Captain said that you are peerless in the whole world, and that this is the opinion they have of you in Rome. Nothing could have made me happier. Since it is now proved that my judgment was not wrong, cease denying that you are peerless when I write it; I have too many witnesses who agree with me, and there is a painting of yours here, God be praised, which wins credence for me with everyone who has eyes.

September 4, 1525

Messer Giovan Francesco Fattucci—I wrote to you people in Rome that since I am old, if I were to start working for Pope Clement on projects that require a long time, I would not be able to attend to them; and for this reason, not being allowed to finish

---

[59] Literal translation, godfather, a pet name.

With regard to the affairs of Julius II, I am willing to make a tomb like that of Pius in St. Peter's,[65] as you write me, and I shall have it made here little by little, now one piece and now another, and I will pay for it out of my own money, since I am to keep the pension and the house; namely, the house in which I lived in Rome, with the marbles and the things I have there. Provided, that is to say, I shall not have to restore to the heirs of Julius, to be quit of his tomb, anything which I have hitherto received, except a tomb like the one of Pius in St. Peter's. I must be allowed a reasonable period of time to make it, and I shall make the statues myself. If, as I said, my pension is paid to me, I shall never stop working for Pope Clement with all the strength I have, which is not very much, since I am old. At the same time, I must not be vexed as I am now, for such treatment weighs greatly on me. These continuous irritations have prevented me from doing anything I wanted the last few months: for one cannot be busy at one thing with his hands, and at something else with his brain, especially when one works with marble. They say here that these annoyances are meant to spur me on; and I tell you that those are poor spurs which make a horse go backwards. I have not received my pension for over one year, and I have been struggling with poverty. I am left all alone to bear my troubles, and I have so many of them that they keep me busier than does my art; this is because I do not have the means to keep someone to manage my house.

October, 1525

Fattucci in Rome.

Messer Giovan Francesco – Piero Gondi showed me your reply to a letter he wrote you several days ago. Piero wrote you the truth. Lorenzo Morelli[66] is one who tried to know my mind. Francesco da Sangallo[67] came to me and told me that Lorenzo wished to

---

[65] A wall tomb.

[66] Representing the Florentines who wanted a statue of Hercules to match the David.

[67] Nephew of architect Giuliano da Sangallo.

know whether I would work for him. I replied that, in view of their good will and the good will of all the people, I could only show my appreciation by making it as a gift, if the Pope, to whom I was under contract, were willing.[68] Messer Luigi della Stufa also has asked me the same thing, and I have given him the same answer. I was told again recently by certain individuals that the *Operai* have declared that they would not mind waiting two or three years before making it: long enough, that is, until I had finished working for the Pope.

THE ARTIST AND HIS WORK

How can that be, lady, which all men learn
by long experience? Shapes that seem alive,
wrought in hard mountain marble, will survive
their maker, whom the years to dust return!

Thus to effect cause yields. Art hath her turn,
and triumphs over Nature. I, who strive
with Sculpture, know this well; her wonders live
in spite of time and death, those tyrants stern.

So I can give long life to both of us
in either way, by color or by stone,
making the semblance of thy face and mine.

Centuries hence when both are buried, thus
thy beauty and my sadness shall be shown,
and men shall say, 'For her 'twas wise to pine.'

April, 1526

Fattucci in Rome.

Messer Giovan Francesco—Sometime during next week, I shall

---

[68] The Medici opposed the Hercules as a symbol of Florence's independence, but were unable to forbid it. So the Pope commissioned it to Bandinelli, hated in Florence.

have covered the statues in the Sacristy which I have rough-
hewn because I wish to clear the Sacristy for the marble cutters.
I want them to work on the wall of the other tomb, across from
the one which is already built;[69] it is practically all squared. I
thought that while they are working on it, we could make the
vault, and I felt that by employing a large number of men, it
could be finished in two or three months. But I am not a good
judge of this.

As for the recess, four columns were put up during this
week, and one had been put up before. The tabernacles will
delay us somewhat, just the same I think that it will be finished
within four months from today. We would put up the ceiling now,
but the linden timber is not quite ready: we shall try to dry it as
fast as we can.

I work as hard as I can, and within fifteen days I shall
have the other captain[70] started; then the only important things
left will be the four rivers. The four statues on the sarcophagi,[71]
the four figures on the ground which are the rivers, the two captains
and Our Lady, who is to be placed on the tomb at the head,
are the statues I should like to do with my own hand. Of these I
have started six; and I feel that I can finish them in due time,
and also to do some work myself on the others which are not so
important. I have nothing else to say. Remember me to Giovanni
Spina, beg him to write a few lines to Figiovanni[72] asking him not
to deprive us of the cart drivers in order to send them to Pescia,
for we would be left without stones. He should tell him also
not to charm the stonecutters away from us, and win them to his
side by telling them: "They have little consideration of you, for,
now that the nights are very short, they make you work until
evening."

---

[69] The tomb of Lorenzo de' Medici, grandson of *Il Magnifico*.
[70] Giuliano de' Medici, son of *Il Magnifico*.
[71] The Allegories: Dawn, Dusk, Day and Night.
[72] Prior of the Church of San Lorenzo which houses the Medici
Chapel.

It is difficult enough by keeping after them to make one of them work, and even he is spoiled for us by some person without conscience. Patience! May God keep me from disliking something he likes.

November, 1526

Fattucci in Rome.

Messer Giovan Francesco – I know that Spina wrote to Rome a few days ago very hotly about my affairs with regard to the tomb of Julius. If he did wrong, seeing the times in which we live, it was my fault for I begged him urgently to write. Perhaps my indignation made me say more than I ought to. Lately I was informed of how my affairs stand there, and it alarmed me greatly: this is that Julius's relatives are very ill-disposed toward me; and not without reason. I hear that the lawsuit is still on, and that they ask of me such an amount of interest and reparations that one hundred of my sort could not meet the claims. This worries me a great deal, and makes me realize that I would be lost if the Pope failed me: I could not go on living. This is what made me write the letter I have mentioned above. Now, I only want what is agreeable to the Pope. I know that he does not want my ruin and my disgrace. Here the work on the wall has slowed down, and expenditures are openly diminishing.[73] Furthermore, I see that they pay rent for a house for me at San Lorenzo, and that they pay me an allowance, which is not a small expenditure. If they could curtail even this disbursement, and give me permission to begin something either here or in Rome for the tomb of Julius, it would please me very much. I desire to free myself from this obligation more than to live. Just the same, I shall never depart from the Pope's will, as long as I am informed of it. Therefore, since you know what my mind is, I beg you to write me and let me know

---

[73] Papal funds were diminishing because the Pope started a war with the German Holy Roman Empire.

what the Pope's will is. I beg you to learn this from his own lips, and to write me in his behalf; thus I shall be better able and willing to obey, and should it be necessary for me to justify myself one day, I shall be able to do so with your letters.

If I am unable to make myself clear to you, do not be surprised, for I am completely out of my mind. You know how I feel. You will find out from him who must be obeyed. Reply, please.

November 10, 1526

Giovanni Spina – I am of the opinion that we should dismiss Piero Buonacorsi,[74] for we no longer need him here. If you want to keep him to do him a service, keep him as long as you like. I write you this because I do not want the responsibility of keeping him, nor do I want to be, as it has been said, the one who throws away the Pope's money.

July, 1527

In Settignano.

Buonarroto – I went to see Messer Antonio Vespucci. He told me that according to the law I cannot let someone else do what I was appointed to do, and that although one can let someone else do it, it is done because that is the practice, not because it is legal. He told me also that if I want to take the risk of accepting it[75] and letting someone else do it, that I am free to take such risk, but that I could be accused secretly and get into trouble. Therefore, it is my opinion that I should refuse it, not so much for this reason, as for the plague which seems to be getting worse all the time, and for the sake of forty ducats I shouldn't want to put your life in danger. I will help you as much as I can.

Do not touch with your bare hands the letters I send you.

---

[74] A stonecutter.

[75] A modest post offered him by the Republic, which he tried to turn over to his brother.

August 22, 1527

In Settignano.

Buonarroto–Today I received an appointment: clerk extraordinary to the Cinque del Contado.[76] It is supposed to last one year, the fee is four ducats per month, and I can appoint whomever I want to carry it out. I do not know enough about it, and I cannot attend to it. I must either refuse it or have someone else do it. Think over whether it's what you want . . . for, during these times, I do not advise you to return to Florence now. Just the same, I wanted you to know about it, before I refuse it, for I have fourteen days' time. Answer.

(July 2, 1528)[77]

1529

Ser Marcantonio del Cartolaio[78]

Ser Marcantonio–I am sure that you will choose a fine and competent man, much better than I could do myself.[79] Therefore, I give you the authority to speak for me, with the understanding that enough authority will be left over to make it possible for me to give my opinion later.

September 25, 1529

Battista della Palla[80] in Florence.

Battista, my dearest friend–As I think you know, I left Florence to go to France.[81] When I arrived in Venice I inquired about the

---

[76] Magistrates of the small farms office.

[77] Buonarroto, Michelangelo's favorite brother, dies.

[78] Secretary of the Nine of the Militia—charged with preparing the defense of Florence against siege.

[79] To superintend the fortifications.

[80] Agent of the French King, Francis I.

[81] Michelangelo had been appointed defense engineer while Florence was under siege of Pope Clement VII and the Holy Roman Emperor. He did a superb job of fortifying the walls facing the encamped army, then became overwrought and ill, fleeing the city.

road, and I was told that going from here one must cross German territory, and that it is a difficult and dangerous journey. I thought, therefore, of asking you to be so kind as to let me know whether you would still like to go; I beg you to consider it, and to inform me where you would like me to wait for you: thus we shall go together. I left without saying a word to my friends and in great confusion; the fact is, as you know, that I had made up my mind to go to France at all costs, and had several times asked for leave, without getting it, I was determined, and without any fear, to wait and see the outcome of the war first. However, on Tuesday morning, September twenty-first, a man came to see me outside of the San Niccolò gate where I was attending to the bastions, and whispered into my ear that I should not remain in Florence any longer if I wanted to save my life. He came with me to my house, and dined with me. He brought me horses, and never left me until he got me out of Florence, convincing me that this was best for me. I do not know whether it was God or a devil.

I beg you to reply to the first part of my letter as soon as you can, for I am burning with impatience to go. Please write me even if you no longer care to go, so that I may provide to go by myself as well as I can.

June 26, 1531

Sebastiano del Piombo[82] in Rome.

My dear Sebastiano – I bother you too much: bear it in peace, and pretend that you are to derive more glory from resuscitating the dead than from painting lifelike figures. At your suggestion, I have thought several times about Julius's tomb, and I am of the opinion that there are two ways I can free myself from my commitment: one is to make it, the other is to give them back their money so that they can have it made themselves. Of these two solutions, one should take only the one that meets with the Pope's pleasure. I do not think the Pope would like me to make it, for I

---

[82] His friend, Sebastiano Luciani, has been appointed Keeper of the Seal (piombo).

could not attend to his things. Therefore, the thing to do would be to persuade them to take the money and have it made themselves. I would turn over to them the designs, the models, and whatever they wanted, along with the blocks of marbles which have already been worked upon. By adding two thousand ducats, it seems to me that they could have a fine tomb completed. There are some young artists who would make it better than I. If they were to take this suggestion of accepting the money and have it made themselves, I could pay them one thousand gold ducats now, and I would find a way of paying them the other thousand later. Provided they decide to do something which meets with the Pope's pleasure.

I do not write you in detail about myself, for it is unimportant. I only wish to tell you this, that of the three thousand ducats I took to Venice in gold and coins, I only had fifty left when I returned to Florence, and the City took from me about fifteen hundred.[83] So I do not know what to do; but we will find some way; seeing that the Pope promises me his patronage,[84] I am optimistic. Sebastiano, my dearest friend, I beg you to go to the bottom of this matter.

March, 1532

Sebastiano del Piombo – I entreat you to tell or, if you wish, to beg Messer Lodovico del Milanese to send Ser Giovan Francesco Fattucci his allowance. You will do me a great favor, and even a greater one to him, for he has to pay out a great deal of money and he does not have the means. I beg you.

April, 1532

Giovansimone – This morning I have to go to Rome for something

---

[83] Fine imposed by Florence for his flight to Venice.

[84] Pope Clement VII regained control of Florence when the city capitulated to his siege. He forgave Michelangelo for his part in the city's resistance and commanded him into service.

of great importance to me,[85] therefore I am sending you four ducats with Monna Margherita,[86] so that they may help you get along. If you need something while I am not here, let me know, and I will help you from wherever I may be. Pray God for me, and be of as good cheer as you can.

May, 1532

Andrea Quaratesi[87] in Pisa.

My dear Andrea – About one month ago, I wrote you that I had the house looked at and appraised, and that I had found out how much one could ask for it these days. I told you also that I did not believe you would be able to sell it. I believed this because, since I had to return two thousand ducats for that matter of mine in Rome, which will probably come to three thousand with certain other things I have to settle, and since I did not wish to be left completely stripped, I decided to sell houses and other possessions, and give the lira for ten soldi, and yet I have been unable until now to find a buyer. For this reason, I think it would be better to wait rather than to give one's things away.

January 1, 1533

Messer Tommaso de' Cavalieri[88] in Rome.

Without due consideration, Messer Tommaso, my dearest Lord, I was moved to write to your Lordship, not in answer to any letter that I might have received from you, but the first one to write,

---

[85] New Julius II tomb contract, April 29, 1532. He was charged to repay two thousand ducats to the heirs.

[86] Longtime family servant.

[87] Rich Florentine banker and friend.

[88] Talented young Roman nobleman, reputed to have had the most perfect face and body of his age. Michelangelo met him on a visit to Rome. They later became close friends and companions. Tommaso cared for Michelangelo during his last illness and comforted him at his death.

as if I had thought of walking with dry soles right across a rivulet, or a narrow fording place. Now that I have left the shore, I realize that I have before me not a tiny river, but rather the ocean with its towering waves: so that, if I could, to avoid being completely overcome by them, I would gladly return to the shore whence I departed. But since I have proceeded this far, I shall be brave and continue, and if I lack the art of navigating over the waves of your great talent, I beg you to forgive me, and not to take offense at my inferior skill, nor expect from me that which I do not possess: for, he who excels in everything, cannot expect to have peers in anything. Therefore, if your Lordship, unequaled splendor of our age in the whole world, should find to his liking some of the works I hope and promise to make, I shall deem said work more fortunate than good. And if, as I said, I should ever be certain to please your Lordship in anything, I will devote to him the present time and all the time the future has in store for me. Indeed, I shall be very sorry not to be able to regain the past, and thus serve your Lordship for a longer period of time than the short span that is left to me now. I am so old,[89] that it cannot be very much. I have no more to say. Read in my heart, not merely my words, for "the pen cannot follow closely the good intention."

I must apologize if in my first letter I show wondrous amazement at your rare genius, for I realize the error in which I was: for it is much the same to wonder at God's working miracles, as to wonder at Rome producing divine men. And the universe can testify to that.

January 1, 1533

Messer Tommaso de' Cavalieri in Rome.
Without due consideration I began to write to your Lordship, and I was presumptuous to be the first one to do so, for I had not received a letter from your Lordship, which it was duty to answer.

---

[89] Fifty-seven.

Later I became all the more aware of my error, when, your Lordship be praised, I read and enjoyed your letter. And from what you write me, you do not give me the impression of just being born, but that you have been in this world a thousand other times; and I would consider myself not born, nay born dead, and in disfavor of heaven and earth, if I had not learned from your letter that your Lordship is willing to accept some of my works: this caused me much amazement and much joy. If it is true that, as you write me, you sincerely appreciate my works; if it so happens that I can make one as I wish, and you do like it, I will consider said work more fortunate than good.[90] I will say no more. On January first, a happy day for me.

––––––◆◆––––––

To Tommaso de' Cavalieri

LOVE THE LIGHT-GIVER

With your fair eyes a charming light I see,
for which my own blind eyes would peer in vain;
stayed by your feet the burden I sustain
which my lame feet find all too strong for me;

wingless upon your pinions forth I fly;
heavenward your spirit stirreth me to strain;
e'en as you will I blush and blanch again,
freeze in the sun, burn 'neath a frosty sky.

Your will includes and is the lord of mine;
life to my thoughts within your heart is given;
my words begin to breathe upon your breath:

like to the moon am I, that cannot shine
alone; for lo! our eyes see nought in heaven
save what the living sun illumineth.

---

[90] He gave De' Cavalieri two drawings, probably Tityos and Ganymede.

1533

At Settignano.

Giovansimone – Monna Margherita did not understand correctly. The other morning, speaking of you and of Gismondo in the presence of Messer Giovan Francesco Fattucci, I said I had always done more for all of you than for myself; and that I had endured many hardships so that you wouldn't have to endure them yourselves; and I added that all you people ever did in return was to slander me all over Florence. That's what I said: and would that it were not true for your sake! You have won yourselves the reputation of being great fools. Concerning your stay there, I am glad of it; take your time and concentrate on recovering; for, I shall never fail to help you in whatever I can, since I heed more my debt than your words. I would be very happy if you brought someone to sleep there, so that Monna Margherita too might stay there. Since, just before dying, my father asked me to look after her, I shall never abandon her.

1533

Giovansimone – I have met a young man who would like to marry Cecca.[91] He belongs to the Sacchetti family and his first name is Benedetto. One of his brothers is married to a Medici girl; another is a prisoner in the citadel of Pisa; he had a third one named Albizo, who died in Rome. If you know them, before you do anything else, I'd like you to let me know what you think of them. You may send me the information through Monna Margherita, and do not speak of it with anybody.

March, 1533

Francesco Galluzzi.[92]

Francesco – The bearer of this is Bernardo Basso, master mason of

---

[91] His niece, Francesca, daughter of Buonarroto.
[92] Tenant in his house on Via Ghibellina.

the Opera di San Lorenzo, to whom I beg you to pay the rent you owe me. I am in very great need of it.

July, 1533

Sebastiano del Piombo in Rome.

My dear Godfather – I received the two madrigals, and Ser Giovan Francesco has had them sung several times. According to what I am told, the music is said to be wonderful: the words certainly did not deserve it.[93] That's the way you wanted it, and I was very happy over it; I beg you to instruct me how I should behave toward the one who composed the music,[94] so that I may seem as little as possible ungrateful and ignorant.

I shall write no more about my work here for the time being.[95] I have done my best to imitate the manner and style of Figiovanni[96] in every detail, for it seems to me very suitable to one who wishes to say many things. Do not show this letter.

You gave the copy of the above-mentioned madrigals to Messer Tommaso; I am much obliged to you for it. If you see him remember me to him most heartily; and when you write me, tell me something about him so that I can keep thinking about him, for, if I forgot, I think I would drop dead.

July 28, 1533

Messer Tommaso de' Cavalieri in Rome.

My dear Lord – If I did not believe I had assured you of the very great, nay boundless love I bear, I would not think it odd, nor would I be amazed at the serious doubt that your letter indicates you had that I have forgotten you merely because I had not written

---

[93] Del Piombo had words of two madrigals by Michelangelo set to music.

[94] Costonzo Festa and Concilion.

[95] Last of Medici Chapel.

[96] Letter-writing style of the Prior of San Lorenzo.

you. But since many things follow the opposite course from what they should, it is neither strange nor amazing that the present matter should move in the wrong direction; for, I ought to tell your Lordship the very thing your Lordship tells me; but perhaps you do it to tempt me, or to kindle a new and greater fire, if a greater one is possible. But be it as it may, I know very well that he who loves has a very good memory, and he can no more forget the things he fervently loves, than a hungry person can the food which keeps him alive. Nay, I could forget sooner the food whereby I live, which only nourishes miserably my body, than your name which nourishes both my body and my soul, the former with great sobriety, the latter with sweet tranquility and with the expectation of eternal salvation. As long as I have you in mind, I can feel neither boredom nor fear of death. Think of what my condition would be if the eyes had also their portion.

October 11, 1533

Bartolomeo Angiolini.[97]

Since first I gave my soul, and my heart to Messer Tommaso, you may consider how it is, being so far from him. . . . Therefore, if I wish without respite day or night to be there, it is only to live again, which cannot be without the soul: and since the heart is indeed the abode of the soul, it is only natural to return my soul to its proper abode.

My dear Bartolomeo, although it may seem that I am joking, I want you to know that I am speaking in dead earnest, for, since I have been here, I have aged twenty years, and lost twenty pounds; and if the Pope leaves Rome, I do not know what he will want to do with me, nor where he will want me to be.

---

[97] Roman friend now handling some of his business affairs.

October 15, 1533

Figiovanni[98] in Florence.

Dear master, Messer Giovanbattista – At the end of this month it will be four months since I arrived in Florence in behalf of the Pope. During the first of the said four months, you brought me my salary; I refused to take it, and I told you to save it for me. You replied to me that if you had to write the Pope, you would tell him that I had received it; I told you to write the truth. Later you showed me a letter from the Pope which said that you should not pay attention to my words and that you should give it to me. Now I should like to make all the money I can in order to settle my business in Rome.[99] Tomorrow evening I shall have finished two small models I am making for Tribolo,[100] and on Tuesday I shall leave at all costs. For this reason, I beg you to give me the salary I told you to save for me; namely, the salary for two months; I shall make the Pope a present of the other two months.

December 15, 1533

Febo[101] – Although you hate me intensely, I do not know why. I do not believe it is because I am fond of you, but because of what other people tell you. Tomorrow morning I am leaving for Pescia, where I am going to visit Cardinal de Cesis and Messer Baldassarre.[102] I shall go with them as far as Pisa, and then I shall go to Rome, and I shall never return here. I want you to

---

[98] Prior of San Lorenzo.

[99] Money he must pay toward Julius's Tomb.

[100] An assistant on the Medici Chapel who began the statue of Earth.

[101] A young friend.

[102] Baldassarre Turini.

know that, as long as I live, wherever I may be, I shall always serve you faithfully and lovingly, as well as you might be served by any other friend you may have in the whole world.

I pray God that he may open your eyes otherwise, so that you will realize that he who wishes your own good more than his own health, knows how to love and not to hate like an enemy.

Michelangelo's reasons for leaving Florence for Rome were many. His father had died, breaking that strong tie. He had signed a new contract April 29, 1532, agreeing to work two months a year in Rome on Julius's Tomb. Florence was prostrate under the heel of the ignorant and brutal tyrant, Duke Alessandro, an illegitimate Medici, who hated Michelangelo and was strangling art as well as political liberty. All of Michelangelo's artist friends were gone. Florence was exhausted after its long defensive war against the Medici Pope, Clement VII, and was impoverished as well as embittered.

Michelangelo too was exhausted from the long years of work in the damp Medici Chapel, which had made him seriously ill. He had completed everything that he would, or could, for the *cappella*: Night and Day, Dusk and Dawn, Madonna and Child, the two Medici tombs, and the figures of the young Medici, Giuliano and Lorenzo. It is possible that he had come to realize that these seven pieces were enough sculpture for the small chapel; that any further carvings would crowd the limited space and detract from the great central figures.

He wanted to get back to his home in Rome, long neglected, to his old and loyal companions there, to new young ones including Tommaso de' Cavalieri. Clement VII had forgiven him for helping defend Florence against Papal troops.

Michelangelo found the Pope in bed, and dying (he died two days later on September 25, 1534), but carrying on an animated conversation with Cellini. At Michelangelo's appearance, Clement VII insisted that he must paint a Last Judgment on the enormous altar wall of the Sistine Chapel.

ROME

1534–1563

There is a lapse of three and a half years, 1534–1537, after Michelangelo reached Rome, during which we have no letters; and then, after the one satiric answer to Aretino, another gap of almost three years. Michelangelo probably wrote to his brothers and friends in Florence during this period, but no one has proffered an explanation of what happened to the correspondence.

These were the years during which he prepared the altar wall and painted the Last Judgment in the Sistine Chapel. He did no sculpting during this period, despite the fact that he was harassed by the Duke of Urbino, the legal heir of Julius II, to complete the tomb. Of the greatest importance to his personal happiness was the finding of two of the deepest and most rewarding loves of his life: Tommaso de' Cavalieri, the young Roman nobleman, who became his closest companion and confidant; and Vittoria Colonna, poet, noblewoman, beauty and near-saint, who returned a considerable part of Michelangelo's love. She was one of the most influential and brilliant women of her age. Though she spent a large portion of her time in convents, she and Michelangelo had a strong influence on each other. They kept up a steady exchange of poetry, among which are some of Michelangelo's finest sonnets.

To Vittoria Colonna
THE MODEL AND THE STATUE

When divine Art conceives a form and face,
she bids the craftsman for his first essay
to shape a simple model in mere clay:
this is the earliest birth of Art's embrace.

From the live marble in the second place
his mallet brings into the light of day
a thing so beautiful that who can say
when time shall conquer that immortal grace?

Thus my own model I was born to be—
the model of that nobler self, whereto
schooled by your pity, lady, I shall grow.

Each overplus and each deficiency
you will make good. What penance then is due
for my fierce heat, chastened and taught by you?

———◆◆———

September 15, 1537

Messer Pietro Aretino[1] in Venice.

Magnificent Messer Pietro, my Lord and brother – When I received your letter I experienced both joy and grief at the same time: I rejoiced exceedingly because it came from you, whose talent is unique in the world. Yet, at the same time I grieved because, since I have completed a large section of my fresco, I cannot put to use your conception, which is such that, if the day of judgment had already taken place, and you had witnessed it, your words could not have depicted it better. In reply to your asking me whether you can write about me, I tell you that not only am I happy over it, but I implore you to do it, since both Kings and Emperors consider it a great favor to be mentioned by your pen. Meanwhile, if I have anything at all that would

[1] Writer famous for his vicious pen when crossed.

please you, I offer it you with all my heart. Finally, by all means do not change your decision not to come to Rome just for the sake of seeing my work, for that would be too much.

June, 1540

Gismondo – I gave here to Bartolomeo Angiolini twenty ducats of seven lire each, so that he have Bonifazio Fazi pay them to you in Florence. Therefore, when you have read this letter, go to collect them. Keep ten of them for yourself, and give five to Monna Margherita. Give the remaining five to Lionardo,[2] if he behaves well, otherwise spend them on household needs.

June, 1540

Lionardo of Buonarroto Simoni in Florence.

Lionardo – I have in my hands a letter from Gismondo who says that I should ask my agents in Florence to give him nine bushels of wheat. I do not know who my agents are in Florence, but I know perfectly well that I have not shown favoritism in sharing what belongs to me. Therefore, tell Monna Margherita to give him something from what can be spared, and tell him for me that his having become a farmer does us little honor. Furthermore, tell Monna Margherita not to give anything in my name to anybody except the members of our family; for I shouldn't want someone to go to her with the excuse that he was doing some business for me, and get something out of her. I have in mind such individuals as Donato del Sera, who never did the slightest thing for me without getting a scudo from me.

July, 1540

Lionardo – I received along with your letter, three shirts. I am amazed indeed that you sent them to me, because they are so coarse that here you couldn't find a peasant who wouldn't be ashamed to wear them. But even if they were lightweight, I wish

---

[2] His nephew, son of Buonarroto, aged twenty.

you hadn't sent them, for when I need them I will send the money with which to buy them. Concerning the Pozzolatico farm,[3] within fifteen or twenty days I shall remit to Bonifazio Fazi seven hundred ducats to get possession of it; but first we must see what security Michele[4] gives, so that, should the necessity arise, your sister could at any time get out of it the dowry she has given. Help Monna Margherita to be in good spirits, and treat her well in words and deeds; and see that you behave like a good man, otherwise I want you to know that you will not get anything out of me.

August 7, 1540

Giovansimone – This morning, I counted out to Bartolomeo Angiolini six hundred and fifty gold scudi, so that he may remit them to Bonifazio Fazi to get the Pozzolatico farm. Therefore, you can take possession of the farm at once. So, you and the priest[5] may go to talk to Bonifazio and he will tell you what is needed.

I want you to know also that, since I have been in Rome, I sent to Florence about two thousand ducats including the last ones mentioned. All I sent I gave in cash to Bartolomeo Angiolini so, since I do not have any sort of receipt for anything, and since we are mortals and new people come on the scene, for the sake of those of us who remain behind, I would like some permanent proof that said money came from me. Be kind to Monna Margherita and tell her that if we get those two farms back, she will be able to keep a maid.

November, 1540

Lionardo – I heard about the death of Monna Margherita, and I am sad indeed; this news caused me more grief than if she had

---

[3] He had given the farm as dowry for his niece, Cecca, in 1537 and is now buying it back.

[4] Michele di Niccolò Guicciardini, Cecca's husband and son of the Florentine historian.

[5] Chaplain Giovan Francesco Fattucci.

been my sister, because she was a good woman and because she had grown old in our house, and also because her welfare had been entrusted to me by our father. The Lord knows that I was ready to do some good to her. Real soon. It did not please God that she wait for it: one must have patience. As for managing the house, you will have to think about it yourselves and not depend on me, for I am old[6] and it is difficult enough for me to take care of myself. If you live peacefully together, you have enough to keep a good housemaid and to lead an irreproachable life. Insofar as I am concerned, I will help you as long as I am alive; but should you behave in an unworthy manner, I will wash my hands of you.

1541

Lionardo – I gave Bartolomeo Angiolini fifty ducats of seven lire each so that he may remit them through the Fazi. The first thing you will do is to have the bank return to him the money which he disbursed for me when I bought the field; and have the bank write down the reason why I am returning said sum to him; thus the money will be returned through a third party, and it will be clear what he has done all along. Have what is left paid to Michele Guicciardini in the same fashion, so that the reason is evident. I will send him the balance of what I owe him when I have the opportunity of sending other money, for I have no such opportunity now.

1541

Lionardo – I received six pairs of raviggiuoli,[7] and I am sure that when you sent them they were lovely, but when I got them they were badly spoiled. Therefore, it is not advisable to send such perishable things.

I am happy to learn that everything is fine with the property and the shop. We must thank God for it, and strive to do good.

---

[6] Sixty-five.

[7] Thin soft white cheeses.

August, 1541

Lionardo – I would like you to go to Michele Guicciardini and tell him that I heard through his letter that he is well, and that he is very pleased with the three sons he has. That gives me a great deal of pleasure; and although, as he writes, Francesca[8] is not in good spirits, tell her for me that in this world one cannot be completely happy, and that she should have patience.

August 25, 1541

Lionardo – You tell me that you want to come to Rome this September with Guicciardini. I say to you that it is not time yet, for this would only add new weariness to the troubles I already have.[9] This goes for Michele also, for I am so busy that I have no time to pay attention to you, and every little thing, even the writing of this letter, vexes me greatly. You will have to wait till the coming Lent; then I will send for you, and I will send you money to prepare for the journey, so that you will not have to come here like a dog. I wrote to Michele also not to come until Lent, especially since Urbino,[10] who stays with me, is leaving for Urbino in September, and leaves me here alone with all my troubles. All I need is to have to cook for you two. Learn to write, for it seems to me that you are constantly getting worse.

January 19, 1542

Lionardo – I am enclosing, unsealed, a letter for the priest,[11] and from it you will learn how I am sending you fifty gold ducats and what you must do with them if you want to come to Rome. And if you do not want to come, you must save them until I

---

[8] Cecca.

[9] Finishing the Last Judgment.

[10] Francesco Amadori called Urbino from the town of Castel Durante, moved into Michelangelo's house, and became apprenticed to him in 1530.

[11] Chaplain Fattucci.

send you another fifty. You will find the bill of exchange in this letter; take it to the Salviati, and they will cash it. Make out a correct receipt.

Read the priest's letter and then give it to him, or else give it to him first, and he will read it to you. If you plan to come, let me know in advance, so that I will speak here with some fine mule driver to have you come with him. Also, see that Michele Guicciardini does not find out, for, as you will see when you come, I do not have the facilities to welcome him in my quarters.

January 20, 1542

Niccolò Martelli[12] in Florence.

Messer Niccolò – Messer Vicenzo Perini delivered to me a letter from you with two sonnets and a madrigal. The letter and the sonnet addressed to me are truly marvelous, indeed they are such that no one could be so faultless as to find any fault in them. Actually, they praise me so much, that if I had Paradise in my bosom, much less praise would suffice. I see that you have come to the conclusion that I am just as God wished I would be. I am a poor man, and of little merit, who plods along in the art which God gave me, in order to lengthen my life as much as I can. Such as I am, I am your servant and of the whole Martelli family. I thank you for the letter and the sonnets, but not as much as I ought to, for I cannot rise to such heights of courtesy. Ever at your service.

February 4, 1542

Lionardo – You write me that you are going to save the fifty scudi until I send the other fifty in order to put them toward a shop.[13] I am ready to send them, but first I want the opinion of Giovansimone and of Gismondo: I want things to be done properly, and through their hands, and with their consent for they are my brothers.

---

[12] Florentine merchant and amateur poet.
[13] A wool shop.

1542

Luigi del Riccio[14] in Rome.
I sent this madrigal some time ago to Florence. Now, since I rewrote it more appropriately, I send it to you so that, if you like it, you may give it to the fire, namely to the fire that consumes me. I'd like to ask another favor of you, and it is this: that you get me out of a dilemma in which I got caught last night; for, as I was greeting our idol in my dream, it seemed to me that he [or she][15] threatened me while smiling at me. Since I do not know to which of the two things to give importance, I beg you to learn it from him [or her], and to tell me about it next Sunday when we see each other.

As always, I am deeply obliged to you.

If you like it, have it copied neatly, and give it to those ropes which bind men without discretion, and remember me to Messer Donato Giannotti.[16]

1542

Luigi del Riccio.
Dearest friend – I am sending you a bagful of written papers, in order that your Lordship may decide which is the one that should be sent to Cortese.[17]

I also beg your Lordship to send me my note and Perino's, and also the sonnet I sent you, so that I may fix it up and, as you suggested to me, make two eyes for it.

---

[14] Close friend in Rome, who assisted him also in his business affairs.

[15] Symonds and Papini suggest it may have been Cecchino Bracci, nephew of Luigi del Riccio, around whom del Riccio was attempting to build a cult. The ambiguity arises from the fact that the personal pronoun in Italian refers to "idol," which gives no clue to the sex of the person involved.

[16] Exiled Secretary of State for Florentine Republic.

[17] Unidentified friend.

CARNAL AND SPIRITUAL LOVE

Swift through the eyes unto the heart within
all lovely forms that thrall our spirit stray;
so smooth and broad and open is the way
that thousands and not hundreds enter in.

Burdened with scruples and weighed down with sin,
these mortal beauties fill me with dismay;
nor find I one that doth not strive to stay
my soul on transient joy, or lets me win

the heaven I yearn for. Lo, when erring love—
who fills the world, howe'er his power we shun,
else were the world a grave and we undone—

assails the soul, if grace refuse to fan
our purged desires and make them soar above,
what grief it were to have been born a man!

———◆◆———

1542

Luigi del Riccio.
My dear Lord and faithful friend—My love has ratified the contract which I have made with him about myself, but I do not
know what to think of the other ratification you know about.[18]
Therefore I recommend myself to you, to Messer Donato
Giannotti and to the third one, or in the inverse succession, as
you wish.

1542

Luigi del Riccio.
Messer Luigi—I beg you, you who are endowed with a poetic
spirit, to abbreviate and patch up the one of these madrigals
which seems least wretched to you, for I must give it to a common
friend.

---

[18] New Tomb contract, still unratified by Julius's heirs.

LOVE'S EXPOSTULATION

If love be chaste, if virtue conquer ill,
if fortune bind both lovers in one bond,
if either at the other's grief despond,
if both be governed by one life, one will;

if in two bodies one soul triumph still,
raising the twain from earth to heaven beyond,
if Love with one blow and one golden wand
have power both smitten breasts to pierce and thrill;

If each the other love, himself forgoing,
with such delight, such savor, and so well,
that both to one sole end their wills combine;

if thousands of these thoughts, all thought outgoing,
fail the least part of their firm love to tell:
say, can mere angry spite this knot untwine?

———————◆◆———————

1542

Luigi del Riccio.

My dear Lord – The song of Arcadelt[19] is esteemed very lovely; and since, from what I hear, he intended to please me as much as you, who asked for it, I should like to show him my gratitude. Therefore, I beg you to think of some present to give him, either in cloth or money, and to let me know, and I shall do it by all means. I recommend myself to you, and to Messer Donato, and also to Heaven and earth.

1542

Luigi del Riccio.

Messer Luigi – I have in the house a piece of satin for a coat, which Messer Girolamo got for me. If you agree, I shall send it to you so that you may give it him.[19]

---

[19] Jacob Arcadelt, Flemish musician who included one of Michelangelo's madrigals in his published works.

Luigi del Riccio.

Dearest friend – He who is poor and does not have someone to serve him makes such errors. Yesterday I was unable either to come or to answer your letter because my friends returned home late. Therefore, I beg your pardon, and I beg you to make my apologies to Messer Silvestro.[20]

July, 1542

Luigi, my dear Lord – I am sending you with Urbino, who lives with me, twenty scudi in order that your Lordship may give them to Master Giovanni[21] for the work[22] you know. Since I am also taking Urbino out of the work, I'll have to give him another twenty, and that will make forty; which means that I'll have spent one hundred and forty scudi already, whereas the work has not progressed sixty scudi's worth. Master Giovanni will have received seventy-five scudi, of which he has actually earned thirty; and the rest of the hundred which I paid out first, that is the difference between one hundred and the fifty-five which Master Giovanni took, were spent by Urbino on wages and marbles, for the company split up. Urbino has not received anything for two months, and actually as I removed him from the job, he ought to receive the same pay as Master Giovanni, namely, thirty scudi; but he will be satisfied with twenty.

Since the amount of work done on the above-mentioned enterprise was estimated and recorded, I surveyed it myself, and I find that not even the tenth part has been completed. I am happy, however, that the men who estimated it said in order to keep Messer Giovanni from complaining, that the seventh part

---

[20] Da Montauto, banker in Rome.

[21] De' Marchesi.

[22] Construction of upper story of Julius's Tomb subcontracted to Giovanni and Michelangelo's assistant, Urbino. They squabbled, and Michelangelo appealed to Riccio to moderate.

had been done. But there is no remedy: and if anybody should complain, I would be more justified than anyone else, for, by getting mixed up with them, I lost two months' time over it . . . but I grieve more over the Pope's anger, than over two hundred scudi.

I am taking too much liberty with your Lordship. May God grant that I repay you for it.

Master Giovanni has to release the marbles left on the Capitoline Hill; the same ones he did not release after he was paid for them. This was one of the things that started the quarrel between them, and in the same way, he must put an end to everything else.

July, 1542

Messer Luigi, my dear Lord – Your Lordship has handled this disagreement which arose between Urbino and Master Giovanni, and since you are not directly interested in it, you will be able to pass fair judgment on it. In order to benefit both of them, I entrusted to them the work you know about. Now, since the one is too stingy, and the other equally crazy, such misunderstanding has arisen between them that it might end up scandalously in bloodshed or even in death. And if such a thing were to befall either the one or the other, I would be very sorry about Master Giovanni, but much more about Urbino since I brought him up. Therefore I would be of the opinion, if reason bears it, to throw out both of them, so that I am left free to carry out the enterprise as I see fit, without being ruined by their bad judgment. And since it has been suggested that I divide the work up, and give one part of it to one, and the other to the other, the fact is that I cannot do that; and if I were to give it only to one of the two, I would insult the other.

As for the one hundred scudi I paid out, and their labor, let them fix it among themselves in such a way that I do not suffer a loss. And since perhaps one of them will try to show that he is completely responsible for the little bit which has been accomplished, and that, besides the money he has received, he has

more coming; if that comes to pass, I myself will be able to show
that in the enterprise I lost a month's time because of their ignorance and stupidity, and delayed the Pope's work, for a total loss
of over two hundred scudi.

Messer Luigi, I have put this speech to your Lordship in
writing, because if I were to deliver it orally in the presence of
those men, I would get so worked up that I would have no voice
left to speak.

July 20, 1542

Petition to Pope Paul III.

A long time ago Messer Michelagnolo Buonarroti undertook, with
certain pacts and agreements, to make the tomb of Pope Julius
in San Pietro in Vincoli; this is shown by a contract drawn up by
Messer Bartolomeo Cappello on April eighteenth, fifteen hundred and thirty-two. Later, however, upon being asked and compelled by His Holiness Paul III[23] to work and paint in his new
chapel,[24] finding it impossible to attend to the execution of both
the tomb[25] and the chapel, through the mediation of His Holiness, he came to a new agreement with the most illustrious Duke
of Urbino,[26] to whom is left the custody of the mentioned tomb:
of the six statues intended for the tomb, the said Messer Michelagnolo could delegate three to a good and renowned master, who
would execute them and erect them in the mentioned tomb; the
remaining three statues, including the Moses, he would execute
with his own hands, and he would also be responsible for the completion of the quadrangle, that is the rest of the decoration of the

---

[23] Alessandro Farnese (1534–49), elected October 13, 1534 to
succeed Clement VII.

[24] Frescoes of the Crucifixion of Peter and the Conversion of
Paul in the Pauline Chapel.

[25] Julius's.

[26] Heir of Julius.

tomb, along the lines it had been started. Therefore, in order to carry out the said agreement, the mentioned Messer Michelagnolo delegated the execution of the three mentioned statues, which were well along, namely, a standing Madonna with the Child in her arms, and a seated Prophet and Sibyl, to Raffaello da Monte-lupo, a Florentine artist who is considered one of the best masters of these days, for four hundred scudi, as is recorded in the contract they signed among themselves. The rest of the framework and decoration of the tomb, except the last frontispiece, he commis-sioned likewise to Master Giovanni de' Marchesi and to Francesco da Urbino, stonecutters and carvers, for seven hundred scudi, as is indicated by their contracts.

He had left the execution of the three statues by his own hand, namely a Moses and two prisoners.[27] These three statues are almost finished. But since the two prisoners mentioned were made when the whole structure had been planned much larger, and with many more statues—which in the later contract was cut down and reduced, so that they do not become this plan, and in no wise would look well in it—the mentioned Messer Michel-agnolo, not to sully his honor, started two other statues which will go on either side of Moses, Contemplative and Active Life,[28] which are fairly well along, so that they can be easily completed by other masters.

Now, since the said Messer Michelagnolo is again asked and solicited by His Holiness Pope Paul III who is determined to have him work and execute his chapel, as is stated above; and since the said Messer Michelagnolo is old,[29] and wishes to serve His Holiness with all his strength, but is unable to carry out the request of His Holiness unless he is completely relieved from this project of Pope Julius, which keeps him troubled in mind and body; he entreats His Holiness to deal with the most illus-

---

[27] The Dying and Heroic Slaves.
[28] Also called Rachel and Leah.
[29] Sixty-seven.

trious Lord Duke of Urbino, and free him completely from said tomb, canceling and annulling every obligation between them with the following honest pacts. First, the said Messer Michelagnolo wants the authority to commission the other two unfinished statues to the mentioned Raffaello da Montelupo, or to anyone else to the liking of his Excellency; for an honest price, and that should be possible, which he thinks will be about two hundred scudi. He insists on delivering Moses completely finished by his own hands. Furthermore, he wants to deposit the whole sum of money needed to bring the tomb to its completion, even if this inconveniences him, and he has already spent a great deal in said enterprise; namely, the rest of what he would have had to pay Raffaello da Montelupo to execute the three statues he had delegated to him, which is about three hundred scudi; the rest of what he would have paid for the completion of the structure and decoration, which is about five hundred scudi; the two hundred scudi, or what it will take to execute the last two statues, and moreover one hundred ducats which will pay for the execution of the last frontispiece for the decoration of the tomb: a total of from eleven to twelve hundred scudi. He will deposit said amount in Rome at a suitable bank in the name of the mentioned most illustrious Lord the Duke, in his name and in that of the tomb, with the explicit understanding that it is to be spent for the completion of said work, and nothing else; and that it cannot be touched or withdrawn for anything else. Furthermore, he will be happy to do all he can to see that the statues and decoration of the tomb are carried out with the required diligence. Thus, his Excellency will have the assurance that the work will be executed, and will know where the money to that end is; he will be able to have his agents continually solicit it and have it completed: which is to be desired, since Messer Michelagnolo is busy with such an undertaking that, let alone doing anything else, he will hardly have enough time to finish that one.

Thus Messer Michelagnolo will remain completely free, and

he will be able to serve and gratify the desire of your Holiness, whom he begs to have someone write his Excellency the Duke to give the appropriate order and send the required power of attorney to free him from every contract and obligation existing between them.

August, 1542

Luigi del Riccio.

Messer Luigi, dear Lord – I beseech you to do me a very great favor: that is to look over a paper which Cortese wrote for me, for I do not understand it, and, as Urbino will tell you, cannot go there. Please forgive me my excessive boldness.

October 15, 1542

Messer Luigi, dear friend – Messer Pier Giovanni[30] urges me to begin to paint. As anyone can see, the plaster is not yet dry, and I do not think I will be able to get started for another four or six days. But there is another thing which bothers me more than the plaster, and which, let alone painting, does not let me live in peace; this is the ratification[31] which has not come yet, so that I realize that I was fed a lot of words, and I am in the deepest despair. I have made the great sacrifice of paying fourteen hundred scudi,[32] which would have allowed me to work for seven years, and finished not one but two tombs. This I did in order to be able to live peacefully, and to serve Pope Paul with all my heart. Now I find myself without the money, and with more troubles and grief than ever. I disposed of the money as I did, because I had the Duke's consent, and the contract for my release; and now the ratification does not come. It is easy to see what this means, without spelling it out. Evidently, my thirty-

---

[30] Aliotti, Pope Paul's Chamberlain.
[31] Release from Julius's tomb by Duke's ratification of new contract.
[32] As outlined previously by him, on deposit to guarantee completion of tomb by others.

six-year-long faithfulness, and my submission to others of my own free will, does not make me worthy of anything else: painting and sculpture, fatigue and faithfulness have ruined me, and things keep going from bad to worse. It would have been better if in my young years I had started making matches, for now I wouldn't be so full of grief.

I write this to your Lordship because you are kindly disposed toward me and know the truth by having been involved in this matter. I beg you to inform the Pope of this, in order that he may know that I have no peace at all and I cannot paint. If I gave any hope that I would begin, I did it for I was hoping in said ratification: it should have arrived over one month ago. I refuse to remain under this weight and to be insulted every day as a cheat by those who have taken my life and my honor. Only death or the Pope can free me from this.

October, 1542

Monsignor[33] – Your Lordship sends me word that I start painting, and that I have no anxiety. I reply that one paints with his brain and not with his hands; and he who does not have his brain under control, shames himself. Therefore, until my business is settled, I cannot do anything good. The ratification of the last contract has not come, and on the strength of the other[34] made before Clement, I am lapidated every day as if I had crucified Christ. It happened that on the same day Clement sent me to Florence, the ambassador Gianmaria da Modena was with the notary, and he had it drawn up in his own way; so that, when I returned and received the copy, I found that it read one thousand ducats more than we had agreed. I found that it included the house in which I lived, and certain other snares that would ruin me. I knew that Clement would not have tolerated

---

[33] The Bishop Vigerio of Sinigaglia, a mediator in the tomb dispute.

[34] Contract of 1532.

9. Moses, 1513-1516. (*Courtesy of Alinari*)

10. Night, *circa* 1530. (*Courtesy of Alinari*)

them, and brother Sebastiano[35] wanted me to inform the Pope, and have the notary hanged. I refused, because I did not feel obliged to something which I could not have done if I had been permitted.

I swear that I am not aware of having received the money mentioned in said contract, and which Gianmaria said he found I had received. But let us suppose that I have received it, and also other money, if more can be found, and let us total the entire thing up, and see what I have done for Pope Julius at Bologna, at Florence and at Rome, in bronze, marble, and painting, and the whole period of time I was with him, which was as long as he was Pope: then we shall determine what I deserve. I say in all honesty that, according to the pension[36] paid me by Pope Paul, the heirs of Pope Julius owe me five thousand scudi. And I'd like to say this too: that if I receive this reward for my labors for Pope Julius, it is my own fault, for I did not manage myself properly; and if it weren't for what Pope Paul has given me, today I would be starving. And to think that according to these ambassadors it would seem that I have become rich, and that I robbed the altar. They are certainly making a lot of noise. I could find a way to make them keep quiet, but I am no good at such things.

Gianmaria, who was ambassador at the time of the old Duke,[37] when I returned from Florence and began the work for Julius's tomb, told me that if I wanted to do the Duke a big favor, I should pick up and go, for he did not care about the tomb, and that he was hurt that I was working for Pope Paul. Then I realized why he had put the house in the contract: to drive me away and to take possession of it with that authority. I see that I lost all my youth tied to this tomb. With all the

---

[35] Del Piombo, now a monk and keeper of the Papal Seal.

[36] Twelve hundred gold scudi yearly, half from the Papal Treasury, half from a toll station near Piacenza.

[37] Francesco della Rovere, Duke of Urbino, and heir of Julius II.

protection I secured from Pope Leo and Clement, my excessive faithfulness, which they refused to recognize, has ruined me. That's the way my fate has decreed! I see many people who, with an income of two and three thousand scudi, are taking it easy, whereas I am trying very hard to impoverish myself.

But to return to the subject of painting, I cannot deny Pope Paul anything. I will paint in a dissatisfied mood, and I will turn out unsatisfactory things. I wrote the above to your Lordship so that, when the opportunity arises, he may be in a better position to tell the truth to the Pope. I should like the Pope to hear about it, so that I may know what he considers to be the reason of this war which is waged against me. Let him who wants to understand, do so.

I am at your Lordship's service.

I have other things to say: namely, that this ambassador[38] says that I lent the money of Pope Julius at an exorbitant rate,[39] and that I have become rich thereby, as if Pope Julius had advanced me eight thousand ducats. The money I received for the tomb was the expenses incurred at that time for the tomb. When he commissioned the tomb to me, I spent eight months at Carrara quarrying marbles, and I brought them to St. Peter's square, where I had my lodgings behind Santa Caterina. Afterwards the Pope decided not to build his tomb during his lifetime, and started me painting. Then he kept me two years at Bologna casting his statue in bronze, which has been destroyed. Then I returned to Rome and stayed with him until his death, always running my house, without any income at all, always living on the money for the tomb. Then, after the death of Julius, Aginensis[40] wanted to go on with the tomb, but on a larger scale. Wherefore, I brought the marbles to the Macello dei Corvi,[41] and had that

---

[38] Girolamo Tiranno.

[39] Accused by Julius's heirs of usury with the commission money.

[40] Lionardo della Rovere, cousin of Julius.

[41] His own house and workshop in Rome.

portion executed which is now walled in at San Pietro in Vincoli; furthermore, I made the figures which I have at home.[42] Meanwhile, Pope Leo, not wishing me to work at the tomb, pretended that he wanted to complete the facade of San Lorenzo in Florence, and asked Aginensis for me. Wherefore, he was forced to give me leave, with the understanding that I would execute the said tomb of Pope Julius in Florence.

After I was in Florence for the completion of the facade of San Lorenzo, I returned to Carrara and remained there thirteen months. I brought all the marbles for the tomb to Florence, I built a yard in which to carry it out, and I began to work. At this time, Aginensis sent Messer Francesco Pallavicini, who is now bishop of Aleria, to me. He saw the place where I was working, and all the marbles and blocked-out figures for the tomb, which are still there today.[43] Cardinal Medici, who was in Florence, and who later became Pope Clement, saw that I was working on the tomb, and he did not let me continue. And so I was at a loss until Cardinal Medici became Pope Clement: whereupon, we drew up in his presence the contract previous[44] to the present one. And I wish to confess a sin to your Lordship, namely, that during the thirteen months I was at Carrara, finding myself without money, I spent one thousand ducats for marbles for the tomb; money which had been sent to me by Pope Leo for the facade of San Lorenzo, or better, to keep me busy. I did not explain this to him, I merely pretended having difficulties. I did all this for the love I had for this work. Now I am repaid for it by being told that I am a thief and a usurer by ignorant fellows who were not yet born.

I am writing this story to your Lordship because I wish to justify myself with you, almost as if I were justifying myself with the Pope, to whom bad things are told about me—according to

---

[42] The two Slaves.
[43] The unfinished Giants (Accademia, Florence)
[44] Contract of 1532.

what Messer Pier Giovanni[45] writes me, who says he has had to come to my defense. Also, I hope that if your Lordship has the opportunity of saying a word in my defense, you will do it, for I am writing the truth. Before men, I do not say before God, I consider myself an honest man, because I never deceived anybody, and also because in order to defend myself against bad people it is necessary sometimes to become crazy, as you see.

I beg your Lordship to read this report, when you have a spare moment, and I want your Lordship to know that there are still witnesses who can testify to a great many of the things I have written down. Also, I would be very happy if the Pope saw this account, nay if the whole world saw it; for I write the truth, even if not the whole truth, and I am not a thieving usurer, but a Florentine citizen, noble, and the son of an honest man, and I am not from Cagli.

After I wrote the above, I received a message from the Ambassador of Urbino, that if I want the ratification, I must clean my conscience. I say that he has fashioned himself a Michelangelo in his own heart with the same ingredients he has inside of it.

To continue with my account of the tomb of Pope Julius, I say that after he changed his mind, namely of building it in his lifetime, some shiploads of marbles arrived at Ripa, and since I could not get money from the Pope to pay the freight, I had to borrow two hundred ducats from Baldassarre Balducci, that is, from the bank of Jacopo Galli. I kept on urging the Pope with all my power to go on with the project, and one morning when I went to speak to him on the matter, he had me driven away by a groom. A Lucchese bishop who witnessed this, said to the groom: "Don't you know who he is?" And the groom said to me: "Pardon me, sir, I have orders to do this." I went home, and wrote the Pope as follows: "Most Blessed Father, this morning I was turned out of the Palace by your orders; therefore, I give you notice that from now on, if you want me, you will have to

---

[45] Aliotti, Pope Paul's Chamberlain.

look for me elsewhere than in Rome." I sent this letter to Messer Agostino, the steward, to give it to the Pope.

At my house I called a carpenter named Cosimo, who lived with me and attended to my household chores, and a stonecutter, who lived with me also, and I said to them: "Sell everything in the house, and then come to Florence." Then I left, took the post, and went toward Florence. When the Pope had received my letter, he sent five horsemen after me, who caught up with me at Poggibonsi about three hours after dark, and gave me a letter from the Pope, which read: "As soon as you have read this letter, return at once to Rome, under penalty of our displeasure." The said horsemen insisted that I reply, in order to prove that they had found me. I replied to the Pope that if he was willing to keep the conditions of our agreement, I would return; otherwise he must never expect to see me again.

Later, while I was in Florence, Julius sent three briefs to the Signory. At last the Signory sent for me and said to me: "We do not want to start a war with the Pope because of you. You must leave; and if you wish to return to him, we will write a letter of such authority that, should he do you harm, he would be doing it to this Signory." And so they did. And I returned to the Pope; but it would take long to recount what followed. Suffice it to say that this matter cost me more than one thousand ducats, for, after I left Rome, a scandal ensued to the Pope's shame; and almost all the marbles I had on St. Peter's square were damaged, especially the small blocks; wherefore, I had to do them over.

And so, I say and claim that either in damages or in interest the heirs of Pope Julius owe me five thousand ducats. And to think that those who have taken from me my youth, my honor, and my possessions call me a thief! And, as I said above, the Ambassador from Urbino has written me that first I must clean my conscience, and then I will get the Duke's ratification. He did not say this before he had me deposit the fourteen hundred ducats!

I beg your Lordship, for the love of God and of the truth, to read these things so that when the occasion presents itself you may defend me before the Pope from those who speak evil of me, without possessing any information, and who, by using false information, have painted me in the Duke's mind as an arch rogue. All the dissensions between Pope Julius and me arose from the envy of Bramante[46] and Raffaello da Urbino:[46] and this was the cause of his not going on with the tomb in his lifetime. They wanted to ruin me; and Raffaello had a good reason indeed, for all he had of art, he had from me.

October, 1542

Messer Luigi, dear friend – Since I have seen that the ratification is not coming, I have decided to stay home to finish the three figures[47] as I agreed with the Duke. This is more convenient for me than to drag myself every day to the Vatican: and let him who wants to get angry, be angry. I am satisfied with having conducted myself in such a way that the Pope cannot complain about me. The ratification would have done His Holiness a favor, not me, since he wanted me to paint. And that's that.

October 17, 1542

Reverend and Magnificent Monsignor Datary[48] – I have eight months' pay coming from the regular pension of fifty ducats a month which our Lord gives me, namely, from February to the present. It is a total of four hundred Italian gold ducats. Please pay them for me to Silvestro da Montauto and Company. In the same manner, you will continue to pay to them every month the

---

[46] Bramante da Urbino was the architect of St. Peter's appointed by Julius II. He and his successor, Raphael, the painter, were hostile competitors of Michelangelo.

[47] Moses, Rachel and Leah.

[48] Tommaso Cortesi from Prato.

usual amount, and get a receipt for it. It is a trustworthy company, and I am satisfied with this arrangement.

December 16, 1542

Gismondo – I am sending you fifty gold ducats, which I deposited today, here in Rome at the bank of Messer Silvestro da Montauto. Spend them on your needs, and let me know that you have received them.

1543

Luigi del Riccio, friend, nay, honorable master in Rome.

My dear Messer Luigi – Because I know that you are a master of social manners, whereas I am completely unskilled in such matters, and since I received from the Monsignor of Todi[49] the present Urbino will tell you about, I beg you to thank him in my name, with those compliments which come so easily to you, and with so much difficulty to me, and make me your debtor of a few pastries.

April 14, 1543

Lionardo – I am informed by your letter and the priest's,[50] where you brought the contract to have it sent to me. It did not get here, therefore, I am of the opinion that it was held up by the bank where you left it. If you want me to get it, give it to Francesco d'Antonio Salvetti[51] and have him address it here to Luigi del Riccio, and it will be delivered at once. And when you write me, do not write on the envelope: Michelagnolo Simoni, nor sculptor; it is enough to write: Michelagnolo Buonarroti, for that's how they know me here. And tell the priest to do the same thing.

---

[49] Federigo Cesi, later Cardinal of San Pancrazio.
[50] Chaplain Fattucci.
[51] A relative of del Riccio.

February 26, 1544

Castellan of Sant'Angelo.[52]

My Lord Castellan – Concerning the model[53] which was discussed yesterday, I did not express entirely my opinion, because I thought I might offend certain people of whom I am very fond. I mean Captain Giovan Francesco,[54] with whom I am not in agreement on certain points; for, it is my opinion that the bastions which have been started can, with reason and power, be defended and continued. If that is not done, I am afraid it is going to be much worse; and result in little honor for His Holiness. Therefore, I favor the continuation of what has been started, I do not mean in every detail, but in connection with the fortification of the mountain, with a few improvements, so as to have the opportunity of removing the present management,[55] if what they say about it is true, and to put in charge the said Captain Giovan Francesco, whom I consider capable and honest in everything. If this is done, I offer myself to him in honor of the Pope, for I have been asked several times, not as a partner, but as a helper in everything.

From the Spinelli to the Castle I would only make a ditch, for the corridor is sufficient, if it is properly restored.

March 29, 1544

Lionardo – I learn from your letter that the marbles[56] were valued at one hundred and seventy scudi, and also what we must do with the money when it is paid to you. It seems to me that, if my brothers approve, the money should be invested for you in a shop of their liking, and that you get from it an honest interest, and furthermore that without their permission you may not

---

[52] Warden of the fortress castle.
[53] Of the fortifications ordered by Pope Paul III of the area involving the Vatican.
[54] Montemellino, engineer and officer of artillery.
[55] The commission under Paul III's son, Pierluigi.
[56] From Michelangelo's Florence workshop.

dispose of the money otherwise. Also, it seems to me that you should sell the yard where the marbles are located, and that, with the same condition, you invest the money you get from it in the same place. Later I will be able to add more money to it, according to how well you behave; for it seems to me that you have not yet learned how to write.

I replied to Giovan Francesco[57] that I cannot attend to the head of the Duke.[58] That is the truth both because of the worries that beset me, and even more because of my old age,[59] for I can't see.

Concerning the purchasing of Luigi Gerardi's farm, I do not think it is a good idea for me to own in Florence any more than I already do, for if one has too much, one only gets troubles from it. Therefore, it seems to me that we ought to buy something elsewhere, so that I could also derive some interest from it in my old age, for, if I cannot be of use, I might be deprived of what the Pope gave me. As a matter of fact, I have had to fight for it twice already.[60] I have nothing else to tell you. Try to do well.

July 11, 1544

Lionardo – I was ill:[61] and you, upon request of Giovan Francesco, dealt me a deadly blow, and tried to find out whether I was leaving anything.[62]

Isn't there enough of my property in Florence to last you? You cannot deny resembling your father, who chased me from

---

[57] Chaplain Fattucci.

[58] A proposed commission.

[59] He was sixty-nine.

[60] His income from the ferry on the Po had been twice halted by a rival ferry.

[61] He became gravely ill in June, probably from a kidney disorder that plagued him in later life.

[62] During the illness, his nephew Lionardo came to Rome, which Michelangelo interpreted as concern for his inheritance.

my own house in Florence. I want you to know that I have my will in such a way that you may as well forget all about what I have in Rome. Therefore God be with you, do not come to see me any more and never write me again.

Pope Paul III.

Most Blessed Father – As you gathered from the chapter of Vitruvius,[63] architecture is nothing but order and disposition, a fine style, and a suitable harmony amongst the parts of the composition, and fitness and distribution.

First: here there is no order of any kind; for, order is a quaint suitability of the elements of the work separately and universally placed, coherently arranged. On the contrary, there is nothing but disorder here, for the elements of said cornice are out of proportion one with the other, nor do they harmonize with one another.

Second: there is no sign of disposition. Disposition is a certain collocation elegantly composed according to the quality and effect of the work. Here there is no quality for the completed work, carried out according to the rules of Vitruvius; and this cornice reveals rather an outlandish or peculiar quality.

Third: a fine style in the convenience of the composition of the members. In the present no such convenience is evident, rather, complete inconvenience. The first inconvenience is that it forebodes such a great expense as to interfere with the completion of said work. The second inconvenience is that it threatens to pull down to the ground the entire facade of the palace. Next, the cornice can be of three styles: doric, ionic or corinthian. The one in question belongs to none of the three, in fact it is bastard.

Fourth: in the composition and its parts there must be a suitable harmony, so that the components correspond separately

---

[63] Ancient author of a treatise on architecture, which he included with his report to the Pope on the Farnese Palace being built by Antonio da Sangallo.

to the whole style of the figure, with the confirmed part. In the said cornice there is no component which corresponds with the confirmed part, to the whole of the cornice, for the corbels are small and far apart for such large size, the frieze is small, and the lower support is too small for such volume.

Fifth: decorum is an aspect in the works to prove that they are composed with authority called propriety. In this cornice there is no propriety, rather there prevails a general impropriety: first, there appears that large head on a small facade, and the head is larger than the rest; and such large head does not become such little height. The other is that the head of the model does not correspond to the hand of the body; it is something quite different.

Sixth: distribution: the distribution according to the abundance of things is a comfortable apportionment of places. Here nothing is well apportioned; everything is apportioned at random, according to the whim of the moment; in one place he has been generous, in another sparing. It will be another type of distribution when the work is done according to the wont of the father of the family. According to the abundance of money, his elegance and dignity, the buildings will be ordered high; for one can see that the city palaces and the country houses, where the harvest is stored, must be built differently. They are not built in the same fashion for usurers, the rich, the refined or powerful people who, with their decisions rule the republic. They must be built suitable for each purpose. The construction of buildings must be executed according to the station of the various people.

This is what I have to tell your Holiness about this matter. I humbly kiss your Holiness's feet; if I do not come myself before your Holiness, it is because of my illness, for every time I have gone out of doors, I have had a relapse.

December 6, 1544

Giovansimone and Gismondo—I have been thinking for a long time to invest for Lionardo gradually up to a thousand scudi in a wool shop, as long as he behaves well; with this condition, however, that without your permission he cannot take the money out or do anything with it. I am ready to launch on this venture with two hundred scudi. If you are of the opinion that I should do it, take care that this money is not invested in a risky venture, for I did not find it in the street. Let me know what you think should be done. You are in a better position than I to know and see Lionardo's behavior, and whether it is worthwhile to get mixed up in this.

December 27, 1544

Lionardo – I have deposited here with the Covoni bank two hundred gold scudi which will be paid to you in Florence. It is my intention that Giovansimone and Gismondo put it in their name for you in the wool shop, for you are of the opinion that that is a safe investment. I am not to be named at all in this connection; with this condition: that the interest is yours, but that said money cannot be disposed of, withdrawn, or used for anything, unless the three of you, that is Giovansimone, Gismondo and you, are in agreement. So that no mistake is made in the drawing up of the papers, when you go to invest the money in the shop, I would like you to ask Michele Guicciardini[64] to be present along with Giovansimone and Gismondo; I think he knows about these things. Then, have Giovansimone and Gismondo write me a receipt for said money.

Send me a copy of the note you will have drawn up by the firm where you will invest the money.

January, 1545

Luigi del Riccio.

Messer Luigi, my dear Lord – I am sending Gabriello, who lives with me, to your Lordship in order that you give him the money you know about. He is trustworthy, and you can give it to him safely. I have recovered,[65] and I hope to live a few more years

---

[64] His niece's husband.
[65] From a recurrent kidney ailment.

yet, since Heaven has placed my health in the hands of Master Baccio,[66] and in care of the trebbiano wine of the Ulivieri.[67]

January, 1545

Lionardo – I received Giovansimone's and your receipt of the two hundred scudi. I cannot advise you on whether to invest them in one place rather than in another because I am not there and I am not a good judge of such things. Francesco Salvetti, a relative of Messer Luigi del Riccio here, wrote here that your advisers are very safe and honest men; yet, do what you think is safest.

January 25, 1545

Messers Silvestro da Montauto and Company, formerly of Rome, and through them Antonio Covoni and friends – You will please pay to the sculptor Raffaello da Montelupo fifty silver scudi at the rate of ten giuli to the scudo, which constitute the entire balance of what he could ask for the execution of the three marble statues which were completed and placed in San Pietro in Vincoli in the tomb of Pope Julius: namely, for a Madonna with Child in her arms, a Sibyl and a Prophet, for which, according to the agreement, he would have coming another hundred and seventy scudi; but since he was ill and unable to work, and the work was carried on by others, we agreed to give him these fifty scudi in total payment. That's how the receipt will have to be worded, and you will pay them out of the account of the one hundred and seventy scudi which you have left on deposit.

January 26, 1545

Messer Luigi del Riccio – If at times I did not express myself, albeit grammatically incorrect, it would be disgraceful of me, since I am on such familiar terms with you. I think that Messer Donato's[68] sonnet is as lovely as anything written in our day; but

---

[66] Rontini, a physician.
[67] Florentine merchants at the Strozzi bank in Rome.
[68] Giannotti.

since I have bad taste, I cannot esteem less a new suit, although of rough wool, than the second-hand silk and gold clothes which, properly tailored, make anyone look good.

Write to him about it, tell him about it, and reward him for it, and give him my best regards.

February 3, 1545

Messers Silvestro and Company, formerly of Rome – As is known to you, when I was busy in the service of our Lord Pope Paul III, painting his new chapel,[69] I could not carry to completion the tomb of Pope Julius II in San Pietro in Vincoli, so with the intervention of the aforesaid Holiness our Lord, we agreed and drew up a pact with the magnificent Girolamo Tiranno, orator of the most illustrious Lord Duke of Urbino. In accordance with this pact,[70] which was later ratified by his Excellency, I deposited with you various sums of money for the execution of said work, of which Raffaello da Montelupo was to receive four hundred and forty-five scudi at the rate of ten giuli per scudo, as balance of five hundred and fifty such scudi. This, for the completion of five marble statues which I had begun and roughhewn and which had been commissioned to him by the Ambassador of the Duke of Urbino: namely, a Madonna with Child in her arms, a Sibyl, a Prophet, an Active Life and a Contemplative Life, as indicated in the contract drawn up by Messer Bartolomeo Cappello, apostolic notary, under the date of August 21, 1542. Of these five statues, since our Lord upon my request and also to please me had granted me a little time, I finished two with my own hand, to wit the Contemplative and the Active Life,[71] for the same sum contracted with Raffaello, and from the same fund from which he was to be paid. Later, Raffaello finished the

---

[69] Pauline Chapel in St. Peter's, with the frescoes of Crucifixion of Peter and Conversion of Paul.
[70] Contract of 1542.
[71] Known as Rachel and Leah.

other three and set them in their places, as can be seen in the mentioned tomb.[72] For this work you will pay him, at his request, one hundred and seventy silver scudi[73] at the rate of ten giuli to the scudo, which you have left from said sum, securing from him a receipt in full drawn up also from the same notary, in which he will specify that he is satisfied with said work, and paid in full. And charge it to the account of the said sum you still have on hand.

February 15, 1545

Lionardo – I learn from your letters that you have not yet found a place to invest the money I sent you, because, according to what you write me, he who can manage his business alone, does not want the money of others. So that if someone accepts the money of others, this is an indication that he does not know how to handle his own: therefore he is a dangerous individual. For this reason I am happy that you are taking your time in investing the money, as long as you do not mishandle it, for this would be your own loss. As I wrote you, whenever I can, a little at a time, I will send you up to one thousand scudi; then I will have to think of myself, for I am old and I cannot work as hard as I used to. I want to give up the harbor the Pope gave me,[74] for I am making too many people uncomfortable,[75] and I do not think it is a good idea for me to hold on to it. For this reason I must secure myself an income here which will permit

---

[72] At San Pietro in Vincoli, Rome.

[73] This letter supersedes the one of January 25. Evidently Montelupo's delivery of the three statues constituted full completion of his contract, and he paid off the men who had helped him finish it.

[74] The ferry at Piacenza.

[75] A lawsuit had been brought against him claiming prior rights to the ferry.

me to live better than I am doing. Therefore, manage properly what you have, for I can help you no longer.

I hear that a boy was born to Michele, and that both he and Francesca are well. I am very happy over it. I think he has four now: may God grant that he derives a great deal of consolation from them. Remember me to him, and thank him for the trouble I am giving him, which grieves me very much.

March 13, 1545

Messer Luigi del Riccio – Today, I received one hundred scudi from Melighino[76] for my salary of January and February past.

April 5, 1545

Lionardo – I thought of sending another sum of money like the previous one in a couple of months, but I am not in favor of your keeping it in the house, because it is dangerous. If you think you can do with it something safer and more useful, do as you wish. I'll try to send you the whole sum I promised you within one year.

May 9, 1545

Lionardo – I do not think one can keep money anywhere at interest which cannot be called usury, unless one takes a great risk. I meant you to buy something like the land of Nicoló della Buca or something else of your choice, not to put it in any bank, for they are all unsafe.

You write me about the appointment you have received;[77] I tell you that you are young and have little experience. I remind you that in Florence it is worse to go ahead than to go backwards.

Tell Giovansimone that a new commentary on Dante prepared by a scholar from Lucca[78] and now available, is not much

---

[76] A mediocre architect favored by Paul III.

[77] Unknown.

[78] By Alessandro Vellutello.

praised by those who know, and that one shouldn't think too much of it. There are no other new ones to my knowledge.

Remember me to Michele Guicciardini, and tell him that I am in good health, but with so many worries that I haven't the time to eat. Therefore, make my apologies to him for not replying. Tell Francesca to pray God for me.

May 13, 1545

Lionardo–Today, I gave the Covoni in Rome two hundred gold scudi, which will be paid to you in Florence. Make out a receipt and send me a copy.

1545

Lionardo–I wrote you last Saturday that I would have appreciated more two flasks of trebbiano wine than the eight shirts you sent me. Now I wish to inform you that I received a load of trebbiano, namely forty-four flasks, of which I sent six to the Pope and to other friends, so much so that I have disposed of almost all of them, for I cannot drink any. There is no reason why you should send me one thing instead of another, or why you should send me anything. All I am interested in is that you be a fine man, and that you do honor to yourself and to all of us.

July, 1545

Lionardo–I wrote you not to send me anything unless I request something of you. I repeat that now. Concerning the investment of the money, if one goes slowly there is less of a chance of making mistakes. You have enough to live on, and no one is chasing you. Therefore you must be patient and hold your tongue, so no one will take your money away from you.

1545

Luigi del Riccio.

Messer Luigi–I beg you to send me the last madrigal which you do not understand, so that I may revise it, for the messenger, who is Urbino, was so quick that he did not allow me to revise it.

As for being with you tomorrow, I make my apologies to you, for the weather is bad and I have something to do here at home. We shall do what we had planned for tomorrow, the coming Lent, at Lunghezza,[79] with a large tench.[80]

1545

Messer Luigi – I recommend myself to you and to those you love. I am at the service of Messer Giuliano[81] and Messer Roberto,[82] of whom you write me, and if I do not do what I should, I am fleeing creditors, because I am deeply indebted and I have little money.

1545

Messer Luigi, dear friend – I beg you to do to me when I come and call on you, what I do to you when you come and call on me. You allow me to come and bother you, and you do not let people tell me; so that I am considered a brazen ox even by the servants.

I think that on Thursday, I will give the order to have the statues[83] taken to San Pietro in Vincoli, and since I want to pay for the carriage with the money you have left for the statues, I think I will write a release for the money and have it signed by the ambassador,[84] so that neither you nor I will ever be asked for it. Therefore, I beg you to draw up a rough draft of how the release should be worded.

Yesterday morning I did not recognize the son of Messer

---

[79] Strozzi villa near Rome.

[80] A freshwater fish.

[81] Giuliano de' Medici of the Cosimo branch exiled in France after his brother murdered the Duke of Florence.

[82] Roberto Strozzi, an exiled Republican.

[83] For Julius's tomb.

[84] For the Duke of Urbino.

Bindo Altoviti, and if you wanted to bring him here, you should have felt free to say so, for I am at the service of Messer Bindo and all his relatives.

1545

Messer Luigi – You know that the fire has uncovered a part of the Chapel:[85] therefore, it seems to me that it should be recovered the way it was as fast as possible, crudely, if necessary, until the weather changes, because the rains not only spoil frescoes, but disturb the walls. And since it is deteriorating under normal conditions, the rain would not help it at all. I write this, hoping that the Pope has not embarked on an expensive undertaking which would be more useful to others than to the Chapel. Therefore I beg you to explain this to the Pope when you speak to him, or to have Messer Aurelio[86] do it, to whom I beg you also to give my best regards.

1545

Vittoria Colonna, Marchioness of Pescara in Rome.
Before accepting the things which your Ladyship has several times wanted to give me, in order to be as little as possible unworthy of them, I wished, Lady, to do something for you with my own hands.[87] Thereafter I realized that the grace of God cannot be purchased, and that it is a grievous sin to keep it waiting; I acknowledge my error, and I accept said things willingly. And when I have them, not because they will be in my house, but because I will be in their house, I will believe to be in Paradise. And for this I will be more obliged to your Ladyship, if it is possible to be more than I already am.

The bearer of this letter is Urbino, who lives with me; your Ladyship may tell him when you want me to come and see the head you promised to show me.

---

[85] The roof of the Pauline Chapel.
[86] A steward.
[87] A crucifix he designed for her as a surprise.

THE TRANSFIGURATION OF BEAUTY
A Dialogue with Love

Nay, prithee tell me, Love, when I behold
my lady, do mine eyes her beauty see
in truth, or dwells that loveliness in me
which multiplies her grace a thousandfold?

Thou needs must know; for thou with her of old
comest to stir my soul's tranquility;
yet would I not seek one sigh less, or be
by loss of that loved flame more simply cold.—

The beauty thou decernest, all is hers;
but grows in radiance as it soars on high
through mortal eyes unto the soul above:

'tis there transfigured; for the soul confers
on what she holds, her own divinity:
and this transfigured beauty wins thy love.

———————◆◆———————

1545

Vittoria Colonna.

Lady Marchioness—Since I am in Rome, it does not seem fitting,
in order to do you a favor, to leave the Crucifix in Messer Tommaso de' Cavalieri's hands,[88] and make him an intermediary between your Ladyship and me, your servant; all the more since it
has been my desire to do more for you than for anyone I ever
knew in the world. But the absorbing tasks which have kept me
busy every moment, have prevented me from letting you know
this. And since I know that you know that love does not want
a master, and that he who loves does not sleep, I thought even
less of using go-betweens. And although it seemed that I had
forgotten, I was working on something I was not talking about
in order to come to you with a thing you did not expect. My
plan has been spoiled: *He sins who so much faith soon forgets.*

---

[88] She found out about the crucifix and asked him to send it by
De' Cavalieri.

A PRAYER TO NATURE
Amor Redivivus

That thy great beauty on our earth may be
shrined in a lady softer and more kind,
I call on nature to collect and bind
all those delights the slow years steal from thee,

and save them to restore the radiancy
of thy bright face in some fair form designed
by heaven; and may Love ever bear in mind
to mould her heart of grace and courtesy.

I call on nature too to keep my sighs,
my scattered tears to take and recombine,
and give to him who loves that fair again:

more happy he perchance shall move those eyes
to mercy by the griefs wherewith I pine,
nor lose the kindness that from me is ta'en!

————◆◆————

December, 1545

Luigi del Riccio in Lyons.[89]

Messer Luigi, dear friend – All your friends, above all Messer
Donato[90] and myself, are sorry that you are not well, especially
since they cannot help you. We hope that it is a very minor thing,
and may it so please God.

I wrote you that if you did not return soon, I was thinking
of coming to see you myself. I repeat that, for, since I lost the
port of Piacenza,[91] and since it is impossible to live in Rome without an income, I would prefer to spend what I have left in inns,

---

[89] He is visiting his employer Strozzi in France.
[90] Giannotti.
[91] The lawsuit continues but he knows it is lost.

than to shiver in Rome like a rogue. Therefore, if nothing else comes up, I am ready to go to St. James of Compostela[92] after Easter, and if you haven't returned by that time, to follow the route that takes me through where you may happen to be.

Urbino has spoken to Messer Aurelio; judging by what he tells me, you will obtain the spot you wish for Cecchino's[93] tomb. Said tomb is almost finished, and it will be very beautiful.

1545

Messer Luigi del Riccio – Our departed friend[94] speaks and says: if Heaven deprived of beauty all the other men in the world in order to make only me beautiful, as he did; and if through divine law on the day of judgment I am to become again the same as I was before, it follows that he cannot return the beauty he gave me to those from whom he took it, and that I must be in eternity more handsome than the others, and that they must be homely. And this is the contrary of the concept about which you spoke to me yesterday, and one is a fable, and the other the truth.

December 31, 1545

Lionardo – You write me of several houses that can be bought, among them one that once belonged to Zanobi Buondelmonti, and this one seems to me more decorous than the others. Therefore, if there is good security we should take it. However, do not trust Bernardo Basso. Pretend to have faith in him, but believe nothing he says, for he is a great traitor. I'd like very much to buy in our zone on Ghibellina street,[95] but every year there the cellars flood. Therefore, seek good counsel, and when you and my brothers have reached a decision, let me know the expense and I will see that you get all the money that is needed.

---

[92] In Galicia, a famous shrine.

[93] Michelangelo designed the tomb for Riccio's nephew, Cecchino Bracci.

[94] Bracci.

[95] He remained partial to his home quarter of Santa Croce, where he went to live at the age of ten.

HEAVEN-BORN BEAUTY

As one who will reseek her home of light,
thy form immortal to this prison-house
descended, like an angel piteous,
to heal all hearts and make the whole world bright.

'Tis this that thralls my soul in love's delight,
not thy clear face of beauty glorious;
for he who harbours virtue, still will choose
to love what neither years nor death can blight.

So fares it ever with things high and rare
wrought in the sweat of nature; heaven above
showers on their birth the blessings of her prime:

nor hath God designed to show Himself elsewhere
more clearly than in human forms sublime;
which, since they image him, alone I love.

———————✦✦———————

January 9, 1546

My dearest Lionardo Buonarroti as a son in Florence.
Lionardo – Today, I gave to Luigi del Riccio six hundred gold
scudi, which he will remit to you in Florence: this will complete
the total of one thousand scudi I promised you.

Messer Luigi will write here below my intentions toward
you, for I am not well and I cannot write any more. However, I
have recovered and I will no longer be ill, God be praised. Thus
I pray to him, and you will do the same.

I have decided, over and above the mentioned money, to
endow Giovansimone, Gismondo and you with three thousand
gold scudi, namely one thousand scudi each, but to all together;
with the condition that they be invested in real estate or in something else which will be useful to you, and which will remain
to the family. Therefore, give some thought to investing them in
something durable and good, and when you find something which

you deem appropriate, let me know, and I will send you the money. This letter is meant for the three of you. My love to all of you.

January 16, 1546

Dearest Lionardo – A close friend of mine here informs me that the landed property of Francesco Corboli is for sale. He lives in Venice. I am told that his property consists of an old house located in Florence in the Santo Spirito district, and of certain farms one next to the other with six pairs of oxen and a good house or farm cottage located at Monte Spertoli. Therefore, I would like Giovansimone and you to find out what the taxes are, how good they are and what income they yield; how they are set up, whether they are involved in any litigation or entanglement, and how much you think they are worth. Reply to all these questions as soon as you can.

February 6, 1546

Lionardo – You were very quick in informing me about the Corboli's property. Are you afraid I might change my mind, as someone may have put it into your head? I tell you that I want to proceed cautiously, for I have earned my money here by dint of all the hard work that cannot be understood by one who was born clothed and shod as you were.

As for your coming to Rome in such haste, I wonder whether you would have come so fast if I were in want and I had nothing to eat. All you are interested in is to throw away the money you have not earned yourself. You are ever so anxious not to miss out in this inheritance! You tell me that it was your duty to come here out of your love for me. The love of the woodworm! If you really loved me, you would have written me now: *Michelangelo, spend those three thousand scudi there on yourself, for you have given us enough already. We care more for your life than for your property.*

11. Tomb of Lorenzo de' Medici, 1520-1534. *(Courtesy of Alinari)*

12. The Medici Madonna, *circa* 1530-1534. *(Courtesy of Alinari)*

You have lived off my earnings for forty years, and I have never received from you as much as one good word.

It is true that last year I reprimanded and rebuked you so much that out of shame you sent me a load of trebbiano wine. I wish you had never sent it.

I am not writing you this because I do not have the intention of buying. I do want to buy in order to assure myself an income, for I cannot work any longer; but I want to proceed cautiously so as not to acquire a lot of grief. Therefore, do not be overanxious.

If in Florence you are told or asked anything in my name, unless you see a paragraph in my own hand, do not believe anyone.

February 15, 1546

Lionardo – As to whether you should use the money I sent you to make a purchase or to invest it in a shop, take counsel among yourselves, for I am not a good judge.

Concerning the Corboli's property I found out one thing that I do not like, that there is a tax of twenty-five scudi. If this is true, that's all I would need on top of all my other troubles. Furthermore, I am told that certain relatives of theirs have some interest on it.

Therefore, keep after them and let me know what it is estimated to be worth. I have nothing else to say.

1546

Messer Luigi del Riccio – You think I should answer you what you wish, when it is quite the contrary. You give me what I have denied you, and you deny me what I have asked you. And you are not guilty of ignorance by sending it to me through Ercole, since you are ashamed to give it to me personally.

He who has snatched me from death[96] can certainly shame

---

[96] Del Riccio nursed him through his illness of June, 1544.

me. But I am not quite sure what is more oppressing, shame or death. Therefore, I beg you and entreat you for the true friendship which exists between us that you should allow that plate to be destroyed, and those which have been printed to be burned,[97] and that if you carry on a trade with me, you do not let others do the same. If you cut me into a thousand pieces, I shall do the same, not with you, but with your things.

Not a painter, nor a sculptor, nor an architect, but whatever you wish. However, not a drunkard, as I told you at home.

March 6, 1546

Lionardo – You write me that you and my brothers have found a certain Palagio and others who are willing to form a company with you. I do not know nor have I any way of informing myself of such a thing; but since nowadays one meets with nothing but fraud, and one cannot trust anybody, I advise you to be cautious, especially since you do not lack bread to eat.

I have heard various things of the Corboli's lands; and since because of my long experience I am suspicious of them, I have let them go, in order to avoid in my old age to get into trouble, and after my death leave someone else in it.

April 26, 1546

The Most Christian King of France.[98]

Sacred Majesty – I do not know which is greater, the favor or my astonishment, that your Majesty has deigned to write to a man of my sort, and still more to ask him for things done by him which are not even worthy of the name of your Majesty. But be they what they may, I wish your Majesty to know that for a long time I have wished to serve you; but for want of an opportunity, since

---

[97] Milanesi says this is probably an engraving made from the Last Judgment by Vico or by Bonasone.

[98] Francis I.

conditions were not favorable to my art in Italy, I have been unable to do so. I have been busy for several months with the commissions of Pope Paul;[99] but if after this engagement I have some years of life left, I will do my best to fulfill the desire which, as I have said, I have had for a long time to do something for your Majesty; namely, one work in marble, one in bronze, and one in painting. And if death interrupts this wish of mine, and it is possible to make statues or paint in the other world, I shall not fail to do it there, where one ceases to grow old. And I pray God that He grant your Majesty a long and happy life.

April 29, 1546

Lionardo – I do not like the house on Via de' Martegli, because I do not think that it is a street for us.[100] The one of the Wool Guild on Via de' Servi, since there is good security, is all right, and if it suits us insofar as rooms and everything else is concerned, you ought to take it. Let me know the money you lack, and I will send it to you. But be sure you are not duped, and that the rumor about your wanting to buy a house does not make the auction tricky. It seems to me that you ought to examine it carefully in advance, then if you see that the price is not right, leave it to whoever wants it, for money does not grow on trees.

April 30, 1546

Lionardo – I received the shirts.

I learned from another letter of yours about the income of a mill which could be bought, and recently you wrote me about another property near Florence. I did not like the mill, for I do not trust an income based on water, and I think also that the

---

[99] Architecture of Farnese Palace; Roman Capitol and Pauline Chapel frescoes.

[100] He wants to obtain a house for his nephew worthy of the family.

property is too close to the city gates. If we could find something eight or ten miles away, I would like that better, but there is no rush. So do not talk too much about it. I have nothing else to tell you.

May 26, 1546

Lionardo – I have received the contract[101] and I find it correct. Therefore, thank Messer Giovan Francesco, for he has done me a great favor, and beg him to thank Bernardo Bini, and give him my regards.

June 5, 1546

Lionardo – I had the rough draft of the power of attorney copied without even seeing it, and since I am giving you power of attorney, I am sending it to you. If it is the way you like it, that's all I want, for I have other things to think about besides powers of attorney. And stop writing me, for every time I get one of your letters I get feverish, so hard is it for me to read them! I think that if you had to write to the greatest ass in the world, you would write with more diligence. Therefore, do not add troubles to those I already have, and believe me I have enough.

September 4, 1546

Lionardo – You certainly wrote me an endless sermon for a little trifle! All this does is to bother me.

November 13, 1546

Lionardo – I did not write you, since you informed me that you were in the process of setting up a shop. I tell you not to be in haste. I have been thinking these last few days that it would be well to buy in Florence a suitable house of about fifteen hundred scudi; for, since you are to be married,[102] the one in which

---

[101] Not identified.
[102] A suitable match is being sought. He is now twenty-seven.

you boys[103] live now is not large enough, and also because I am old and should invest this money in something.

December 4, 1546

Lionardo – I received sixteen marzolini cheeses, and I paid the driver four giuli. You must have received the letter I wrote you concerning the purchase of a fine house, of fifteen hundred or two thousand scudi preferably located in our district.[104] I say this because a fine house in town does one a great deal of honor, for people can see it better than they can your other possessions. After all, we too are burghers who have descended from very noble stock.[105] I have always done my best to uphold our name, but I have not had the right kind of brothers for that. Therefore, try to do what I tell you, and have Gismondo come back to live in Florence, so that people here will no longer say to my great shame that I have a brother in Settignano who tends oxen. And after you have bought the house, we shall also buy other things.

Some day when I have time, I will inform you of our origin, and of when and whence we came to Florence, for perhaps you do not know it. For this reason we should not deprive ourselves of what God has given us.

December, 1546

Lionardo – About one year ago I chanced to pick up a book of Florentine chronicles written by hand. There I found that two hundred years ago, if I recall correctly, a Buonarroto Simoni was several times in public office, then a Simone Buonarroti, then a Michele di Buonarroto Simoni, then a Francesco Buonarroti. I did not find there our father Lodovico's father Lionardo, who

---

[103] Giovansimone is sixty-seven; Gismondo is sixty-five.

[104] Santa Croce.

[105] A letter of October 8, 1520, from the Count of Canossa had claimed kinship with Michelangelo, which he sometimes believed. Modern sources do not.

was one of the Signori, because those chronicles did not come that close to our time. Therefore, it seems to me that you should sign your name *Lionardo of Buonarroto Buonarroti Simoni.*

1547[106]

Giovansimone – I have received several letters from Ser Giovan Francesco Fattucci concerning your illness. I was very sorry to hear about it, all the more since I was not there to help you, as I have always tried to do. Just the same, I shall do my best to see that you lack nothing. I am enclosing ten scudi, and I promise you that in the future I shall see to it that you get everything I can provide you with while I am here. Therefore, take courage and try to get well, and do not worry about anything else, for as long as I am not in need, neither will you. And as far as I can tell, at the end there will be more goods than men. Pray to God, for he can help you more than I can.

January 22, 1547

Lionardo – I learn from your letter that you have hired a broker in connection with the Buondelmonti house, and that you understand the cost to be twenty-four scudi. It seems like a lot of money to me, and, if they are trying to sell, I do not think that these days they will get it in cash as they would from me. So, keep up with any developments and in the meantime you can look for something else. As I wrote you, I would like to find something in our neighborhood, but the fact that the cellars get flooded does not seem unimportant to me. As for starting to send you money, I would like to send it the usual way, as in the days of Messer Luigi.[107] Therefore, if you can find out from the

---

[106] On January 1, 1547, he was appointed architect of St. Peter's, succeeding Antonio da Sangallo, who died October 3, 1546. He was then seventy-one.

[107] Del Riccio died late in 1546.

Capponi, let me know, and I will begin sending money little by little for the above-mentioned house.

February 11, 1547

Lionardo – Today I took five hundred gold scudi to Messer Bindo Altoviti, and asked that the sum be paid to you in Florence. It will be paid to you by the Capponi. When you write me, address the letters to Messer Girolamo Ubaldini, and, if you keep the money in the house, do not let the right hand know what the left one is doing because it is very dangerous.

March 5, 1547

Lionardo – This morning, I took another five hundred gold scudi to Messer Bindo Altoviti, who will have them paid there by the Capponi either to you or to Gismondo, or to the both of you. After you have purchased the house I will send you what is lacking, and I think that it would be a good thing for when one dies without heirs, everything goes to the Hospital.[108] Remember me to the priest.

March, 1547

Lionardo – I received the receipt of the scudi which the Capponi gave you, and I am surprised that Gismondo did not go with you to receive payment either of the first remittance or of the last, for I send the money to them as well as to you. And you write me and thank me for the good I do you, Lionardo, whereas you ought to write me: *we thank you for the good you do us.* I sent the last sum of money with the same condition I wrote you about when I sent you the money to invest in a shop: namely, that you do nothing without the consent of my brothers.

I already wrote you in regards to buying a house, for whenever you decide to get yourself a wife, as I think you should, the

---

[108] Of Santa Maria Nuova.

house in which you are living is not large enough for your needs. And if you should not find a suitable thing to purchase, I think that the house where you are living on Via Ghibellina could be enlarged, namely, by buying the little house below, if that will be enough, and by bringing the consoles of the house out to the corner and turning them toward the other street. However, if you succeed in making a safe and good purchase, I think that that would be better; and I will send you what you lack.

Concerning your taking a wife, here in Rome people have mentioned several names: some I like, some I do not. I am sure that they have spoken to you about them too. Therefore, if you feel like getting married, let me know; and if you like one better than the other, I will tell you my opinion. I have nothing more to say.

1547

Lionardo – The bearer of this letter is a stoneworker from Settignano named Jacopo, and he says that he wants to sell certain lands near ours, a place called Fraschetta. Therefore, tell Gismondo. If they are a good buy and have good security, and if by buying them we would not get tangled up in a lawsuit, let me know. I will send you the money.

1547

Lionardo – You write me that the house on Via de' Servi was sold at auction, and that, after all, it was not what we wanted. I think that the house of Giovanni Corsi about which you write me now is the one on a corner in Piazza Santa Croce, right across from the Orlandini house. I like it, but if it were sold, I have some strong doubts about the security. Therefore, if we plan to buy it we must keep our eyes good and open. I know that it is an old house, and I think that inside it is badly arranged.

I received a load of trebbiano wine, but only thirty-eight out of the forty-four flasks: three were broken, and three were left at the customhouse. I sent ten of them to the Pope.[109] I hope it is good.

September, 1547

Lionardo – Concerning the Corsi house, I was told the last time you wrote me about it, that there was a rich neighbor who was going to buy it; I shouldn't want you to acquire a lawsuit. Concerning the charity, I am satisfied to know that you gave it, and it is sufficient to get the receipt from the Monastery; you do not have to mention my name. I was as sorry about Guicciardini's baby[110] as if he had been my own. Comfort them and give them my love. Give my regards to Giovan Francesco and tell him please to excuse me if I do not do for him what I should, for I am laden down with troubles, especially now that I lost the port[111] and that I am forced to live on my capital. God help us. Tell him to remember me to Bugiardino,[112] if he is still alive.

1547

Lionardo – Concerning the Corsi house, it seems to me that, if the outside walls are good and sound, and if there is good security, we ought to take it for the sake of investing that money. We can fix the interior later, a little at a time. Furthermore, it seems to me that in Florence families have lasted out only if they had real estate. Therefore, think it over carefully, for whatever you do, you will do it for yourselves.

I think you are neglecting the giving of alms far too much. If you do not give away what belongs to me for the repose of your father's soul, you would give even less of what belongs to you. As for finding you a wife, I am waiting for a friend of mine

---

[109] Paul III.

[110] His niece has lost a child.

[111] When Emperor Charles V obtained Piacenza, Michelangelo permanently lost the ferry.

[112] Friend and fellow apprentice at Ghirlandaio's.

who is out of Rome. He wants to talk to me about three or four possibilities. I will let you know about them. We shall see whether he has something that will do for us.

1547

Lionardo – As far as I can tell from your last letter, it seems to me that there are more bad features than good ones in the Corsi house; unless one gets a good bargain, one should not buy these old houses. For, as soon as one starts fixing them up, one comes across more and more bad material, so that it would be better to build one from scratch. The only good thing about it is the security it offers. If you have made up your mind to take it, have somebody examine it carefully, and try to get it for as low a price as you can.

1547

Lionardo – I wrote you concerning your getting married. I told you about three young women who had been mentioned to me here: one is the daughter of Alamanno de' Medici, another is the daughter of Domenico Gugni, and the other is the daughter of Cherubin Fortini. I do not know any one of them, therefore I cannot say either good or bad things about them, nor can I advise you to choose one rather than another. However, if Michele Guicciardini were willing to take some pains for us, he could find out about them and let us know; and likewise if he knew about anything else.

But above all it takes God's counsel, for it is an important matter. And remember also that between the husband and the wife there must always be at least ten years difference, and be sure that besides being good she is also healthy.

Concerning the purchase of the house, I think that it is necessary before you get married, for I know that the one in which you fellows live now is not large enough.

1547

Lionardo – I received fourteen marzolini cheeses, and I am telling you again what I told you other times, namely not to send me anything unless I ask for it.

Concerning the Corsi house I have a feeling that the impression they are giving you that someone else wants to buy it is merely a ruse to put pressure on you.

Concerning the house which you say is in the direction of the Alberti corner, it seems to me that, considering the size and the fact that it is not finished yet, they are asking too much. But I repeat that I cannot pass judgment on things which are so far from me. I give you a similar answer for the setting up of a shop: it is not my profession. You must be responsible for the good or the bad you will do.

1547

Lionardo – I have the receipt for the charitable donation you made, and I am happy over it. Thank Messer Giovan Francesco for me, for I am much obliged to him. Also, tell him that that good man who replied to him that I am not a statesman, can only be kind and discreet, for he said the truth. I only wish that my business here in Rome bothered me as little as the affairs of State!

I never receive a letter from you without losing my patience before I get through reading it: I'll never know where you learned to write. You certainly care little to learn!

July, 1547

Lionardo – You say that you think the house of Zanobi Buondelmonti will be for sale. I would like it as much as that of the Corsi's. At any rate, whichever we can get of the two, it seems to me that we should take it and not let one hundred scudi stand in the way. Should you want to get married, out of respect, it would be best for you to do it while I am alive rather than after my death. I am beset by troubles.

I should like you to get, through Messer Giovan Francesco, the height of the dome of Santa Maria del Fiore,[113] from the

---

[113] He is beginning to plan the dome of St. Peter's.

beginning of the lantern to the ground; and then, the height of the whole lantern, and send these measurements to me. Mark for me in the letter one-third of the Florentine braccio.[114]

August 6, 1547

Lionardo – I am sending five hundred and fifty gold scudi on account for what is still lacking to the thousand I sent you to buy the house. Make out a correct receipt. Give four or six of the scudi to that woman[115] whose letter you enclosed in your last one to me.

August, 1547

Lionardo – I received with your letter the receipt of the five hundred and fifty gold scudi which I sent you through Bettini. You tell me that for the love of God you will give four of them to that woman. I like that. Also for the love of God, I want that the rest of the fifty scudi be given part for the soul of your father Buonarroto and part for mine. Therefore, try to learn the name of some needy citizen who has daughters to marry off or to put in a convent, and give the money to him, but secretly. But be sure you are not fooled, have him give you a receipt and send it to me, for I know that there are some citizens who are in need but who are ashamed to go begging.

You sent me a brass arm,[116] as if I were a mason or a carpenter and had to carry it about with me. I was ashamed to have it around the house and gave it away.

Francesca writes me that she is not in very good health and that she has four children, and that as a result she has a lot of trouble. I am very sorry to hear that; otherwise, I do not think she lacks anything. As for troubles, I think I have more

---

[114] A unit of measure, also the word for "arm."

[115] A needy person.

[116] Lionardo misunderstood Michelangelo's request in July; he meant *braccio*, the measure. Lionardo sent a workman's tool.

than she; moreover, old age[117] is with me and I have no time to entertain my relatives.

See that you sleep with your eyes open.

December 17, 1547

Lionardo – I learn from your letter that a lawsuit has been brought against us for certain lands at Settignano,[118] and that I should send you a power of attorney so that you may defend them. I think I will have to send you a book of contracts which I had properly drawn up by Ser Giovanni da Romena, and which cost me eighteen ducats. I am sure that in it you will find the contract of said lands. I shall send several contracts and corrections and other writings which concern my worldly possessions. There- fore, I should like you to find a dependable driver, and that you send him to me when he comes to Rome. I will give him a bundle of the said documents, which will weigh about twenty pounds. Make an agreement with him, and do not haggle over half a scudo,[119] so that he will take the bundle to you safely.

January, 1548

Lionardo – There came to see me today with a letter from you a fellow who says he is the son of the driver Lorenzo del Cione. I do not know him, but thinking that he is the one you are sending to me for said contracts, I am giving them to him, even if with a certain amount of suspicion, for they are very important. I have placed the bundle in a box, and I have carefully wrapped the box twice in a waxed cloth and tied it crossways so that the rain will not damage it. I do not know the date, but today is the Epiphany.

---

[117] Seventy-two.

[118] A bank which gave security at Settignano for a purchase now wishes to use that security to buy the land.

[119] A coin roughly equivalent to a florin.

January, 1548

Lionardo – I learn from your last letter about the death of Giovansimone.[120] It grieved me greatly because, although I am old, I was hoping to see him before he died, and before I died. That's the way God wanted it: faith! I should like to know in detail about his death, and whether he died after having confessed himself and received communion with all the ritual prescribed by the Church; for if I know that he received the last sacraments, I will not feel so badly.

January, 1548

Lionardo – I gather from your letter that you received the box with the book of contracts at a very opportune moment. I also thought you needed it.

You pass over the death of Giovansimone very lightly, for you give me no details of anything nor of what he left behind. I remind you that he was my brother and, whatever he was, there is no reason to think that I am not sorry about his death, and that I shouldn't want to do for the rest of his soul what I did for your father's soul. Therefore, be sure not to be ungrateful for what has been done for you, who didn't have a single thing to your name. I am amazed that Gismondo hasn't written me a word about it, for what Giovansimone left belongs to him as well as to me. To you belongs only what we decide and nothing else.

February, 1548

Lionardo – After I wrote you last, I found a letter at home in which you tell me about all that was found belonging to Giovansimone. Then I received another which informs me in detail of his death. Concerning what is left that belonged to him you might have informed me in the first letter, so that I wouldn't have had to wait and find out from someone else, as it happened: and that made

[120] January 9, 1548.

me very angry. Concerning his death, you tell me that, although he did not receive all the sacraments of the Church, he had a good contrition. If that is the case, that's all that is needed for one's salvation. As for what he left, since he did not make a will, it is logical that everything goes to Gismondo; and my advice to you two is that you use it to do all the good you can for his soul, and do not spare the money, for I shall not fail you in whatever you will do.

February 28, 1548

Lionardo – It's up to you whether you should get married or not, and whether you should choose one rather than another, as long as she is noble and well-bred, and, for the sake of harmony, it would be better if she had no dowry at all rather than too much.

March, 1548

Lionardo – I am glad you informed me about the proclamation,[121] for, if I have abstained until now from talking and consorting with the exiles, I shall be even more careful in the future. Concerning my having been at the Strozzi house while I was ill, I do not look upon it as having been in their house,[122] but rather in the bedroom of Luigi del Riccio, who was my close friend, and after the death of Bartolomeo Angiolini I couldn't have found anybody to take care of my things better or more faithfully than he.[123] The whole city of Rome can testify to the fact that after his death I have never set foot in that house, and also to the kind of existence I am leading, for I am always alone. I do not go around much, and I do not speak to anybody, most of all about Florentines. Logically, if someone greets me in the street, I cannot

---

[121] Duke Cosimo de' Medici issued a proclamation March 11, 1548, against all conspirators and rebels (The Republicans), and their dependents.

[122] During June, 1544.

[123] Del Riccio.

help replying in a civil manner; but then I go on my way; and if I knew who are the exiles, I would not reply to them under any circumstances. As I said, from now on I shall be very careful, especially since I have so many other cares,[124] that I find it hard to keep alive.

———◆◆———

After the Death of Vittoria Colonna

A WASTED BRAND

If being near the fire I burned with it,
now that its flame is quenched and doth not show,
what wonder if I waste within and glow,
dwindling away to cinders bit by bit?

While still it burned, I saw so brightly lit
that splendor whence I drew my grievous woe,
that from its sight alone could pleasure flow,
and death and torment both seemed exquisite.

But now that heaven hath robbed me of the blaze
of that great fire which burned and nourished me,
a coal that smoulders 'neath the ash am I.

Unless Love furnish wood fresh flames to raise,
I shall expire with not one spark to see,
so quickly into embers do I die!

———◆◆———

April 7, 1548

Lionardo – Concerning your getting married, if you think you should let this summer go by, so do I. As for going to Loreto[125] for your father, if it was a vow I think that you should keep it at all costs. If it is for the good you want to do his soul, I

---

[124] Recurrent illness; death of Vittoria Colonna in 1547, loss of his toll revenue, conflict with Sangallo's disciples over St. Peter's.

[125] House of the Virgin, a shrine. Loreto is near Ancona.

would rather donate what the journey would cost you there in Florence, for the love of God and for his; for the Lord knows what priests do with the money one takes to them. Furthermore, since you are running a shop, I do not think it would be a good idea to waste your time. For, if you want to profit, you must be a slave to your job, and set aside the amenities of youth. I can't think of anything else.

April 14, 1548

Lionardo – I received in one of your letters the copy of the deed of the company of the Wool Guild which you formed. Concerning what you write me about the Santa Caterina property, do what you boys think best. It is true that the Tornabuoni house is out of our district, yet the price and the security could make up for everything. I should like you to send me my birth certificate, just as you did once before, exactly as it is recorded in our father's book, for I lost it.

April 28, 1548

Lionardo – In this letter you will find a contract to the effect that I refuse Giovansimone's inheritance.

May 2, 1548

Lionardo – I received the little barrel with eighty-six pears; I sent thirty-three of them to the Pope. He thought they were lovely and he appreciated them very much. Concerning the little barrel of cheese, the Customs Office says that that driver is a rogue, and that he never brought it into the Customs House. Therefore, when I find out that he is in Rome, I'll see that he gets what he deserves, not because of the cheese, but to teach him to have more consideration for his fellow men. I was very ill the last few days from not being able to urinate, for I am afflicted with that difficulty;[126] but now I am better. I am writing you

---

[126] Kidney stones. Treated by his friend, the physician Realdo Colombo, whom he later helped prepare a book on anatomy.

this, lest some chatterbox should write you a thousand lies to worry you. Tell the priest not to address his letters to me as *Michelangelo sculptor*, for I am known only as Michelangelo Buonarroti, and also that if there is a Florentine who wants an altarpiece painted, he ought to find a painter, for I never was a painter nor a sculptor such as one who runs a shop. I have always refrained from it for the honor of my father and my brothers, even if I have worked for three Popes. That could not be helped. I have nothing else to say. You must have found out from my last letter how I feel about your getting married. Do not tell the priest what I said above about him, for I want to pretend not to have received his letter.

June, 1548

Lionardo – I was very happy to receive a load of trebbiano wine. Just the same, I tell you not to send me anything unless I ask for it, for I will send you the money to buy what I want. I would like you to let me know how the shop is coming along.

July 28, 1548

Lionardo – You write me that they want you to buy the Buondelmonti house, and on what terms. I reply that I like the house, but the way of buying it seems to consist merely of loaning some money on it. Therefore, I should dismiss whoever proposes it to you, for I think that to buy a house without knowing whether one is going to keep it or not is sheer madness.

August 10, 1548

Lionardo – You write me that you are considering a farm costing thirteen hundred florins outside of Porta al Prato.[127] It seems to me that, if it is good, you ought to get it by all means, provided you have good security, so that we will not have any legal difficulties over it. Also, you should verify that it is located where

---

[127] City gate leading to Prato.

the Arno River cannot cause any damage to it. If we could find some expensive property, of three or four thousand scudi, ten or fifteen miles out of Florence, I would take it, provided I would be entitled to the income derived from it; for, since I lost the port, I must assure myself an income which cannot be taken away from me. And I would rather have it in Florence than elsewhere.

August, 1548

Lionardo – Since I was unable to make out your last letter, I threw it into the fire, therefore I cannot answer it. I have told you several times that every time I receive a letter of yours I go crazy before I learn to decipher it. For this reason I tell you not to write me any more from now on, and if you have something to tell me, hire someone who can write, for I have other things to do than to lose my temper on your letters. Messer Giovan Francesco[128] writes me that you would like to come to Rome for a few days. I am somewhat amazed, for, since as you write me you formed a company, I do not understand how you could leave. Therefore, take care not to throw away the money I sent you, for a person who has not earned his money does not appreciate it. This is proven by experience, for the greatest part of those who are born wealthy, throw their money away and die bankrupt. So, open your eyes, and consider and realize what misery and hardship I endure, being old as I am.

Recently, a Florentine citizen came to talk to me of one of the Ginori's daughters. He says that you too have been approached about her, and that you like her. I certainly would not like you to marry a girl whose father would not give her to you if he had a suitable dowry to give her. I would like you to marry a girl whose father would give her to you for your sake, and not for your money. It seems to me that it is up to you to look for a girl who does not have much of a dowry, and not up to others to offer you a girl

---

[128] Fattucci.

because she does not have a dowry. For, you should seek only the soundness of mind and body and the nobility of blood; and furthermore, you should consider her manners and her relatives; for that is very important.

September 15, 1548

Lionardo – I have been in low spirits because I was unable to urinate, but now I feel better. Let me know how your shop is coming along, and if someone from here comes to Florence and brings any messages from me, do not believe him unless he is the bearer of one of my letters.

October 20, 1548

Lionardo – I learn from your letter about the property which is for sale in the vicinity of San Miniato al Tedesco.[129] I say that there is no place in the Florentine countryside which I like less, for many reasons. I have little time to write.

December 29, 1548

Lionardo – Recently, in connection with giving you a wife, I have been approached again about two young women; one of them is the daughter of Alamanno de' Medici, the other of Cherubino Fortini. I think that the Medici girl does not have much money, and that she is too old. I can say even less about the other, so that I can hardly advise you about either one of them, for I know little about them. Just the same, I am convinced that, since you are the only one of us who can do so, you should get married. However, these days one ought to keep his eyes wide open for various reasons. Therefore, think about it. I have had more than once the notion of setting up an income for myself in Florence so that I may be able to live here without working too hard, for I am exhausted: however, during the last month I almost lost interest

---

[129] A town in the province of Pisa.

in it.[130] I will find some other way to assure myself a livelihood, and I hope that God will help me.

January 18, 1549

Lionardo – As you know I am old, and since I may die at any time, I shouldn't want the little capital I have to go to waste, for I have earned it by working very hard. For this reason I thought that if it were safe to put it in Santa Maria Nuova, I should make up my mind to do so, as long as I could use it in case of need, such as illness or other necessities, and as long as I wouldn't be deprived of it.

Tell Messer Giovan Francesco that during the last month I haven't gone around very much because I have not been feeling very well, but that I will look up Bettino[131] who knows his way about the court better than I, and that the two of us together will do all we can for him. I do not have too many contacts in Rome, and I am not acquainted with the people who can help him; furthermore, if I ask one of these people a favor, they ask one thousand of me. For this reason, I must associate with few people; just the same, I will do what I can.

January 25, 1549

Lionardo – I have not received the cheese which you mention in your letter. I think that the driver who brought it sold it to someone else, for I have sent several times to the customhouse for it in vain. Therefore, do not send me anything else ever, for I get more grief than usefulness out of it.

Concerning your taking a wife, this morning I was informed of several young women who are looking for a husband. Although he has not signed his name, I believe that the man who wrote me is a middleman, who can only be a man of little wisdom, for,

---

[130] He had not been feeling well.
[131] Bartolomeo Bettini, a friend, for whom he made the cartoon for Venus and Cupid.

since I have been living continuously in Rome for sixteen or seventeen years, he should have realized that I know very little of Florentine families.

For this reason I tell you that, if you want to get married, you should not worry about me; all I can tell you is not to chase after money, and to take into consideration only goodness and a good reputation.

I believe that in Florence there must be many noble poor families; it would be a kind thing to marry into one of them, if one were sure that there is no dowry, for there wouldn't be any pride involved. You need someone to live with you and whom you can order around; one who is not too ostentatious, and does not want to go everyday to dinners and weddings; for, it is easy to lose one's virtues at parties, especially for one who has no relatives. And you should not pay any attention if people say that you do it because you want to become a nobleman, for it is known that we are old Florentine citizens, and as noble as the next family; therefore, ask for God's help, and pray him that he prepare for you a suitable partner. And I shall be very grateful to you if, when you find a girl, you inform me of it before you marry her.

I have been advised against what I wrote you concerning Santa Maria Nuova,[132] so forget it.

February 1, 1549

Lionardo – I sent Urbino several times to the customhouse in connection with the cheese you sent me. The Customs Officers say that the driver sold it at the inn, or else left it behind in Florence, for he brought into Customs only five little casks of cheese, all of which were delivered by the Customs Officers to their rightful owners. There is no question that the driver is a rascal of the worst sort, for here in Rome he did his best to avoid Urbino until he finally left. But if he should return, let me know.

---

[132] Placing his money there.

February 9, 1549

Lionardo – Bartolomeo Bettini began to urge me to give you his niece. Now he has tried to put pressure on me through a friend of mine. I replied that you are courting a girl whom you like, and that you have almost declared your intentions, and that I do not feel like steering you in another direction. I am warning you so that you will know what to answer, for I think that he will have someone speak to you very enthusiastically there in Florence. I will leave you so much that you will not be in need. Bartolomeo is a fine, obliging and capable man, but he is not our equal, and your sister is married to a Guicciardini. I know that you know that honor is worth more than possessions. Give my regards to Guicciardini and to Francesca, and tell her for me to try to console herself, for she is not the only one suffering, especially these days when the best people suffer the most.

March 15, 1549

Lionardo – I have been very ill with my old trouble of not being able to urinate; I moaned day and night without being able to sleep or take the slightest rest. The doctors say that I am afflicted with kidney stones. I am not sure of it yet, all the same I am taking medicines for this ailment, and I have been reassured that I will be all right. Nonetheless, since I am old and afflicted with such painful illness, I cannot take any chances. I was advised to go to the Baths of Viterbo, but one cannot go there before the beginning of May; meanwhile, I will bide my time as well as I can, and I may be lucky to discover that I do not suffer from the said ailment, or I will find some good remedy. So tell Francesca to pray for me. As for the rest of my body, I am much the same as I was at thirty years of age. This illness has come upon me through the great hardships I have endured and the disregard I have always had for my own life. Patience! With the help of God, I will come out of this better than I think; and if it should turn out otherwise, I will let you know, for I want to take care of my spiritual and temporal things, and you will have to be here for that. When I feel that the time has come, I will inform you. And whatever anyone says do not start out unless I write you.

If you hear of some noble family being very hard up—and there must be—tell me who it is; for I will send you up to fifty scudi which you will distribute in return for prayers for my soul. This will not cut at all into what I have planned leaving you: so do it by all means.

March 23, 1549

Lionardo – In my last letter I wrote you about my suffering with a kidney stone; it is extremely painful, as those who experienced it well know. Since then, after I was given a certain type of water to drink, I passed a lot of white, thick mucus with my urine, and also some fragments of the stone, so that I feel much better; and we hope that shortly I will be rid of it. I thank God and some good person who has prayed for me.

This illness of mine has made me think of settling my spiritual and temporal matters more than I would have done otherwise.

March 29, 1549

Lionardo – This morning I sent with Urbino fifty gold ducats to Bartolomeo Bettini. You notified me of a member of the Cerretani family who is going to place one of his daughters in a convent.[133] See that the money is given to someone who needs it, and not because of friendship or kinship, but for the love of God. Try to get a receipt, and do not reveal where the money is coming from.

April 5, 1549

Lionardo – When I wrote you concerning my intention of set-

---

[133] Daughter of Niccolò Cerretani requires a customary dowry on entering a convent.

13. (At right) Sketches for the Sistine Chapel and the Tomb of Julius II, 1506-1512. *(Courtesy of Ashmolean Museum)*

14. (Below) Study for the Last Judgment, 1537-1538. *(Courtesy of British Museum)*

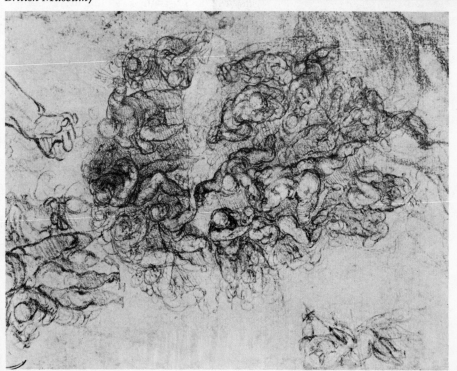

15. The Last Judgment, 1536-1541. (*Courtesy of Alinari-Anderson*)

tling my affairs, I merely meant that I thought I should write my will. And my will is this: namely, to leave you and Gismondo what I have, as follows: that both Gismondo my brother, and you my nephew, be equally responsible for it, and that neither of you can reach a decision without the consent of the other. If you think that this should be written down by a notary, I will be willing to sign it.

As for my illness, I now feel much better. We are sure that I have a stone, but it is a small one, and through the mercy of God and the virtue of the water I am drinking, it is wearing down little by little, so that I hope to get rid of it. Just the same, I would like to keep in Florence the cash I have here, and when I no longer need it leave it to you. This amounts to about four thousand scudi. I feel that especially now that I have to go to the spas I want to be as unhampered as possible.

This morning a friend of mine called on me and begged me to bring to your attention a daughter of Lionardo Ginori, whose mother is a Soderini. I can tell you that I was begged to do so. When you have made up your mind answer me so that I may tell my friend either yes or no.

Before you took a wife I should like you to buy a larger and finer house than the one in which you now live, and I would send you the money.

April 13, 1549

Lionardo – I have in my hands the receipt for the fifty scudi you gave the convent. I think I will have to go to the Baths, for the doctors advise me to do so. I received with your letter one from Bugiardino:[134] next time do not enclose anyone else's letters in yours, for appearances' sake.[135] Bugiardino is a good but simple man: and that's enough of that. If someone should ask you to enclose his letter in yours, say that you are not planning

---

[134] The painter.

[135] With reference to exiles.

to write me. Concerning the house near the Proconsolo, I wish to tell you that I do not like its location as well as the one on Via del Cocomero. If we had been able to get that one with good security, I think we could have found no better.

April 19, 1549

Benvenuto Olivieri in Rome.

Magnificent Messer Benvenuto and Co.[136] – You will please pay Messer Bartolomeo Bettini and Company twenty-two gold scudi every month, beginning with the first wages for this past month of January, for I make use of Bettini's services every month. The twenty-two gold scudi are the same which are remitted to you every month from my notary's office of Romagna. May it please your Lordship to continue with this arrangement until further notice.

April 19, 1549

Lionardo – Concerning the Chianti farm, I say that I prefer to make a purchase rather than to keep the money around.

As for my illness, to the amazement of many people, I feel much better, and I am very hopeful. People thought I was as good as dead, and so did I. I had a good physician,[137] but I have more faith in prayers than in medicines.

As regards the daughter of Lionardo Ginori, you answered me, reminding me that I wrote you about this matter last year. I wrote that to you because I am frightened by the pomp and foolishness so dear to such noble families, and to keep you from becoming the slave of a woman. However, if you like this woman, do not be influenced by what I write, for I know nothing about the Florentines. You are the one who must like the girl; if you are satisfied with her, so will I be.

---

[136] Florentine bankers in Rome.
[137] Colombo.

May 11, 1549

Lionardo—You write me again about the Monte Spertoli farm, and about a shop which is for sale at Porta Rossa. I tell you in return that, if there is good security, you go ahead and buy both the farm and the shop; feel free to spend up to four thousand scudi, and worry only about the security. This is much better than keeping money in the banks, for I do not trust any of them.

May 25, 1549

Lionardo—I learn from your last letter that you got the Chianti property. I think you say for two thousand three hundred florins of seven lire each. If, as you say, it is good property, you did well not to worry about the cost. I took to Bartolomeo Bettini five hundred gold scudi, which you will receive in Florence as a first payment; next Saturday I will send an additional five hundred through the Altoviti. When Urbino, who went home to Urbino several days ago, returns, which ought to be within eight or ten days, I will send you the rest. The gold scudi I am sending you are worth here eleven giuli each.

June 1, 1549

Lionardo—This morning, I took one thousand gold scudi to the Altoviti, and five hundred to Bartolomeo Bettini, in order that they be paid to you in Florence for the payment of the Chianti farm. Let me know how much is lacking, so that we may expedite matters for the sake of the harvest. As for my ailment, I am feeling much better than anyone would have believed.

June 8, 1549

Lionardo—This morning, I took one thousand gold scudi to the honest that you should pay for it four hundred scudi more than it is worth. I suspect that you are making it obvious that you are eager to get it, and so they are trying to rush you into making up your mind. I do not think there is anyone who would pay that much more than it is worth. One should not be stopped by fifty or one hundred scudi; all the same, I leave it up to you. I received the trebbiano wine. For about two months I have been drinking, morning and evening, a spring water that comes from a place forty miles from Rome. This water breaks up stones. I must store a lot of it in my house, and use no other water for drinking and cooking purposes. Also, I am forced to lead a different life from what I used to.

1549

Messer Benedetto Varchi.[138]

Messer Benedetto – So that it may be evident that I have received your little book, I shall reply to what you ask me, even if ignorantly. I say that painting is to be considered the better, the more it approaches relief, and relief is to be considered the worse, the more it approaches painting. And so I used to be of the opinion that sculpture is the lamp of painting, and that between them there is the same difference that there is between the sun and the moon. Now that I have read your essay, in which you say that, philosophically speaking, those things which have an identical goal, are one and the same thing, I have changed my mind. And so I say that if greater judgment and difficulty, impediment and labor, do not constitute higher nobility, then painting and sculpture are essentially the same. And in order that this be upheld, every painter should think no less of painting than of sculpture. By sculpture I understand that art which operates by taking away. That art which operates by laying on, is similar to painting. Suffice it to say that, since both emanate from one and the same intelligence, sculpture and painting can be made to live in harmony together, and give up so many lengthy arguments, for, these arguments take up more time than the actual practice of both arts. The man who wrote that painting was

---

[138] Consul of the Florentine Academy. He solicited the opinions of many artists on the relative merits of the arts, for inclusion in a book of his lectures.

more noble than sculpture did not know what he was writing about, and if he understood the other things about which he was writing no better, I am sure that my housemaid would have written more intelligently about them. There are infinite points not yet expressed which could be voiced on similar sciences; but, as I said, it would require too much time, and I have but little of it, for, not only am I old, but almost to be numbered among the dead. Therefore, I beg you to forgive me. Finally, I thank you from the bottom of my heart for the too great honor you have done me, which is more than I deserve.

1549

Messer Luca Martini.[139]
Magnificent Messer Luca – I received from Messer Bartolomeo Bettini a letter of yours, with a little book, containing a commentary on a sonnet of mine. The sonnet comes indeed from me, but the commentary comes from Heaven;[140] and it is truly a marvelous thing, not only in my own judgment, but in that of competent men, and especially of Messer Donato Giannotti, who is never tired of reading it. Concerning the sonnet, I know its true merit; but be that what it may, I cannot help experiencing a little vainglory upon the realization that it was the cause of so beautiful and learned commentary. And since I gather from the words and praises of its author that he thinks more highly of me than I deserve, I beg you to express my gratitude to him with words corresponding to so much love, affection and courtesy. I beg you to do this, because I feel myself inadequate, and one who is held in high esteem should not tempt fortune. It is better to keep silent than to fall from a lofty place. I am old, and death has deprived me of the thoughts of my youth; and let him who does not know what old age is, wait till it arrives, for he cannot know it before. Remember me to Varchi, with deep af-

---

[139] Florentine merchant.

[140] Varchi's book contained a lecture on one of Michelangelo's sonnets.

fection for him and his fine qualities, and as his servant wherever I may be.

Yours, and at your service in whatever I can do.

June 15, 1549

Lionardo – I received the roll of serge: it is very beautiful, but it would have been better if you had given it for the love of God to some poor person. Concerning the contract you write me about, it might be a good idea to have it drawn up in the vulgar tongue,[141] so that anybody can understand it. I thought you would get the money I sent through Bettino right away; instead it is still here, so I do not think we will get this year's harvest.

July 12, 1549

Lionardo – I am of the opinion that, if the security is good, for two hundred and fifty scudi you should take by all means the Chianti property which is near the one you purchased. I have no time to write anything else.

July 19, 1549

Lionardo – In your last letter you inform me of all the expenses incurred in connection with the Chianti property. You did not have to do that, for, if as you say the money was well spent, everything is all right. Recently I received a letter from that weaver's woman, who says she wanted to give you as a wife a girl whose father is a Capponi, and whose mother is a Niccolini, and who is in the Candeli convent. She wrote me an endless letter which ended with a short sermon in which she exhorts me to lead a virtuous life and to distribute alms. She says that she exhorted you to live like a good Christian, and I am sure she told you that she was inspired by God to give you said girl. I say that she would be much better off if she tended to weaving or spin-

---

[141] Italian, instead of customary Latin.

ning, rather than displaying so much holiness. I have the impression that she wants to be another Sister Domenica:[142] so do not trust her.

August 3, 1549

Lionardo – Concerning the house, you say that, if we cannot find one that we can buy, we could fix up our own for sixty scudi. I say that, if you think it should be done, go right ahead and do it. However, since the house is poorly located in regards to the river, and since we have to buy another one, I do not think we should spend much on it.

December, 1549

Lionardo – In reply to your last letter, I say that it is true that the death of the Pope[143] has filled me with grief and has done me great harm, for His Holiness did me a lot of good, and I was hoping in even more. It was God's will: we must be patient. He died peacefully, and he was conscious till the very end. May God have mercy on his soul. Here we are expecting a new Pope from one moment to the next. God knows the need of his Christians, and that's that.

1550

Fattucci, priest of Santa Maria del Fiore.
Dearest friend in Florence – Although we have not exchanged any letters for many months past, still our long and good friendship has not been forgotten. I wish you well, as I have always done, and I love you with all my heart, also for the countless favors you have done me. Concerning old age, in which both of us are at the present time, I should like to know how yours affects you, for mine does not make me very happy. You know that we

---

[142] A prophetess who counseled the heads of state during the siege of Florence.

[143] Pope Paul III died November 10, 1549.

have a new Pope,[144] and who he is. All Rome is delighted, God be thanked, and everybody expects nothing but the greatest good from him, especially the poor people, for his generosity is well known. As regards my own things, I would appreciate it very much, and you would be doing me a great favor, if you let me know how Lionardo's affairs are; don't let anything stop you from telling me the truth, for he is young[145] and I am very anxious for him, especially since he is alone and without counsel.

I have nothing else to say, except that a few days ago Messer Tommaso de' Cavalieri begged me to thank for him Messer Benedetto Varchi, light and splendor of the Florentine Academy, for a certain admirable little book of his which has been printed, in which he speaks with praise of him, and no less of me.[146] He has given me a sonnet which I wrote for him some time ago, and he begs me to send it to Varchi, by way of justification. If you like it, deliver it; for I believe he is a good friend of yours; if not, give it to the flames. I am struggling with death,[147] and I have other worries in my head.[148] Concerning the honor which, as I said, Messer Benedetto has done me in his sonnets, I beg you to thank him for me.

Since the last few days I was at home very heavy-hearted, while I was searching through certain things of mine, I came across a large number of those trifles[149] which once I used to send you. I am sending you four of them, which I may have sent you at other times. I am sure you will say that I am old and crazy; and I tell you that, in order to remain sane and to suffer less,

---

[144] Giovanni Maria de' Ciocchi del Monte became Julius III. He was made a Cardinal by Pope Paul III, and was a patron of the arts and of liberal reform.

[145] Thirty.

[146] In the Book of Commentaries, Varchi included two of Michelangelo's sonnets, one to De' Cavalieri.

[147] Refers to his spasmodic kidney stone attacks.

[148] St. Peter's.

[149] Madrigals which Fattucci liked to sing.

I can find nothing better than madness. So, do not be amazed.
And I beg you to answer me with a few lines. As ever.

———————————◆◆———————————

LOVE FEEDS THE FLAME OF AGE

When masters bind a slave with cruel chain,
and keep him hope-forlorn in bondage pent,
use tames his temper to imprisonment,
and hardly would he fain be free again.

Use curbs the snake and tiger, and doth train
fierce woodland lions to bear chastisement;
and the young artist, all with toil forspent,
by constant use a giant's strength doth gain.

But with the force of flame it is not so:
for while fire sucks the sap of the green wood,
it warms a frore old man and makes him grow;

with such fine heat of youth and lustihood
filling his heart and teaching it to glow,
that love enfolds him with beatitude.
    If then in playful mood
he sport and jest, old age need no man blame;
for loving things divine implies no shame.

    The soul that knows her aim,
sins not by loving God's own counterfeit—
due measure kept, and bounds, and order meet.

———————————◆◆———————————

February 16, 1550

Lionardo – If you search through my letters you will find that I
wrote you that since I expected the Pope[150] to fail me because of
his old age, I wanted to set up for myself in Florence an income
so that I wouldn't have to go begging in my old age, especially
since I had made others rich while I endured all sorts of hardship.

---

[150] Late Pope Paul III.

Therefore let me know how things stand. I find myself with little capital, and if I spent this little amount I might starve here.

The fact is that if you had found in Florence something to assure me an income of one hundred scudi a year, I would have gone through with it, and I would do it even now if I could or if I thought I could make use of it for my needs.

August 1, 1550

Fattucci in Florence.

Dear friend – Since it so happens that I have to write to Giorgio[151] the painter in Florence, I take the liberty of troubling you a little; namely, I should like you to deliver to him the letter which I enclose in yours, thinking that he is a friend of yours. Not to be too brief in my note to you, since I have nothing else to tell you, I am sending you some of my stories[152] which I used to write to the Marchioness of Pescara,[153] who was very fond of me, and I no less of her. Death has deprived me of a great friend. I have nothing else to say.

I am feeling as usual, bearing patiently the ills of old age. I am sure you are doing likewise.

August 1, 1550

Messer Giorgio Vasari,[154] excellent painter.

Dear friend – Concerning the new foundations at San Pietro in Montorio,[155] since the Pope refused to hear anything about them, I did not write you anything, for I knew that you were already informed by your man here. Now I wish to tell you that yesterday

---

[151] Vasari.

[152] Poems.

[153] Vittoria Colonna.

[154] Vasari was briefly Michelangelo's apprentice in 1525. Later he was his biographer in *Lives of the Painters*.

[155] Michelangelo supervised a chapel and tombs for relatives of the new Pope Julius III in this church outside Rome. Vasari made the designs and Ammannati was to execute them.

morning, the Pope, having gone to Montorio, sent for me. I did
not arrive on time, in fact I met him on his way back on the
bridge. I had a long conversation with him concerning the tombs
which have been commissioned to you, and at the end he told me
that he had decided not to place them on that mountain, but instead in the Church of the Florentines.[156] He asked for my
opinion and for a design, and I encouraged him, thinking that
thus the Church will be finished. As for the three letters I have
received from you, I do not have a pen that can reply worthily
to such lofty words; but if there is one reason why I should like
to be in part as you depict me, it is so that you would have a
worthy servant. But I am not amazed at the fact that, since
you resuscitate the dead,[157] you prolong the life of the living,
indeed that you keep those who are hardly alive for an infinite
time from death. In short, I am all yours, such as I am.

August 7, 1550

Lionardo – I did not have the opportunity of writing you since I
received the trebbiano wine and the shirts.

Now, I need to have here two briefs of Pope Paul,[158] which
contain the income for life given me by His Holiness, while I was
at his service in Rome. I sent the briefs to Florence along with
the other documents in the box you received. I think they are in
certain tin containers: I know you will recognize them. Wrap
them up in some waxed cloth and put them in a well-corded box.
If you see that you can send them with a trustworthy person, so
that they will not get lost, send them to me, and promise him
whatever amount you think is necessary in order that they be
delivered to me. I want to show them to the Pope,[159] so that he

---

[156] A projected church of the Florentines in Rome for which
Michelangelo made the plans.
[157] In Vasari's biographies completed that year.
[158] Of September 1, 1535 and December 18, 1537.
[159] Julius III.

may see that according to them I am his creditor, I think, of more than two thousand scudi: not that this is going to help me any, but for my own satisfaction.

August 16, 1550

Lionardo – You write me in your last letter that Cepperello wants to sell the farm which is next to ours at Settignano, and that concerning that woman who has a right to it for the rest of her life, if Cepperello could sell the farm now, he would take off from the price a suitable amount in accordance with her life-expectancy; after her death, one would take possession of the farm. I do not think it would be wise to purchase it because of the many dangerous complications that might arise while not being in possession of it. Therefore, one must wait until she dies.

As for your taking a wife, you write me that first you want to come here and speak to me; as you will see, I live rather poorly, although I spend a lot of money. I do not mean to imply that because of this you should not come, but it seems to me that you should wait till after the middle of September, and in the meantime you could find a good and neat housekeeper for me. It is not easy, however, for they are all slovenly and filthy. Let me know. I pay ten giuli a month; I live poorly, but I pay well.

Someone called to my attention for you a daughter of Altovito Altoviti: she has neither father nor mother, and she lives at the San Martino convent. I know nothing about her.

August 22, 1550

Lionardo – Recently I wrote you about a housekeeper: I think I found one, therefore do not look for one.

August 22, 1550

Messer Giorgio Vasari – Many days ago I received a letter from you; I did not reply at once in order not to behave like a merchant. Now I wish to tell you this, that if I deserved a single one of the numerous praises you shower on me, I would feel that, if I had given myself to you soul and body, I would have given you something, and I would have repaid you for a tiny particle of what I owe you. For I realize all the time that I owe you much more than I can ever repay you. Since I am old,[160] I have no hope of evening the score in this life, but I hope to be able to do so in the next. Therefore, I beg you to be patient.

August 31, 1550

Lionardo—Concerning the Cepperello's farm, you write me that it might be bought by someone with whom we would not get along. I scoff at that, for I know that in Florence justice is strictly carried out. But since you like it, and since the security is good, take it. I do not know how much money you have, but I am not going to send you any more. I want to employ the capital I have left to set up an income for myself.

Let me know how much he is asking for the farm.

October 4, 1550

Lionardo—You inform me that you are ready to come to Rome, and that before starting out you are waiting to hear from me. As soon as you receive this, leave when it suits you. I am sure that when you arrive in Rome you will be able to find the house, namely, across from Santa Maria del Loreto[161] near the Macello de' Corvi.[162]

October 13, 1550

Vasari—As soon as Bartolomeo[163] arrived here, I went to speak to the Pope. When I saw that he wanted some new foundations at Montorio for the tombs, I looked for a mason from San Pietro.

---

[160] Seventy-five.

[161] Church adjoining Trojan's Forum.

[162] His street called, literally, "Slaughterhouse of the Crows."

[163] Ammannati.

Bishop Somanythings[164] found out, and he insisted on sending one that he liked. In order not to fight against the man who sets the winds in motion, I stepped back, for, since I am light, I shouldn't want to be blown into some thicket. I have a feeling that we must forget all about the Church of the Florentines.[165] Come back soon and safely. I have nothing else to say.

December 20, 1550

Lionardo – I received the marzolini cheeses, twelve of them. They are very beautiful. I will give some to my friends, and I will use the others at home. As I wrote you boys other times, do not send me anything at all, unless I ask for it, especially those things that cost money.

As for your taking a wife, do not pay any attention to dowry, for in this world there is more property than men. As for beauty, since you are not the most handsome man in Florence, you should not worry about that too much, as long as she is not crippled or loathsome.

Yesterday I received a letter from Messer Giovan Francesco[166] who asks me whether I have anything belonging to the Marchioness of Pescara. I do not think I have anything[167] because when I was ill and spent some time away from home, many things were stolen.

I would appreciate it very much if you would inform me when you hear of some noble fellow citizen who is in dire need, especially if it is someone who has daughters around the house, for I should like to do him some good for the salvation of my soul.

February 28, 1551

Lionardo – I learn that you have not as yet done anything about

---

[164] His nickname for Aliotti, who was a busybody.
[165] Project later abandoned.
[166] Fattucci.
[167] Poems.

getting married. I am sorry, for it really is something one should do. If you find a girl who is well brought-up, good, healthy and noble, even if she has no dowry, you can pretend you are marrying her out of charity. Were you to do this, you would not have to put up with the pomp and vanity of women, and peace would reign in your home. After all your rank and appearance do not make you worthy of the greatest beauty in Florence. Ask in your prayers that you do not go astray.

When you came here recently,[168] you brought me a piece of cloth, which I think you said had cost you twenty or twenty-five scudi. It occurred to me then that we could give the money to someone in Florence for the souls of all of us. Since then, because of the great famine going around here, that money was turned into bread, and I am afraid that if some help is not given us, we are all going to starve.

March 7, 1551

Lionardo – I received the pears, namely ninety-seven bronche pears as you call them in Florence.

Recently I was told of a girl of the Alessandri family, but I was not given any details.

About one month ago Messer Giovan Francesco asked me if I had anything that belonged to the Marchioness of Pescara. I have a little parchment book which she gave me as a present about ten years ago[169] containing one hundred and three sonnets, not counting those she sent me later from Viterbo[170] on fine cotton-paper, which are forty. I had these bound with the same booklet and at the time I loaned them to many people, so that one can find them printed everywhere.[171] Furthermore, I have many

---

[168] Lionardo visited for the month of October.

[169] Her *Rime,* first published in 1538.

[170] From a convent into which she withdrew in 1541 from the growing power of Cardinal Caraffa, leader of the Counter Reformation.

[171] The third edition.

letters she used to write me from Orvieto and from Viterbo.
Therefore, show this letter to the priest, and let me know what
he says.

May 8, 1551

Lionardo–I am not sending the booklet of sonnets of the
Marchioness because first I want to have it copied, and then I
will send it. Nothing else occurs to me.

May 22, 1551

Lionardo–I answered you some time ago that I had obtained
some information about the Nasi girl, and that I had discovered
only good things about the family. Since then I have been approached again concerning a daughter of Filippo Girolami, whose
mother is a sister of Bindo Altoviti. I do not know the details; just
the same I did not want to fail telling you about her. If what I
hear here in Rome about the Nasi girl is correct, I like her. Therefore, if you pursue the matter, I will appreciate your keeping me
informed.

June 28, 1551

Lionardo–A week ago I received a load of trebbiano wine, that is,
forty-four flasks; I have given some to several friends. It is
considered the best that came to Rome this year. I thank you,
and that's all I have to say about this.

As for the Nasi matter, you write me that as yet you have
not received an answer from Andrea Quaratesi.[172] I do not
believe that in these matters we should depend too much on him;
with all this waiting time goes by and never returns. It seems to me
that if a noble, virtuous, good and very poor young woman were
to be found, she would be the ideal person with whom to live in
harmony. Thus you would be the benefactor of someone else,
just as someone was for you. But you find yourself rich, and you do
not appreciate it. I do not want to take more time to tell you about

---

[172] A Florentine friend.

the poverty in which I found our family when I began helping them; a whole book wouldn't be enough to recount it; and all I ever got was ungratefulness. Therefore, thank God for your present condition, and do not run after pomp and foolishness.

October 17, 1551

Lionardo – I learn from your last letter that you secured some information about the Girolami girl, and that you hear nothing but good things about her. Therefore, if she possesses the good qualities that one should look for in such matters, I do not believe that the dowry should interfere with the marriage. So, think about it, for it seems like an honorable marriage to me, and I would be very pleased about it, provided, as I said before, she has good qualities, namely good breeding, a good name, and good manners, as one likes in a bride. This you can find out by inquiring diligently, and by believing only a few people. I should very much like that one of you leave an heir.

December 19, 1551

Lionardo – I learn from your last letter about her[178] nearsightedness, which does not seem a small defect to me, for, as you write me, it is hereditary.

I find myself with a little capital, which I would prefer not to spend here. Therefore, if you could find there a good house or property which would be a safe purchase for fifteen hundred scudi, I would be willing to take it.

1552

Benvenuto Cellini.

My Benvenuto – I have known you for many years as the greatest goldsmith of whom the world has ever heard, and now I am to know you as a sculptor of similar ability. I want you to know that Messer Bindo Altoviti took me to see his bust in bronze,[174] and he

---

[178] The Girolami girl.

[174] In the Altoviti house at the foot of Sant'Angelo bridge in Rome.

told me that it was by your hand. I liked it very much, but I was sorry to see it exhibited in a bad light. If it had proper lighting, one would really see what a beautiful piece of work it is.

February 20, 1552

Lionardo – Recently, while I was speaking to her uncle[175] about that thing, he told me that he was quite amazed you had changed your mind, and that he thought some undernourished hog had prevented it in order to acquire that property or to inherit it. I thought I should tell you what he said.

Right after I began writing you this letter, I received one of yours, which informs me of a daughter of Carlo of Giovanni Strozzi. I knew Giovanni Strozzi[176] when I was a boy, and he was a fine person. I can't tell you anything else about him. I met Carlo also, and I think it may be a good match.

I am old, and so, in order to discourage some foolish people entertaining vain hope, I am thinking of making a will, and of leaving what I have in Florence to my brother Gismondo and to you, my nephew, in such a way that neither one of you can dispose of his own share without the consent of the other; and furthermore, should you two leave no legitimate heir,[177] everything will go to San Martino in order that the income may be given for the love of God to the poor citizens of Florence who are ashamed to beg. But you may be able to suggest a better arrangement.

April 1, 1552

Lionardo – I have been told by a friend of mine, that the defect of the Girolami girl being nearsighted which made you change your

---

[175] Altoviti was the uncle of the Girolami girl suspected of nearsightedness.

[176] Scholar who wrote the madrigal to Michelangelo's sculpture of Night in the Medici Chapel.

[177] Gismondo is seventy-one.

mind about her does not exist. A friend of yours told you that, because he wants to give you a relative of his, and since she is not of marriageable age yet, he told you that so that you would wait until she is ready. If, then, that business of the nearsightedness is not true, and if she has no other defects, it seems to me that you ought to go through with it. So be sure you are not duped by people who are much inferior to others. Remember that time goes by fast, and that I would hate to have worked hard my whole life for people I do not know, but I hope my testament will take care of that.

April 23, 1552

Lionardo – Now you answer me that you are certain of that defect, but that if I want you to marry her you will do so. I tell you that since the defect is a reality, we should forget the whole thing, and that you keep looking, as long as the girl is a Florentine and good. Be sure you try to find one who, when the necessity arises, will not be ashamed to wash the dishes and do the other household chores.

June 24, 1552

Lionardo – I received the trebbiano wine, namely forty-four flasks; I thank you for it. It seems very good to me, but I cannot enjoy it for long, for, after I have given my friends a few flasks, whatever I have left turns sour in a few days. Therefore, next year, if I am alive, it will suffice that you send ten flasks, if you find a way, with somebody else's shipment.

Recently Bishop Minerbetti[178] was here, and when I met him with Giorgio[179] the painter, he asked me about you and about giving you a wife. We spoke of that, and he told me that he had a good prospect in mind, and also that you would not have to marry her for the love of God. Now you write me that a member of her family

---

[178] Of Arezzo.
[179] Vasari.

spoke to you and urged you to get married, saying that I am very anxious for you to do so. You already know that, and I repeat it now so that our family does not end with us. It is true that that would not be the end of the world, but just the same every animal tries to preserve its species. Therefore I want you to take a wife, provided you find a suitable wife. And if you feel that your body is not healthy enough to justify your taking a wife, it is better to try and keep in good condition than to kill oneself for the sake of procreating others. I added this last statement because I see that you are taking a long time in making up your mind, and I shouldn't want you to do for my sake something against your wishes, for you would never be happy and neither would I.

As for my finding you here something worthwhile, I do not want you to count on me any more than if I were dead, for I have very few contacts, especially with Florentines.

October, 1552

Lionardo – Since you are not sure which of the two girls you saw together is the one they are talking about, take care that they do not give you one for another, as happened to a friend of mine. As for the dowry, I will guarantee it and will do what you tell me. However, I was told here that there is no dowry of any kind. Therefore, proceed with extreme caution, for you could never turn back, and I would be heartbroken if either because of the dowry or anything else you wouldn't be happy. I like the match, and since she has the qualities one desires in a wife, you shouldn't mind if the dowry is not what you would like. One must pray, and ask others to pray too, in order that everything will turn out for the best, for such things are done only once.

October 28, 1552

Lionardo – I am enclosing the reply I give Michele Guicciardini concerning your getting married. I am ready to guarantee the dowry with my possessions, and he will show you how I think the guarantee should be handled. I warn you not to buy a pig in a poke; take a good look with your own eyes, for she could be lame or sick, and you would never be happy. Therefore, put all your heart in this matter. Since I have not been in Florence for a long time, I do not have any information on Florentine families; but I have so much faith in Guicciardini that I do not believe he would suggest something which was not suitable. Also, I said that you should try to see her with your own eyes.

Should you find a house that you could buy for one thousand, or even up to two thousand scudi, please let me know.

November 21, 1552

Lionardo – It seems to me that things which begin badly cannot end well. I hear from your last letter that they failed to keep the promise they had made you. I say to you that, although I have written you many times not to worry about the money, just the same it does not seem right to me that they should not keep their promises to you. And since anger is very powerful, it seems to me that we should forget the whole thing; unless you see so many other things that answer your need, that you do not think we should be concerned with such trifles. We should ask for God's help; I am sure that with his grace everything will be settled.

I am not answering Guicciardini because I have not been able to make out his letter. I do not know where you people learned to write.

December 17, 1552

Lionardo – You write me of two matches which have been placed before you: I like them much better than the previous one, but since I do not know anyone from whom I can get any information about them, I cannot say anything in particular about them.

March 18, 1553

Lionardo – You already wrote me in the past about a daughter of

Donato Ridolfi,[180] whose mother is of Benino's family; and now you mention her again to me in the letter you wrote Urbino. I cannot give you either favorable or unfavorable advice, because here I do not associate with Florentines; but since Guicciardini spoke to you about it, considering that he is a relative of ours and a genuinely conscientious man, I judge that it may be the very thing you are looking for. Therefore, I ask you to beg him on my behalf that for the love of God he take an interest in the matter, whether it be this Ridolfi girl or another, until we find what we want.

March 18, 1553

Lionardo – I gather from your last letter that you have become interested again in the Ridolfi girl. It must be over four months now since I answered you concerning two other matches you had written me about, and I told you that I liked them; so that I do not understand you at all, and I do not know what is going through your mind. This business has been going on for so long that I am tired of it.[181] As for the Ridolfi girl, if what you hear about her pleases you, take her, and I confirm what I have said other times about the security. And if you do not feel like taking this girl or any other girl, that is entirely up to you. I have been taking care of the affairs of all of you for sixty years; now I am old, and I must think of my own; so, do as you please, for whatever you do is for your sake and not for mine, since I do not expect to live much longer.

April 22, 1553

Lionardo – I learn from your letter that your negotiations for the daughter of Donato Ridolfi were concluded satisfactorily. The

---

[180] Cassandra Ridolfi from a noble Florentine family which married into the Medici.

[181] His letters have dealt with Lionardo's possible marriage for seven years.

Lord be praised. Let us pray Him that He gives us His blessing also after this. I spoke to Lorenzo Ridolfi[182] and I uttered the customary phrases as well as I could. I can't think of anything else at the moment. Later you will write me about the marriage, and I will send something, as one does on such occasions.

April 30, 1553

Lionardo – As soon as I received your letter informing me that the marriage had taken place, I sent you the power of attorney to enable you to guarantee the dowry with my property; namely, one thousand five hundred ducats of seven lire each. The notary who prepared it is an important man, for he is the notary of the Florentines' Consulate and of the Treasury.

I gather from your last letter that both sides are happy with the marriage; I thank God for this. As soon as Urbino returns from Urbino, which will be in fifteen days, I shall do my duty.[183]

May 20, 1553

Lionardo – I gather from your last letter that you have a wife in your house and that you are very satisfied with her, and also that you send me her regards, and that you have not yet settled the dowry. I am very happy that you are satisfied with her. As for settling the dowry, if you have not done so, do not do it and keep your eyes open, for these money problems always give rise to disagreements. I am not a good judge of such things, but it seems to me that you should have settled everything before getting married.

As for her sending me her regards, thank her and tell her on my behalf what you think I should, for you can tell her better by word of mouth than I would be able to say on paper. I want people to see how I feel about the wife of a nephew of mine, but I have not been able to give evidence of it because Urbino was out

---

[182] A son of Contessina de' Medici.
[183] Send a gift to the bride.

of Rome. He has been back two days, and now I am thinking of giving some token of my love. I have been told that a valuable pearl necklace would be becoming. I have asked a jeweler friend of Urbino to look for me, and I hope to find it, but do not tell her anything yet: and if you think I should send something else, let me know. Take care of yourself and reflect and weigh things well, for the number of widows is always larger than that of widowers.

June 21, 1553

Lionardo – I received the shipment of trebbiano wine you sent me, namely forty-four flasks: it is very good, but it is too much, for I have no one to give it to, as I used to. So, if I am still alive next year, do not send any.

I have bought two rings for Cassandra, one with a diamond and the other with a ruby; I do not know with whom to send them to you. Urbino told me that after the feast of St. John[184] a friend of yours, Lattanzio da San Gimignano, is leaving Rome. I thought of sending them to you with him; otherwise, let me know of some trustworthy individual, so that they will not be replaced by others or get lost. When you get them, I wish you to have them appraised to see whether I have been duped, for I am not a good judge of such things.

July, 1553

Lionardo – I am sending you the two rings with the postman, one is a diamond and one is a ruby. As you wrote me, I am sending them in a corded little box. You will give the postman three giuli for the carrying charges; I promised to give him three giuli myself if he brings me a receipt. So, make out a receipt to him.

August 5, 1553

Lionardo – I received the shirts, namely eight shirts: they are a

---

[184] June 24. John was patron saint of Florence.

16. The Conversion of St. Paul, 1542-1545. *(Courtesy of Alinari)*

17. Dome of St. Peters, 1546-1564. *(Courtesy of Alinari)*

lovely thing, especially the material. I like them very much. Nevertheless, I am sorry that you give up so much for me, for I do not lack anything. Thank Cassandra for me, and ask her what I can send her from here, typically Roman things, or anything else, for I shall be glad to send them. I have in my possession the receipt for the two rings and the appraisal of their value. I am happy, for I am certain I was not deceived; and although I sent a little thing, some other time, I will make it up with something to her liking, in accordance with what you will suggest to me. Take care of yourself and live happily.

October 24, 1553

Lionardo – I gather from your letter that Cassandra is pregnant; that makes me very happy, for I hope that we will leave behind some heir, be it a boy or a girl; and we must thank God for everything. Recently Cepperello returned from Florence, and he told Urbino that he wants to talk to me; I imagine it is concerning his farm which is next to ours. Let me know whether he has mentioned it at all to you boys in Florence, for, if we could get it, it would be to our advantage.

March, 1554

Lionardo – I received a letter which you wrote last week in which you tell me how happy you are with Cassandra. We must thank God for this, all the more since it is a rare thing. Thank her, and remember me to her; and if she should like anything from here, let me know. As for finding a name for the children you are expecting, it seems to me that you should name them after your father and your mother, depending on whether it is a boy or a girl, namely Buonarroto and Francesca.

April, 1554

Lionardo – I gather from your letter that Cassandra is about to give birth to a child, and that you would like to have my opinion concerning your children's names. If it is going to be a girl, you tell me that in view of your wife's good behavior, you have already made up your mind; if it should be a boy, I do not know what to say. I feel strongly that the name Buonarroto should remain in the family, since we have had it for three hundred years already. I have nothing else to say, and writing is a great chore for me. I am managing to keep alive.

April, 1554

Vasari.

Dear friend – Your letter filled me with joy, seeing that you still remember the poor old man, and even more because you were present at the triumph you tell me, namely of seeing another Buonarroto born. I thank you from the bottom of my heart for this news; however, I disapprove of so much pomp, for man should not laugh when the whole world is weeping. So, I do not think Lionardo has much judgment, especially in making such a celebration for the birth of a child, with that gladness which ought to be reserved for the death of one who has lived well. I am deeply grateful to you for your love for me, although I am not worthy of it. Here things are unchanged.

April, I do not know on what day.

April 21, 1554

Lionardo – I learn that Cassandra gave birth to a fine boy, that she is doing well, and that you will name the boy Buonarroto. All this made me extremely happy. The Lord be praised; may He make him good, so that he will do us honor and keep the family going.

September 19, 1554

Vasari.

Dear friend – You will undoubtedly say that I am old and mad to make sonnets;[185] but since many say that I am doting, I have wanted to act my part. I see from your letter that you have much

---

[185] Enclosed was his sonnet called "On the Brink of Death."

affection for me. I want you to know for certain that I'd like very much to place these weak bones of mine next to those of my father, as you beg me to do. However, if I left here now,[186] I would cause a great deal of harm to the construction of St. Peter's, a great deal of shame, and a very serious sin. But as soon as the whole composition has been established in such a way that it cannot be changed, I hope I will be able to do as you write me, if it isn't already a sin to make life unpleasant for several covetous individuals who are expecting me to leave soon.[187]

————◆◆————

WAITING FOR DEATH

My death must come; but when, I do not know:
life's short, and little life remains for me:
fain would my flesh abide; my soul would flee
heavenward, for still she calls on me to go.

Blind is the world; and evil here below
o'erwhelms and triumphs over honesty:
the light is quenched; quenched too is bravery:
lies reign, and truth hath ceased her face to show.

————◆◆————

December 8, 1554

Lionardo – I received the cheeses you sent me, namely twelve marzolini; they are very beautiful and good. I gave some to my friends, and I am keeping the rest to be used here at home. As for my health, it seems to me that, considering my age,[188] I am not faring any worse than other people of the same age. I hope you are

---

[186] Vasari on behalf of Duke Cosimo requested his return to Florence.

[187] The followers of Antonio da Sangallo continue to harass him. In 1551 they induced the Pope to call an inquiry into Michelangelo's plan, at which time he vindicated himself and exposed their ignorance of his design.

[188] Seventy-nine.

all well, including Cassandra. Tell her that I pray God that she will have another baby boy. Nothing further occurs to me.

January 26, 1555

Lionardo – I sent Urbino with one hundred gold scudi to Messer Bartolomeo Bussotti[189] in Rome. With this money, I'd like you to buy nineteen spans of dark red serge, the most beautiful you can find, for a dress for Urbino's wife.[190] With what is left over, I should like you to distribute alms, wherever you think they are needed most, and especially for young girls.

February 9, 1555

Lionardo – As for the child you are expecting, you write me that you are of the opinion of naming him Michelangelo. I say that if that's the way you like it, so do I; but if it should be a girl, I do not know what to say. Do as you wish, especially as Cassandra wishes, and remember me to her. As for the alms I am writing you about, do not talk too much of them.

March 2, 1555

Lionardo – I received the serge: it is very lovely. If I had bought it here, it would have cost much more, and it would not have been so beautiful. Urbino thanks you very much for it. People say here that in Florence there is a great famine and much misery. It is time, therefore, that one should do his best to work for the salvation of his soul.

March, 1555

Lionardo – Your last letter informs me of the death of Michelangelo;[191] and just as I was very happy when he was born, now I

---

[189] Banking agent.

[190] In September, 1551, his assistant married Cornelia Colonelli from Castel Durante, and Michelangelo welcomed her into his house.

[191] Lionardo's second son.

grieve over his death; actually, much more. One must be accepting, and think that it is better that he died now, than if he had in his old age. Manage to keep alive yourself, for it would be unfortunate if one had worked so hard to accumulate property and there were no one to enjoy it.

March 30, 1555[192]

Lionardo – Messer Francesco Bandini asked me whether I want to sell the Santa Caterina lands I own, for he has a friend who would be willing to buy them. I told him that everything I own in Florence and surroundings belongs to you boys and that I will approve of everything you do with it. I confirm that once more. Therefore, get together with Gismondo, and see what is more advantageous for you to do, to have the money or to keep the property.

A hod carrier who works at St. Peter's here gave me two gold scudi in order that I send them to his mother. Therefore, read the note I am enclosing, and give the money to the person it says, for I have no other way to send them.

1555

Messer Bartolomeo Ammannati.[193]

Dear friend – It cannot be denied that Bramante was as gifted an architect as anyone else from the times of the ancients until now. He laid the first plan for St. Peter's, not filled with confusion, but clear and pure, full of light and isolated from its surroundings, so that it did not interfere with any part of the Palace. It was considered a very fine thing, and it is evident even now; so that, whoever departed from Bramante's plan, as Sangallo did,[194]

---

[192] Pope Julius III died March 23, 1555. He was succeeded by Marcellus II, who died of apoplexy April 30. Cardinal Caraffa became Paul IV on May 23.

[193] Florentine sculptor who worked on tombs of Julius III which Michelangelo supervised. He became a good friend.

[194] Changing from the central plan of a Greek Cross (equal arms) to the Latin Cross (elongated nave).

departed from truth; and those who consider his model with unprejudiced eyes will see that it is so. The first thing that Sangallo's plan does, with that ring of chapels on the exterior, is to deprive Bramante's plan of all light; and that's not all, but it has no light of its own. And its numerous hiding places, above and below, all dark, lend themselves to innumerable knaveries: such as provide shelter for bandits, for coining money, ravishing nuns, and other rascalities, so that in the evening, when the church is to be closed, it would take twenty-five men to seek out those who are hiding inside, and, because of its peculiar construction, they would be hard to find. Also, there would be this other inconvenience: in carrying out the ring that Sangallo's plan adds to Bramante's, it would be necessary to tear down the Pauline Chapel, the rooms of Piombo[195] and Ruota, and many others. And I think that even the Sistine Chapel would suffer thereby. As for the outworks which have already been executed,[196] which they say cost one hundred thousand scudi, that is not true, because it could be done with sixteen thousand; and by tearing it down little would be lost, because the blocks which have been put up and the foundations which have been made, could be put to good use, and the whole fabric would profit two hundred thousand scudi and three hundred years of time. This is my objective opinion, for to gain a victory here would be a very great loss for me. If you can explain this to the Pope,[197] you will do me a great favor, for I do not feel well.

Looking over Sangallo's model, I'd like to add this: I hope that all the work which was done under my direction will not be destroyed, for it would be a most serious loss.

---

[195] Keeper of the Seal.

[196] For Sangallo's plan.

[197] Paul IV, strict and narrow-minded reformer who had led the Counter Reformation and Inquisition, was indifferent to art and to Michelangelo.

May 11, 1555

Giorgio Vasari – I was forced to participate in the construction of St. Peter's, and I have served for about eight years not only gratis, but with the greatest loss and grief to myself. Now that it has been started and money is available, and I am about ready to vault the cupola,[198] if I left it would be the ruin of the edifice. I would be greatly disgraced throughout all Christendom, and my soul would be in grievous sin. For these reasons, my dear Messer Giorgio, I beg you to thank the Duke[199] in my behalf for his offers, about which you inform me, and please ask his Lordship to give me leave of absence to let me continue here until I can leave with a good reputation and honor, and without sin.

June 22, 1555

Vasari.

Dear friend – A few evenings ago there came to call on me at my house a prudent and fine young man, namely Messer Lionardo, valet of the Duke.[199] With tenderness and affection, on behalf of his Lordship he made to me the same offers that you did in your letter. I gave him the same answer I gave you, that is, to thank the Duke for such wonderful offers as politely as he could in my behalf, and to pray his Lordship to give me leave to continue working here on St. Peter's, until it is at such a point that it could not be altered in its main features;[200] for, if I left before then, I would be responsible for a great calamity, for a great disgrace, and for a great sin. I entreat you for the love of God and of St. Peter to pray the Duke for said leave, and recommend me to his Lordship.

---

[198] The Dome.

[199] Cosimo, still urging his return to Florence and the service of the Medici.

[200] By his enemies of the Sangallo sect, one of whom, Pirro Ligorio, was already appointed Architect of the Vatican.

My dear Messer Giorgio, I know that you can tell from my handwriting that I am on the twenty-fourth hour, and not a single thought is born in me which does not have death engraven within. May God grant that I keep it waiting a few more years.

July 5, 1555

Lionardo – You write me that you have come to an agreement with the Spedalingo of Bonifazio about my Santa Caterina lands, namely, to sell them to him for three hundred and twenty scudi, and that you want me to send you the power of attorney. I was unable to send it before because of a sharp pain I had in one foot, which prevented me from going out of doors, and inconvenienced me in other matters. They say that it is a sort of gout: that's all I needed in my old age! Just the same, now I feel much better. Hold on to that agreement, for I like it very much.

September 28, 1555

Lionardo – I gather that the Duke came to see the two models of San Lorenzo's facade,[201] and that His Lordship asked for them. I say to you that you should have sent them at once wherever His Lordship wanted them, without bothering to write me. And that is what you ought to do, whenever we have something he likes.

I am enclosing an answer to the letter of Messer Giorgio, concerning the Library staircase.[202] I remember it like a dream, and I tell him the little I recall.

I am happy that you, Cassandra and the baby[203] are well, but I am sorry and concerned about Gismondo. I also have many things wrong with me, and I am beset by troubles and inconveniences. In addition to all this, I have had Urbino bedridden and ill for the last three months. This has caused me a great deal

---

[201] Made for Pope Leo X in 1517.

[202] The Laurentian Library planned by Michelangelo for Clement VII in 1524. Vasari is trying to complete it according to Michelangelo's plan.

[203] Their first child.

of grief and anxiety. Comfort Gismondo for me, and help him as much as you can.

November 30, 1555

Lionardo – Your letter informs me of the death of my brother Gismondo,[204] which is a great sorrow for me. One must accept: inasmuch as he died in possession of his faculties and with all the sacraments prescribed by the Church, one should thank God for it.

Urbino is very ill. I do not know what will come of it. It grieves me as much as if he were my own son, for he has been with me twenty-five years and he has always been very faithful. Being old, I do not have the time to train another one as I should like; and so I am deeply afflicted. Therefore, if you know a devout person there, I beg you to have him pray for his recovery.

December 4, 1555

Lionardo – Concerning the effects left by Gismondo, I say that everything is to go to you. See that you carry out his will, and have some prayers recited for the repose of his soul, for we cannot do anything else for him.

I inform you that yesterday, at four o'clock in the afternoon, Francesco called Urbino passed from this life, to my great sorrow. He left me afflicted and troubled, so that I would have preferred to die with him, so much I loved him; and he deserved it, for he had become a capable, faithful, and loyal man. Wherefore, his death has left me lifeless, and I cannot console myself. For this reason, I should like to see you, but I do not know how you could leave your wife and come here. Let me know whether within a month or a month and a half you could come all the way down here, provided, of course, you had the Duke's[205] leave. I said that you should come with the Duke's leave for the sake of appearances;

---

[204] November 13, 1555.
[205] Cosimo is a dictator.

but I do not believe it is necessary. I will write you when you should leave, because first I want Urbino's wife to leave.[206]

January 11, 1556

Lionardo – If you can fix your affairs in Florence in such a way that you can leave them without danger or harm for one month, I would like you to get ready to come. If it should not be convenient for you, either because some harm would ensue, or because you are afraid of the roads, or for some other reason, wait until the opportune moment arrives; and when you think the time has come, come, for I am old and I am anxious to speak with you before I die.

If someone were to write you, do not trust him unless you see my handwriting.

February 23, 1556

Vasari.

Dear friend – I cannot write easily, yet, in answer to your letter I will say something. You know that Urbino is dead. I owe the greatest thanks to God, but my loss is heavy, and my sorrow infinite. I owe God many thanks because, while Urbino gave me life while he was living, with his death he has taught me how to die, not with grief, but with a desire for death. I kept him with me twenty-six years, and found him most sincere and faithful; and now that I had made him rich[207] and that I expected him to be the staff and repose of my old age, he has gone, and I have no other hope left, but to see him in Heaven. God has given me a token of this through the happiness with which Urbino has gone toward death. Even more than dying, it grieved him to leave me alive in this treacherous world, with so many troubles, although

---

[206] She is expecting a child, born in mid-December.

[207] Besides delegating commissions to Urbino and securing him the curatorship of the Sistine frescoes, Michelangelo had given him two thousand scudi for his independence after his own death.

the better part of me is gone with him; nor is anything else left to me but infinite distress. I beg you, if it is not troublesome, to make my apologies to Messer Benvenuto[208] for not replying to his letter. The fact is that I am so engrossed in similar depressing thoughts, that I cannot write. Remember me to him, and my best wishes to you.

March 7, 1556

Lionardo – I gather from your letter that you arrived safely, and that makes me very happy, all the more since Cassandra and the others are well. As for myself, I am here in the same condition you left me.

As for my investing two thousand scudi in Florence either on a house or on lands, I am of the same opinion as when I first wrote you about it. Therefore, if you find something suitable, let me know.

Urbino's wife[209] has sent me word that she would like seven spans of lovely, light, black cloth, and that she will send me at once the money to cover the cost. Therefore, I'd like you to send it to me, and to pay for it, and when I have the opportunity of sending you some money, I will reimburse you.

April 11, 1556

Lionardo – You certainly happened to give that cloth to a great rogue. I am very upset at the thought that I have been waiting for it for a whole month, and that I had someone else waiting for it too. I beg you to investigate what that rascal of a driver did with it, and if it can be found, send it as soon as you can. If it cannot be found, and if we are justified, have that rogue punished. Make him pay for it, and send me another seven spans. That's all I needed! I can't tell you how much grief it has caused me, and it still causes it.

---

[208] Cellini.

[209] Now returned with her children to her family home in Castel Durante.

April 25, 1556

Lionardo – Thank goodness, I finally received the cloth; as soon as I find a trustworthy driver, I will send it to Cornelia.[210]

I never answered you concerning the house you told me we should purchase because I have had other things to worry about. Now I tell you that I do not like a house in that street, because it seems to me that it is too narrow and gloomy. I should like it in a more open and airy place. Don't worry about the cost, and if you can't find a house, look for a lot, for I should like to relieve myself as much as possible of the small capital I have here. I lost a lot of weight since Urbino's death, and I might die at any moment; then, goodness knows what would become of my things. So, give some thought to what I am writing you, for it is very important for you.

May 8, 1556

Lionardo – I received your letter with a lot of receipts. I did not wish to see them, and I was badly hurt, for it seems that you think that I do not trust you. I was anxious to know how you had distributed the alms and to whom, in order to become acquainted with the names of the poor, and all you had to do was to pass on some information to me in a letter.

You tell me that Cassandra is not feeling well; I am very sorry to hear that. Do not fail to do all you can, and if I can do anything let me know, and remember me to her.

May 28, 1556

Vasari.

Dearest friend in Florence – Only the other day I spoke to Messer Salustio,[211] and not before, because he was not in Rome. I think he is willing to do you any favor, but he believes we should wait for the right moment, and he says that since the

---

[210] Urbino's widow.

[211] Peruzzi, architect of the Pope, son of architect Baldassare Peruzzi.

Pope wishes to place your paintings elsewhere,[212] and since His Holiness does not do anything about such things without consulting him, he will decide where it shall be placed. That will be the appropriate moment to speak to him of you; and I am sure that he will be of great help to you, for such is his desire.

May 31, 1556

Lionardo – If the Cepperello farm comes close to a reasonable price, you should take it by all means.

I received a letter from Francesca. She begs me to send ten scudi to her confessor for a poor girl whom he is putting in the Santa Lucia convent. I want to do it out of my love for Francesca, for I know that if it were not a good cause, she would not ask me.

I am very happy that Cassandra is in fine health. Give her my regards, and both of you take good care of yourselves.

June 27, 1556

Lionardo – I received the cask with the white and red chick-peas, the green peas, and with the apples. I did not write you before about this, because I did not think it was a very important matter, and because writing is a great chore for me. Nothing else occurs to me.

I am sending you ten gold scudi through Francesco Bandini.[213] Take the money to Francesca so that she may donate it for that girl about whom she wrote me.

July 4, 1556

Lionardo – I did not write you about the trebbiano wine because I was in a hurry. I received it, namely thirty-six flasks. It is the

---

[212] Paul IV commissioned a painting from Vasari for a chapel in the Vatican, then changed his mind, but eventually returned it to Vasari.

[213] Archbishop of Siena, exiled when Duke Cosimo de' Medici of Florence conquered Siena.

best you ever sent. I thank you for it, but I am sorry that you spent so much money, especially since I lost all of my friends, and there is no one to whom I can give it.

You have shown too much desire to get the Cepperello farm. You did exactly the opposite of what I wrote you from here. That loose widow wants us to believe that she is giving us a treasure; nothing but clumsy wiles that make me laugh. But let's let it be. Do your best, and go ahead and take it, and let me know how and where you want me to send you the money, but do everything as quietly as possible. I am glad you are all well; the Lord be praised.

August 1, 1556

Lionardo – Your haste cost me at least fifty gold scudi. But what hurts me more is the fact that you gave more consideration to a piece of land than to my words. I told you to pretend that I did not want it, and to let them beg us to buy it. Instead, as soon as you got there, you hastily put the brokers to work on it. Now, as long as it is done, take care of yourself and enjoy it.

August 8, 1556

Lionardo – Bastiano[214] has started going out, and on Monday or Tuesday he will go to Bandini to deposit the money, and it will be paid to you there in the manner you wrote me. As for the purchase, you handled it your own way, not mine; it cost me at least fifty scudi. There is no question that vanity deceives all men.

August 15, 1556

Lionardo – You write me about the money which I told you to spend as you saw fit. You know very well that I did not mean on the Cepperello farm, for it is an old matter which had been on the fire over twenty years, and which we had already decided to buy; but you preferred to interpret it and manage it according to your whim.

---

[214] Malenotti of San Gimignano, his new assistant.

September, 1556

Lionardo – Concerning your fulfilling the vow[215] you write me about, I say to you that I do not believe this is the time to go traveling around. As for your naming the child you are expecting Michelangelo, it is all right with me. I'd also approve of another name, as long as it is after someone in our family. The name Giovansimone would do too. I will be happy with whatever you decide to do.

October 31, 1556

Dearest nephew Lionardo – Several days ago I received a letter from you which I did not answer because I did not have the opportunity. Over a month ago, seeing that the construction work of St. Peter's had slowed down, I decided to go to Loreto for a vow of mine.[216] When I arrived at Spoleto somewhat fatigued, I stopped for a while to rest. Thus, I was unable to carry out my plans,[217] for a man was sent after me to ask me to return to Rome. Not to disobey, I returned to Rome, where, by the grace of God, I now am. Here, considering the difficult times, we live as it pleases God. There is good hope for peace.

Yours, like a father.

December 19, 1556

Lionardo – I wrote you about my return to Rome. Later I received a letter of yours, in which you told me that Cassandra had had a baby girl, and that the latter died after a few days. That filled me with grief, but I am not surprised, for we are destined not to have our family multiply in Florence. Therefore, pray God that the child you still have will live, and do your best to keep

---

[215] Lionardo had vowed to his father to visit the shrine at Loreto.
[216] He left Rome because of the threatened invasion of the Spanish Army.
[217] To reach the shrine at Loreto.

in good health yourself, so that the Hospital will not inherit everything we have. Pray God for me, for I need it.

December 28, 1556

Vasari.

Messer Giorgio – I received the booklet of Messer Cosimo,[218] which you sent me. I am enclosing a note of thanks for his Lordship. Recently, although it cost me great discomfort and a lot of money, I rejoiced visiting the hermits in the mountains of Spoleto, so that I came back halfheartedly to Rome; for, indeed, peace can be found only in those woods. I am glad you are sound and happy.

February 6, 1557

My dearest Lionardo – I received your letter and I read what you had to write me about his Excellency,[219] therefore, you will deliver the enclosed letter to Messer Lionardo,[220] and make my apologies; for I am not going to fail to keep my promise to his Excellency[221] as soon as I have the time. However, I cannot do it so soon, since I must first put my things in order here.

February 13, 1557

Lionardo – About two years ago when Messer Lionardo, a man at the service of the Duke of Florence, came to see me here in Rome, he told me that his Lordship would be very happy to see me return to Florence, and he made me many offers on his behalf. I replied to him that I begged his Lordship to grant me enough time to leave the construction of St. Peter's at such a point that my plans would not be subsequently altered without my permission. Not having heard anything further, I continued

---

[218] Bartoli, who sent him a booklet on the language of Florence and Dante by Carlo Lenzoni.

[219] Duke Cosimo.

[220] The Duke's valet.

[221] To return to Florence in the Duke's service.

with my work in said construction, and as yet it has not proceeded to that point. Furthermore, I am faced with the necessity of making a large wood model with the dome and lantern,[222] and to complete it exactly the way the construction is to be finished. All of Rome, and especially the most Reverend Cardinal da Carpi,[223] beg me to do it; so that I think I will have to remain here for not less than one year. I beg the Duke to grant me this period of time for the love of Christ and of St. Peter, so that I may return to Florence without this worry, and with the intention never to have to return to Rome.

As for the rumor that the construction has stopped, it is not true, for, as anybody can see, sixty men between stonecutters, masons, and helpers, are still working there, and hope to continue. If the plan of the construction were changed, as some envious people are trying to do, it would be the same as if I had not done anything at all.

March 28, 1557

Cornelia, Urbino's widow.

I had noticed that you were peeved at me, but I did not know why. Now, after reading your letter, I think I know the reason. When you sent me the cheeses, you wrote me that you wanted to send me other things, but that the handkerchiefs were not ready yet; and I, to prevent you from spending more money on me, wrote you not to send me anything else, but instead to ask *me* for something, for, in doing so, you would be doing me a very great favor, since you knew, nay you must have been certain that I still love Urbino, although he is dead. As for my coming there to see the children, or your sending here Michelangelo,[224] it is necessary that I write you what my household here

---

[222] Now preserved in St. Peter's.

[223] Rodolfo Pio da Carpi, a friend and commissioner of the fabric of St. Peter's.

[224] Her eldest son was his namesake and godson. Under Urbino's will both children were under Michelangelo's guardianship.

is like. I do not think it would be a good idea to send Michelangelo here, since I have no housemaids or anyone to take care of my household affairs. Furthermore, the boy is still too young, and something might happen that would make me very unhappy.

There is this other consideration: for the last month the Duke of Florence, God bless him, is doing his utmost to entice me to return to Florence with very generous offers. I have asked him for enough time to settle my affairs here, and to leave St. Peter's fabric well along, so that I think I will be here the whole summer. After I have settled my things and yours at the Monte della Fede,[225] next winter I shall return to Florence for good, for I am old, and I do not have the time to return to Rome again. On my way, I shall come to see you, and if you wish to let me have Michelangelo, I will keep him with me in Florence, and I will take better care of him than of the children of my nephew Lionardo. As his father wanted him to do, he will learn what I can teach him.

May, 1557

Most Illustrious Lord Cosimo Duke of Florence.
Your Lordship – About three months ago, I informed your Lordship that it was impossible for me at that time to leave the fabric of St. Peter's without great harm for the construction and very great shame for me; and that, if I wished to leave it in the state I desired, I would need no less than one additional year's time. I was given the impression that your Lordship was willing to grant me this span of time. Now I am in possession of another letter from your Lordship, which urges me to return sooner than I expected. This weighs heavily on me, for the affairs of the fabric are giving me more toil and trouble than ever before. This is due to the fact that, since I am old and cannot visit the construction often, an error was made in the vault of the Chapel of the Kings of France, which is an artful and unusual affair, so that I must

---

[225] The fund holding the inheritance for Urbino's children.

undo a large part of what has been done there. Bastiano da San Gimignano, who was a supervisor here, can testify what kind of chapel it is, and how important it is to the rest of the construction. Once the chapel is corrected, which, in my opinion, ought to be completed at the end of this summer; I will have nothing else to do than to leave behind the model of the whole thing, as everybody begs me to do, especially Cardinal Carpi; and return to Florence with the expectation of finding rest in death, with which I try to familiarize myself day and night, so that it will not treat me worse than it does other old people.

Now, I pray your Lordship to grant me the requested time of one year for the fabric, as, in my opinion, you were willing to grant me on a previous occasion.

May, 1557

Vasari.

Dear friend – I call God as a witness that, against my will, Pope Paul forced me ten years ago to work in the construction of St. Peter's.[226] If we had continued to work in said fabric until today as we began at that time, enough progress would have been made so that I would be satisfied with it, and would be able to return to Florence. But, through work stoppages, progress slowed down, and what is more, it is slowing down as we are facing the most exhausting and difficult part; so that, if I abandoned it now, it would amount to a most shameful repudiation of the prize which I have earned during ten years' hard work for the love of God. I made this long speech in reply to your letter, and also because I have in my hands a letter from the Duke which caused great amazement in me, realizing that his Lordship had deigned write with so much sweetness. I thank God and his Excellency from the bottom of my heart.

I wander from my topic, because I have lost my memory and my judgment, and writing is very painful for me, for it is not my

---

[226] When he accepted he refused a salary for the work.

profession. The conclusion is this: to make you understand what would follow if I gave up the fabric, and I left Rome. First of all, I would make many thieves happy, and I would be responsible for its ruin, and perhaps also of its shutting down permanently. Next, I have some obligations, and a house and other things, which amount to a few thousand scudi; and if I departed without leave, I do not know what would become of them. Finally, I am not feeling well, and I am affected with gravel and kidney stones, like all old men; and Doctor Realdo can testify to that, for I owe him my life.[227] Therefore, I have not the courage to come to Florence and then return here; and as for my coming there for good, I need a little time to settle matters in such a way here, that I will not have to worry about them any more.

I pray you to speak of me to the Duke, and give him my apologies, for now I have the courage only to die, and the information I am giving you concerning my state of affairs here is the Gospel truth. If I had felt like riding a horse, I would have come there immediately and then returned, without anybody here knowing anything about it.

May 4, 1557

Lionardo – I am sending you through Messer Francesco Bandini fifty gold scudi, for I want you to send me five yards of the lightest and most beautiful black serge you can find, and one yard of sarcenet.[228] Urbino's wife has asked me to get these things for her. So, send them as soon as you can, and let me know the cost. Distribute what is left of the fifty scudi as alms among the people who need them most.

There are many things the matter with me, so that I feel that death is not far away; for this reason, if I am still alive, I should like you to come down next September in order to settle my own

---

[227] Realdo Colombo diagnosed and treated his kidney stone disorder in March, 1549.
[228] A heavy cotton cloth with a high gloss.

and our affairs. Unless, of course, I come to Florence before then.

In order to make me return to Florence, and perhaps to cover up the dishonor of his departure from here, Bastiano da San Gimignano[229] has told many lies there in Florence, perhaps with a good reason.

June 16, 1557

Lionardo – I received the serge and the sarcenet.

As for myself, I am plagued by all the woes typical of old age; kidney stones prevent me from urinating; my loins and my back hurt so, that often I cannot climb stairs; and what makes matters worse, is that I have many worries and anxieties, so that, if I gave up all the conveniences I have here for my ailments, I would be dead in three days. Yet, I shouldn't want because of this to lose the Duke's favor, nor neglect the construction of St. Peter's or myself. I pray God that he help and counsel me. Should I be taken ill, that is be seized by a dangerous fever, I shall send for you at once. But do not worry about it, and don't you dare come unless I tell you so in my letters.

July 1, 1557

Lionardo – I'd rather be dead than incur the Duke's disfavor. I try to be honest in everything I do, and if I have delayed coming to Florence, as I promised, it was my understanding that I would not leave from here until the construction of St. Peter's would be at such a stage that my plans could not be ruined or changed. The reason why I have always practiced and am still practicing such diligence is because I believe, like many others, that God entrusted me with this work. However, the construction has not reached that stage through lack of money and men. And since I am old and I have nothing else to leave behind, and also because

---

[229] His assistant.

I work for the love of God, in whom I place all my hope, I refused to abandon said construction.

To make it possible for Messer Giorgio to inform the Duke of the cause of my delay, I enclose a little sketch of the error.

August 17, 1557

Vasari – The centering marked in red[230] was taken by the superintendent on the body of the whole vault. Then, as he approached the mezzotondo, which is at the highest point of the vault, he noticed the error made, as can be seen from the enclosed drawing, for he depended entirely on one centering, whereas there must be infinite ones, as is indicated in the drawing by those marked in black. With this error the vault has progressed to such a point that it is necessary to remove a large number of stones, for, instead of masonry, the vault requires travertine blocks exclusively; and the diameter of the tondi (rounds) exclusive of the cornices which enclose them is twenty-two spans. Since I had made an appropriate model, as I do for everything, this error accrued because I was unable to go there often to inspect the work on account of my old age. And whereas I thought said vault would be finished by now, it will not be finished during the whole winter. If one could die of shame or grief, I would not be alive.

August 17, 1557

Lionardo – In your last letter, you urge me to come there; and I tell you that a person who is not here and does not hear or see me, does not understand what my life here is like. So, I must not be importuned. I do the best I can in my condition.

August 17, 1557

Vasari.

Messer Giorgio – In order that you may understand better the difficulty of the vault of which I sent you a drawing, I am send-

---

[230] On the diagram explaining the construction error which delayed work on St. Peter's.

ing you the plan of the vault, in order to follow its birth from the ground up. It was necessary to divide it into three vaults, in place of the lower windows divided by pilasters, which as you see proceed pyramidally to the half-round (mezzotondo) at the highest point of the vault, as does the base and the sides of the vault. Also, they must be governed by an infinite number of centerings, and the circles and the squares which come in the middle of the bases must increase and diminish in so many ways and go through so many points that it is difficult to find the right way. Nevertheless, since they had my model, they should never have made such an error as to let one single centering govern all three shells. As a result, to our shame and with great loss, we have been compelled to undo what has been done: and even now a large number of stones are being taken down. The vault, the dressed stones and the openings are all in travertine, as also everything else at the base: something not done before in Rome.

I am most grateful to the Duke for his leniency, and may God grant that I place at his service my poor person, for there is nothing else left. My memory and intellect went to wait for me elsewhere.

September, 1557

Lionardo – I learned from your letter of the great disaster caused by the flood[231] to bridges, monasteries, and houses, and of the number of dead, and that by comparison with other people, you suffered very little. I had already heard about it, and I imagine you people have heard about what happened here, for the flood of the Tiber caused similar destruction and deaths; and since we live on a hill, we came out of it much better than others. I pray God that he protect us from something worse, as I am afraid will come to pass because of our sins.

My things here are not going too well: I am referring to the construction of St. Peter's, for it is not enough to give the

---

[231] Of the Arno, September 13, 1557.

right instructions, since the superintendents, either through ignorance or through malice, always do the opposite, and I am left to suffer.

December 16, 1557

Lionardo – You write me that if I need a housemaid or anything else for my well-being, I should let you know, and you will send me whatever I need. I tell you that for the time being I do not need anything, because I have two good boys to do what I need.

June 25, 1558

Lionardo – I received the trebbiano wine, and not without deriving from it shame and anger, for I gave some of it as a present without tasting it. If you bought good trebbiano there, there is no question that the mule driver worked out some dirty trick on the way. Later, it made me angry. You shouldn't have sent it, even if it had been good, for these are not times to do such things.

July 2, 1558

Lionardo – You do not have to apologize for the wine. Another time I would much rather you spent that money for charitable deeds, for I believe there are needy people, especially since, according to what they say here, there is a great famine in Florence. There are signs that it is going to spread down here too.

September 28, 1558

Vasari.

Dear friend – Concerning the staircase for the Library,[232] about which I have been asked so much, I want you to believe that if I could recall how I had arranged it, I wouldn't wait to be coaxed. A certain staircase comes to my mind just like a dream, but I do not believe it is exactly like the one I conceived then, for it seems a rather awkward thing to me. Just the same, I shall describe it here: namely, it is as if you took a quantity of oval

---

[232] The Laurentian in Florence.

boxes, one span deep each, but not of the same length and width; and you placed the largest one on the floor, removed from the wall where the door is in accordance with the gentleness or the steepness desired for the staircase; and you placed another box on this one, which should be smaller than the first in every direction, so that below it there should be enough surface needed by the feet to climb; and so on, diminishing them and drawing them toward the door, always with enough space to climb; and the top step should be the same width as the opening of the door. Said oval staircase should have two wings, one on each side, which follow the same steps, but straight and not arched: these for the servants, and the middle one for the Lord. From the middle on up of said staircase, the ends of said wings must go back toward the wall, from the middle down as far as the floor, they must be away from the wall, with the whole staircase about three spans, in such a way that the footing of the recess is not encumbered anywhere and every front is free. What I am writing may sound laughable, but I know well that Messer Bartolomeo[233] and you will find something for the purpose.

Would to God that I could find something lovely to my taste, for I wouldn't let anything stop me from sending it to his Lordship. I beg you to thank his Lordship for the very great offers. I know that I do not deserve them, just the same I treasure them.

December 2, 1558

Lionardo – I heard about the death of the little girl.[234] I am not surprised, for in our family we never had more than one child at the time.[235] I wrote you in the past to buy a fine house in a good district. I feel the same way about it now, for I put about

---

[233] Ammannati, who is helping Vasari on the project.

[234] Another child of Lionardo's dies.

[235] Michelangelo repeats this again and again but actually only Buonarroto had children and Lionardo and Francesca are both alive. And Cecca has three alive at this time.

nine hundred scudi in the bank here, and I would like to take it out, and with the money I would get from my house here, I could buy one in Florence.

I have nothing else to say. I am old, and my hard work here is not appreciated. I do it for the love of God, and I trust in him and in nothing else.

December 2, 1558

Lionardo – Bartolomeo Ammannati, superintendent of the construction work of Santa Maria del Fiore,[236] wrote me on behalf of the Duke for my advice in connection with a certain staircase which is to be built in San Lorenzo's[237] Library. I made a little rough clay model of it, as it seems to me the staircase should be, and I thought of placing it nicely inside a box, and of giving it to someone Ammannati will suggest who can take it to him. Therefore, speak to him and inform him about it as soon as you can.

If I can complete what I promised here before I die, I should like to know that in Florence I have a nest for myself alone and for my close friends. As I wrote you, I have bad luck.

January, 1559

Bartolomeo Ammannati.

Messer Bartolomeo – I wrote you that I had made a small clay model of the Library staircase. I remember that the one I specified in the past was isolated and leaned only against the door of the Library. I have tried to follow the same plan. Concerning the stairs which enclose the main staircase, I should not want them to have balustrades at the end like the main stairway, but a base between every two steps, as is indicated by the decorations. I do not have to tell you about the shape of the supports, and mouldings of those footings, and other cornices, for you are skilled, and, furthermore, since you are on the spot, you will see

---

[236] Cathedral in Florence.
[237] The Medici family church.

the need much better than I. Take up as little space as you can for the height and width, by compressing and enlarging as you will see fit.

I am of the opinion that if said staircase were made of fine walnut, it would look better than in stone, and it would be better suited to the stalls, the ceiling and the door. I have nothing else to tell you. I am all yours, old, blind, and deaf, and in poor agreement with my hands and my person.

July 15, 1559

Lionardo – I received the shirts along with all the other things mentioned in the letter. Do not forget to thank Cassandra for me.

I received two letters in which I am entreated to return to Florence. I do not believe you know that about four months ago, through Cardinal da Carpi, who is one of the supervisors of the construction work at St. Peter's, I obtained the Duke of Florence's permission to continue here in Rome my work at St. Peter's. That made me very happy, and I thanked God for it. Now I cannot understand whether you entreat me to return to Florence because you want me to return there, or because of some other reason. So, throw some light on this matter, for everything upsets me and bothers me.

Writing is very troublesome to my hand, my sight and my memory. That's what old age does to you!

November 1, 1559[238]

Duke Cosimo de' Medici.
Most Illustrious Lord Duke of Florence – The Florentines have repeatedly expressed the desire to build here in Rome a Church of St. John.[239] Now, hoping to find it easier to accomplish during the rule of your Lordship, they have reached a decision, and they

---

[238] Pope Paul IV died August 18, 1559. Giovanni Angelo de' Medici, from an obscure Lombard branch of the family, succeeded him December 25, 1559, as Pius IV.

[239] The long-planned Church of the Florentines.

have formed for this purpose a five-man committee, which has begged me for a design of said church. Being aware of the fact that Pope Leo took the first steps for said church, I replied to them that I did not want to have anything to do with it without the permission and commission of the Duke of Florence. Now, after whatever steps they took, I find myself in possession of a most gracious and kind letter from your most illustrious Lordship, which I consider as an explicit command that I must attend to the above-mentioned church of the Florentines, for you indicate that it would give you great pleasure.

I have made various designs suited to the place where, according to the members of the committee, the church is to be erected.[240] Since they are men of great intelligence and judgment, they chose one which, in truth, seems to me the worthiest.

I am very sorry, in this instance, that I am so old[241] and in such ill health, that I can promise only little help for said construction; yet, I shall do my best while remaining indoors.

Servant of your Excellency

December 16, 1559
Lionardo – I received the twelve marzolini cheeses you sent me: they are very beautiful. I will share them with some friends. Next spring I should like you to come here for various reasons; do not come until I write you to do so, however.

January 7, 1560
Lionardo – Simon del Bernia[242] brought me fifteen marzolini cheeses and fourteen pounds of sausage. I was happy to receive them because there is a scarcity of such things. Just the same I hope you will not spend any money on such things again, for here I get to consume the smallest part for myself.

---

[240] On the Via Giulia.
[241] Eighty-four.
[242] The mule driver.

I wrote you about a house for the sake of transferring there before my death what I own here; I do not know what will come of it, for I am all tied up here.

January 10, 1560

Pier Filippo Vandini[243] at Castel Durante.
Magnificent Messer Pier Filippo – In reply to your letter, I inform you that I too have a counsel of experts, namely, that since it is a fact that the house was turned over to Cornelia[244] not as dotal funds, but as an equivalent of five hundred florins, she is not forced to take the house back. If she wishes, she can have the money. But since I think I know that Cornelia would like to remain in the house and have the five hundred florins, and perhaps take for herself the best lands owned there by those poor wards, and since, in my opinion, she gives evidence in this of being an unloving mother, I incline to think that it is our duty to see to it that the wards' property is not squandered.

Therefore, it might be a good idea to see whether the house can be sold for five hundred florins, and, if possible, for eight hundred, as I hear it is worth. It is to the advantage of the wards to alienate the house and the farms rather than take money from the Monte,[245] where it is accumulating interest and increasing, especially in view of the fact that for three or four scudi a year the wards can rent a fine house.

And perhaps, when Cornelia learns that you wish to sell the house, she will change her mind and will decide to take the house, seeing that her plans and speculations are not meeting with any success. I would also appreciate it if you would come to Rome, as you courteously offer to do, thus we would talk the whole thing over together, and it would be easier for us to find a satisfactory settlement for the affairs of those poor orphans.

---

[243] One of the trustees of Urbino's will who managed his estate under Michelangelo's authority.

[244] Urbino's widow, who has remarried.

[245] The fund holding the inheritance.

March 10, 1560

Lionardo – I received the red and white chick-peas, and the beans. I appreciate them very much, although, old as I am, I am in no condition to observe Lent. I shall be waiting for you after the middle of next May. If you do not feel like coming, or you cannot, inform me.

March 10, 1560

Most Illustrious and Most Excellent Lord Duke of Florence and Siena.[246] Most honorable Lord – The members of the committee on the construction of the Church of the Florentines have decided to send Tiberio Calcagni[247] to your most illustrious Excellency. This pleases me very much, for, through the designs he will show you, you will be better able to see what we shall have to do. If you find these designs satisfactory, with the help of your Excellency, we will be able to begin the foundations, and to go on with this holy enterprise. I felt it was my duty to tell you with these few lines, that, since your Excellency asked me to look after this fabric, I shall not fail to do all I know and can, although because of my age and ill health I shall not be able to do as much as I should like and I ought to do for your Excellency and for my country.[248]

March 5, 1560

Lionardo – I was very happy about the little girl who was born to you, for, as we are alone, it would be a good thing if she will be able to make a good marriage.[249] Therefore, take care of her, although I will not be here when that comes to pass. I want you

---

[246] Cosimo de' Medici.

[247] A disciple of Michelangelo to whom he delegated the plans for the Church of the Florentines.

[248] Tuscany, the Grand Duchy of Cosimo.

[249] There will be available a substantial dowry.

to know that the thing which bothers me most here in Rome, is having to answer letters.

April 11, 1560

Lionardo – You wrote me that this spring you wanted to go to Loreto, and that you would pass by here. It seems to me that it would be better if you went to Loreto first, and then stopped here on the way back. Then you would be able to stay a few days. See that you are in good company, for it does not do any harm at any time.

April 25, 1560

Most illustrious Duke of Florence.

I saw the designs of the rooms painted by Messer Giorgio,[250] and the model of the large hall[251] with Messer Bartolomeo's design of the fountain[252] which is to go in the said place. As for the paintings, I thought I saw some marvelous things, which is typical of all those which are or will be made under the patronage of your Excellency. As regards the model of the hall, as it is now it seems low to me. Since so much money is going to be spent, it should be raised at least twenty-four feet. Concerning the restoration of the palace, judging by the designs I saw, I am of the opinion that it could not be carried out any better. As for the fountain of Messer Bartolomeo, I think it is a beautiful fantasy which will turn out an admirable thing. As regards the fabric of the Florentines[253] here, it grieves me that I am too old and near death to gratify your desire in full.

---

[250] The Geneology of the Gods by Vasari, in the old Palazzo della Signoria, which Cosimo was remodeling.

[251] Hall of the Five Hundred in the Palazzo.

[252] Ammannati had entered the contest for the Fountain of Neptune in the Piazza della Signoria, and sent his designs to Michelangelo for his opinion.

[253] Church of the Florentines in Rome.

May 18, 1560

Lionardo – I gather from your last letter that you returned from Loreto. I was waiting for you in Rome on your way back, but I see that you did not get my letter before you left Florence. Now, since it happened that way, and since we are far from each other, it seems to me for various reasons that it would be preferable to delay your coming until September, and then I shall be waiting for you.

July 27, 1560

Lionardo – A few days ago I received your letter in which you inform me of the death of your daughter Lessandra. It made me very sad: but I would have been surprised if she had lived, for in our family we cannot have more than one child at the time. One must be patient, and take all the better care of those who survive. When the hot weather is over, if you can, come down to Rome.

1560

Cardinal Rodolfo Pio da Carpi.[254]

Most Reverend Monsignor – If a plan has diverse parts, all those which are alike in quality and quantity, must be decorated in the same way and in the same fashion. And the same is true of their counterparts. But when the plan changes form entirely,[255] not only is it permissible, but it is necessary to change the decorative appurtenances, as well as their counterparts. The intermediate parts are always free, as indeed they should be: just like the nose, which is in the middle of the face, is not bound to correspond with either of the eyes, but each hand is certainly bound to be like the other, and each eye like the other, for the sake of the sides and counterparts. And so it is an undeniable thing that the members of an architectural structure follow the members of the human body. He who has not been or is not a good master

---

[254] His friend on the commission of the fabric of St. Peter's.
[255] As St. Peter's did under many architects.

of the nude, and especially of anatomy, cannot understand the principles of architecture.

1560

The Superintendents of the Fabric of St. Peter's.
You know that I told Balduccio[256] not to send his lime if it was not good. Now, since he has sent bad quality, and does not think that he will be forced to take it back, one is led to believe that he is in collusion with the person who accepted it. This does a great favor to those men whom I have dismissed from the fabric for similar reasons. And a person who accepts bad goods, needed for the fabric, when I have forbidden them, is doing nothing else but making friends of people whom I have made my enemies. I believe there will be a new conspiracy. Promises, tips and presents corrupt justice. Therefore, with that authority I have from the Pope, I beg you not to accept anything from now on which is not suitable, even though it comes from Heaven. I do not want to appear partial, for I am not.

September 13, 1560

Cardinal of Carpi.
My Most Illustrious and Reverend Lord and Venerable Master –
Messer Francesco Bandini[257] told me yesterday that the building of St. Peter's could not possibly be faring worse than it is doing. This has grieved me deeply, both because you have not been informed of the truth, and because I, as I must, desire more than anyone else that it should proceed well. And, unless I am deceived, I think I can truly assure you that the work which is now in progress there could not possibly go on better than it is. But since it is possible that my own interests and old age[258] may easily deceive me, and thus, against my will, expose to harm and injury the mentioned fabric of St. Peter's, as soon as I can I

[256] Supplier of material to the fabric.
[257] Archbishop of Siena, now in exile. Michelangelo gave him his Pietà, now in the Duomo in Florence.
[258] He is eighty-five.

intend to ask permission of His Holiness to resign my office. In fact, to save time, I wish to entreat your most illustrious and reverend Lordship to do me the favor to free me from this annoyance, at which, at the orders of the Popes, as you well know, I willingly worked gratis for the past seventeen years. It is easy enough to see how far the said fabric has progressed through my efforts during this period. I entreat you once again to accept my resignation. For once, you could not do me a more singular favor. I reverently and humbly kiss the hand of your most illustrious and reverend Lordship.

October 27, 1560

Lionardo – Several months ago I wrote you that I should like you to come here. Now I gather from your letter that you think you should wait until October. I say that four months more or less do not matter. Therefore, you will do well to wait until the coming spring, when the weather will be better for your journey to and from Rome.

January 12, 1561

Lionardo – Several days ago I received from you twelve marzolini cheeses. They were beautiful and good: I thank you for them. I have nothing else to say. This is not the right time for you to come here, because I am in such a state that it would only add to my troubles and worries. When the times comes, I will let you know.

February 18, 1561

Lionardo – I'll be waiting for you during the Easter holidays. I did not think it was the right time before. So, if it is all right with you, do not fail.

March 22, 1561

Lionardo – See that you travel in good company, and do not take with you anyone who expects to stay at my house, for there are women[259] living here, and I do not have much furniture. After two or three days you will be able to return to Florence, for I will tell you in a few words what I have in mind.

June 22, 1561

Lionardo – Today I received forty-two flasks of trebbiano wine. I thank you for it. It is very good: I'll share it with my friends. The name of the mule driver is Domenico da Figline. I also thank you for the two hats. I would like you to let me know how Francesca[260] is getting along.

July 18, 1561

Lionardo – Now, since I am old, as you know, I should like to distribute some alms in Florence for the good of my soul; for I do not know in what other way I could do some good. For this reason, I should like to send to Florence a certain sum of money, with which you could give out alms where the need is greatest. This sum will consist of about three hundred scudi. I asked Bandino[261] to have the money paid in Florence, and he replied that within four months he will take it there himself. I do not want to wait that long, therefore, if you have some Florentine friend to whom I can entrust said sum, let me know.

September 20, 1561

Lionardo – I should like to look through the papers of our father Lodovico to see if there is the copy of an Apostolic contract which was made for certain statues which I promised I would continue to do for Pope Pius the Second after his death.[262] Since, because

---

[259] He had many female servants. His last was Caterina Mulattieri.

[260] His niece.

[261] Francesco Bandini, banker. (Same as former Archbishop of Siena?)

[262] The contract of 1503 with Cardinal Piccolomini (later Pope Pius III) for an altar in Bologna honoring Pius II. The Piccolomini heirs still claimed Michelangelo owed one hundred ducats on this unfinished work.

of certain misunderstandings, said work was suspended about fifty years ago, and since I am old, I should like to settle this matter in order to avoid their bothering you unjustly after I am dead. I seem to remember that the notary who drew up the contract in the bishop's residence, was named Ser Donato Ciampelli. I am told that all of his papers were left to Ser Lorenzo Violi. So, if you do not find the copy in our house, you might ask the son of said Ser Lorenzo, and get a copy of it regardless of cost.

November, 1561

The Supervisors of the Fabric of St. Peter's.

Lord Supervisors – Being old and seeing that Cesare[263] is so busy with his duties in connection with the construction of St. Peter's, and since men oftentimes lose their heads, I thought it necessary to give Pierluigi[264] as a companion to Cesare, for I know him to be a useful person who will do honor to the fabric; also because he was acquainted with the construction, and because since he lives at my house, he will be able to inform me in the evening of what has been done during the day. Your Lordships will see to it that his stipend is computed from the first of this month, and at the same rate as Cesare's; otherwise I will pay for it with my own money, for, being aware of the needs and interests of the fabric, I am determined that he work there.

November 30, 1561

Lionardo – I received two of your letters, one from Antonio Maria Piccolomini, and the contract. I cannot tell you anything else, for His Eminence the Archbishop, of Siena,[265] started to settle this matter for me, and since he is a fine and capable man, I think he will succeed.

---

[263] De Castel Durante, one of the supervisors.
[264] Gaeta.
[265] Francesco Bandini Piccolomini.

January 12, 1562

Lionardo – Many years ago, since things were very uncertain here in Rome, I sent you a box containing very important papers so that they would not get lost here.[266] Now, for my own welfare and honor, I should show them to the Pope.[267] Therefore, I want you to send them to me as soon as you can with a trustworthy man. Promise the driver whatever you think he should get, for I will see that he gets paid here.

January 31, 1562

Lionardo – I received the box with the papers. I found in it many things that bear on what I want to be able to prove. Nothing further occurs to me.

February 14, 1562

Lionardo – I am not yet returning to you the papers you sent me, because I was unable to do anything I intended to do, both because it is Carnival time and because I have not been feeling well. I have had some very bad colic pains. Now I am well. After I have used the papers, I will keep the copies and return everything to you. Save them.

February 20, 1562

Lionardo – I received a large cask with three little sacks of leguminous plants, red and white chick-peas, and green peas. I thank you for them. I have nothing else to tell you.

June 27, 1562

Dearest Nephew – With this I acknowledge having received the trebbiano wine, that is, forty-three flasks, and, as usual, I appreciate it very much. Do not be surprised if I do not write you boys,[268] for, as you know, I am old and I find writing very

---

[266] Records of his pension.

[267] Pius IV.

[268] Lionardo and his nephew-in-law Michele Guicciardini.

fatiguing. I am in good health, and I hope the same is true of all of you. Pray God for me. If Cassandra has a boy, name him Buonarroto;[269] if she has a girl, name her Francesca. May the good Lord protect us all from evil.

January 31, 1563

Lionardo – Simon del Bernia, the mule driver, brought me the cloth. I thank you. For the moment, if you came to Rome you would only make things more difficult for me. I have nothing else to say.

June, 1563

Lionardo – I received the trebbiano wine with other letters from you and Francesca. I did not reply before because my hand is no longer able to write. I said the same thing to his Lordship the Ambassador of the Duke.[270] I thank you for the letter of Messer Giorgio.[271] Love to all of you.

August 21, 1563

Lionardo – I gather from your letter that you believe certain envious and wretched individuals, who, not being able to twist me around or to rob me, write you many lies. They are a pack of greedy individuals; and you are so foolish as to believe what they tell you about me, as if I were a child. Drive them out like the scandalous, envious rogues they are. You wish to know how I am getting along. As for the household management I tell you that I couldn't wish for anything better, for I couldn't be served or treated more faithfully. As for my being robbed, I tell you that I can fully trust, and not worry in the least about the people

---

[269] He is confused. Lionardo's first-born, still alive, is already named Buonarroto.

[270] Averardo Serristori.

[271] Vasari.

I have in the house.[272] Therefore, relax, and do not worry about my affairs, for I am not a child and if need be I can take care of myself. Keep well.

December 28, 1563

Lionardo – I received your last letter along with twelve excellent marzolini cheeses. I thank you for them. I rejoice knowing that you are in good health, and so am I. In the past I received several letters of yours, and the reason why I did not answer them is because my hand is no longer any good at writing. Therefore, from now on I shall have someone else write, and I will sign my name. I have nothing else to say.

I, Michelangelo, Sculptor in Rome.

THE SPEECH OF NIGHT

Sweet is my sleep, but more to be mere stone,
so long as ruin and dishonor reign;
to bear nought, to feel nought, is my great gain;
then wake me not, speak in an undertone!

---

[272] Catarina Mulattieri and an assistant named Antonio.

EPILOGUE

Michelangelo died in his house in the Macello dei Corvi on February 18, 1564, just a few weeks short of his ninetieth year.

By the end of his life he had become known throughout Europe as "the master of the world." The High Renaissance, of which he was the embodiment, died with him.

When Michelangelo had entered Ghirlandaio's studio at the age of thirteen, the artist, painter and sculptor alike had had little social position, and was regarded as just another artisan who decorated walls or filled niches, even as a cooper made barrels or a tailor sewed cloaks. By the time he died, the artist as a creator had come to enjoy the highest of respect, was widely sought after, and was felt to be not only an interpreter of his age, but one of God's clearest voices.

By actual count, Michelangelo was kept from his beloved marble for a full half of his working life. This is why he sometimes fell into despair, and toward the end thought that he had not accomplished very much. Yet his body of work is formidable, in marble and paint, architecture, engineering and poetry, all of it so magnificently high in quality that one may be justified in thinking of him as the single greatest artist in the history of man.

There have been periods in the past when Michelangelo's work has been severely attacked, his style rejected. One can draw a graph covering four hundred years which shows the rise and fall of his popularity, linked to the taste of the times. Many of the attacks on his sculpture and painting, over the centuries, have been of astounding bitterness. Yet always the work survives, and succeeding generations come back to it with renewed vision and fresh understanding.

INDEX

M.=Michelangelo